EMPOWERING SINGLE PARENTS

TEN WAYS TO INCREASE YOUR EFFECTIVENESS

GREG CYNAUMON, Ph.D.
WITH DANA CYNAUMON

MOODY PRESS
CHICAGO

ISBN: 0-8024-7942-1

1 3 5 7 9 10 8 6 4 2

Printed in the United States of America

To all single moms and dads

CONTENTS

ACKNOWLEDGMENTS

Thanks go to Jan, my beautiful wife of thirteen years, for her unswerving support and unparalleled patience—especially through the "cop" years.

To my kids, Tracy and Matt, who have made being a dad the greatest experience on earth. Thanks for making me laugh as only the two of you can. Please don't spoil it all when you become teenagers.

To Dana, my co-writer, partner, and brother, for his dedication and hard work. I cherish how our relationship has grown through the years. And to his lovely wife, Pam, for her support during the many hours he and I were working on this book.

To my parents, Ed and Myrna, for their love, support, and wonderful role modeling. Thanks for your collaboration on this book, too! And, by the way, stop spoiling the grandchildren!

To my friends and colleagues at the Minirth-Meier Clinic West, especially Jim, Dave, Carolina, Steve, and Pete, for their friendship and encouragement.

And finally, to all single moms and dads, who each day face one of the most difficult jobs on earth. Sit back, relax, and put your feet up. This book is for you.

INTRODUCTION

BLINDSIDED BY THE NINETIES

The 1990s caught many of us with our spirits up, our guard down, and our gold cards fully extended. One decade: it's a new condo, candlelight dinners, and hot tubs. Next decade: it's day care, cup-o'-soup, and custody battles. Were we too busy to see it coming?

We've been busy, all right. Busy juggling a job and a family, crabgrass, crabby bosses, career changes, back-to-school, back to court, back to dating—and all in shrinking increments of time and money. Dozens of plates spinning simultaneously atop dozens of shaky, slender sticks. Neat trick for Chinese acrobats, but for us, it's a different story. We dart back and forth like crazed amateur-hour contestants, giving each plate a spin with only seconds to spare. Now and again we're late: a dish breaks. A lay-off. *Crash.* Trouble with the kids. *Crack.* No biggie. It's not the formal plates yet.

Then, a shattering event. A divorce. And one by one, the fine china falls. You feel helpless, hopeless, angry, out of control—on a good day. But there are bills to pay, so it's back to work. Part-time at first, then full-time, then no time. No time for a bubble bath. No time for a quiet walk or an afternoon with a good novel. No money for the latest perfume whiffed from a magazine while waiting for your son at the dentist. If you're a dad, there's no time for golf or racquetball or an afternoon (or evening) spent watching your favorite sports team. There are other priorities, such as food, shelter, and child care.

And no time for friends—married friends—who seemed to have mysteriously misplaced your phone number of late.

No, it's not your imagination. Life has changed all right. It's harder. Much harder. At the end of the day—when you're stressed, starved, and ready to collapse on the couch—there are still kids to feed and then dishes to be done. There are still baths to take. Laundry to fold. There is still homework to check. Bedtime stories to read. A checkbook to balance. Teens to track down. Rules to enforce. And love and attention to distribute evenly—precious little attention.

After all, you didn't volunteer to be divorced. You didn't sign up to become widowed. You didn't knowingly marry a rat, a liar, an abuser, a cheater, or a drunk. And if you did, you found out the hard way that love alone wouldn't change him (or her).

Now, suddenly, you're a single parent wondering how to keep your family feeling like a family. Perhaps for the first time. You may be also wondering what went wrong and "who is going to clean up this pile of porcelain known as my life?"

This book will provide the broom, the dust pan, and a new set of dishes in the form of special tools—tools that will empower you to reach your potential as successful single parents.

Take heart. I understand how bleak it looks at times, but it can be done!

FROM JELLY DONUTS TO TROUBLED TEENS

It's amazing how one thing leads to another. When I entered the police academy at twenty-one, single-parenting issues were the furthest thing from a mind filled with images of shiny badges, uniforms, chrome-plated pistols, and helping to keep the streets safe for law-abiding folk. Sounds corny, but I probably watched too many "Dragnet" reruns.

The academy taught us how to deal with a long buffet line weighted down with unappetizing human behavior, from robbery to rape. We even mastered the art of eating jelly donuts without staining our neatly pressed uniforms (at least some of the others did). There was no way, however, for the academy to have prepared us for the children. Teens too drunk to drive home. Children stopped for joyriding in a stolen car. Teenagers dead from a drug overdose or a gang-related shooting. As an idealistic rookie cop, it was a rude awakening for me—one that would forever change me as a person.

One of my first assignments was to interview children and teens who had been detained for various reasons. Naturally, I would ask the children whom we should call. All too often they would answer, "I only live with my mother, and she's not home." Or, "My parents are divorced."

Even a rookie could detect a pattern. Where were the parents? Working? Going to school? Drinking? I didn't have a clue. I only knew something was very wrong. But what could I do? After all, I was just one cop. I was married with my own children to worry about. Besides, I rationalized, my job was to catch the "bad guys"—wasn't it?

Although I did force my share of criminal types into early retirement over a ten-year career, I couldn't help but wonder about the path I had chosen. For one, I was gaining a dubious reputation of being a trouble magnet—someone always hip deep in unusual, if not dangerous situations. Bullets, knives, high-speed car chases. It didn't matter. If something serious was "going down," I was usually the closest unit to the hot spot. Believe me, it was a reputation I could have lived without.

A more compelling reason for re-thinking my career in law enforcement was my growing interest in working with troubled children and teens. Sure, I did what I could. I spoke at high schools about the dangers of drugs. I even got involved with the Big Brother Program. Still, I felt that I wasn't doing nearly enough.

SENSITIVITY STRIKES

Doing more meant returning to school. Instead of learning more about cops and robbers, however, I turned my attention to the field of psychology. Problem was, those studies were interfering with my job performance.

The more I studied, the more sensitive I became. Now sensitivity in a police officer is about as appropriate as pyromania in a fireman. It's not the most useful job skill. I found myself providing ten minutes of roadside therapy with each traffic ticket I wrote. "So tell me, sir, how do you feel about this ticket? Have I taken on a parental transference projection in your life?" To which the motorist might respond sarcastically, "Yeah, sure, officer, you're a real father to me!"

I was beginning to feel guilty about the traffic tickets I was writing —except for the most heinous of driving offenses. That was it! Time to leave the world of mace, handcuffs, and donuts. When I graduated from the psychology program I had been enrolled in I accepted a position as program director and counselor of an adolescent psychiatric treatment hospital.

I wondered what I would miss the most about police work? The camaraderie? The brotherhood? The satisfaction? You guessed it— the fresh donuts hitting the shelves every morning at 4:00 A.M.

"BIG GULPS" TO THERAPY

When I speak to groups of single parents, the audience is naturally curious about my parenting status. They ask if I'm a single parent too. The answer, thankfully, is no.

No, I'm not a single parent. Fact is, I'm in awe of single parents. I'm in awe over how one parent can manage to keep together what two parents often can't. (Then again, I'm in awe of anybody who can negotiate downtown traffic without spilling their "Big Gulps"—you know, those 44-ounce convenience store beverages designed to gush all over your trousers the second you hit a bump. Naturally, I arrive at my counseling office resembling a walking Rorschach test. For new patients, it's an excellent ground breaker. "Tell me, does this cherry stain remind you of anything? Perhaps your mother?" Long-term patients who know me simply shake their heads. They wonder why I'm not on the couch too.)

Single parents have what must seem at times an almost overwhelmingly difficult job. My task, as I see it, is to do what I can to make the job of single parenting a little easier for those who find themselves in that role, for whatever reason. I counsel clients in one-on-one sessions or in group sessions, lead seminars, conduct surveys, and write articles and books on the subject.

When I began conducting family group therapy sessions at the hospital, I saw a familiar pattern in the families who came for counsel—one I had seen before as a police officer. Very often, when both parents were supposed to attend the sessions, only one did—usually the mother. The more I looked into the matter, the more I could see that a high percentage of the families in the program were single-parent families.

It was time to dig deeper.

THE FIRST OF THE SINGLE-PARENT SURVEYS

There was plenty of circumstantial evidence to indicate that single parents could use some assistance. But I needed more proof. So, I pulled out my old uniform, jelly donut stains and all, and did a little detective work in the form of two surveys designed to get at the core of single-parent family issues.

The goal was to identify the specific wants and needs of children and teenagers as their families dove headlong into the divorce process. I was determined to smoke out the vulnerabilities and the potential hot spots facing single-parent families in the nineties.

I set out to develop a series of safeguards for single parents—steps that would help them and their children adjust more quickly to the enormous pressures of divorce, a course of action that would reduce the long-term emotional fallout that afflicts children and teenagers when their parents divorce.

The first single-parent family survey featured a series of questions probing several areas. Children and teens were asked some of the following questions:

- What was the most stressful aspect of your parents' divorce?
- Were you tempted to take drugs or drink alcohol during or after your parents' divorce?
- What kinds of problems did you struggle with most after your parents' divorce?
- What advice do you have for other children and teenagers whose parents are going through a divorce?

THE SIZE OF THE FIRST SURVEY
The survey examined 1,000 parents, adolescents, and children representing both two-parent and single-parent families. It was distributed at various inpatient psychiatric hospitals and outpatient therapy clinics.

Its purpose was to examine the short-term (two years or less) similarities and the warning signs of impending problems among children from single-parent families.

WHO PARTICIPATED IN THE FIRST SURVEY?
Of the 1,000 families who took part in the survey, 640 single-parent family members were identified and interviewed. The pool of respondents included the following:

- 288 single parents
- 291 adolescents (ages thirteen through eighteen)
- 61 children (ages eight through twelve)

The 352 adolescents and children who took part in the survey were further divided by sex, and by those who were currently receiving some form of treatment or counseling and those who were not. Interestingly enough, 68 percent of the children and adolescents we surveyed who were currently receiving treatment were males.

The predominance of males in the study to some extent reflects the fact that boys are generally more prone to become involved in activities that might call attention to their need for help. Those activities, along with the most common problems for girls, will be pointed out in later chapters.

The most logical locations for the surveys to be completed were at largely Christian outpatient counseling settings (therapists' offices) and inpatient hospital programs for teens. Those locations were selected because they provided an environment where families were learning about themselves. As a result, the participants were more open to discussing their life stories, successes, and failures.

Most of the families who participated in the survey lived in the the Southern California counties of Los Angeles, Orange, Riverside, and San Diego.

- ✓ 143 teens were interviewed while they were in hospital programs.
- ✓ 209 teens and children were interviewed while they were receiving outpatient counseling.

THE RESULTS OF THE FIRST SURVEY

Are children and teenagers from single parent families more likely to need emotional counseling than those from two parent families? Sadly, the answer was yes.

Of the 1,000 surveys that were completed, a total of 640 respondents were from single-parent families.

Several other critical facts surfaced when we tabulated the results of the survey.

- Nearly three out of four parents believed the divorce led to their children's serious emotional problems.
- Boys are at higher risk than girls of having severe emotional problems.
- Sixty-seven percent of teenage girls have their first sexual relations following the divorce of their parents.
- More frequent visitation plays a significant role in the emotional stability of the child.
- An emotional crisis is most likely to occur with children and teenagers within twenty-four months of the divorce.

Does that mean that all children and teens from single parent families are destined to have emotional problems? Absolutely not —and that is one of the reasons this book was written: to help single parents successfully negotiate the upbringing of their children even though only one parent resides in the home.

Why is it so important for single parents to understand the facts brought out by this first survey? Simple. Awareness make parents less likely to slip into complacency or, worse, denial during and after a divorce. The first survey clearly paved the way to a better understanding of what single parents and their children think and feel during the divorce process and postdivorce period.

THE SECOND SINGLE-PARENT SURVEY

The second survey examined 575 single moms and dads. The questionnaires were distributed to various single-parenting groups at churches and single-parent organizations throughout the state. Although the first survey had proved to be extremely helpful in learning how divorce affects children and teenagers, it did not address the unique needs from the perspective of the single parent. Gaining this valuable perspective was the goal of the second survey.

In this second survey, a series of questions was asked. Some of them are listed below.

- How significant a problem is it that your ex-spouse doesn't support your rules when the children are visiting?
- Do you find it hard to discipline your children now that you are a single parent?
- What do you do when you find your ex-spouse "puts you down" when he's with your children?
- What is it like to set limits and boundaries now that you are a single parent?

As a husband and father in a two-parent family, I could spend the next eighteen years writing books about my own parenting mistakes. If you've read *How to Avoid Alienating Your Kids in 10 Easy Steps* (Moody Press, 1993) you already know about some of the struggles we all endure as parents, regardless of our marital status.

But if you are a single parent the struggles you will experience as you raise your children will be even more intense and hard to overcome, if our survey results are at all accurate.

If you're a single parent and feeling alone, you have something in common with approximately 30 percent of all parents. That's right. Since 1970, single-parent families have mushroomed from 13 percent to 32 percent.[1]

Bookstores are jammed with materials designed to help moms and dads become better parents. But how much has been custom tailored to you, the single parent? Your issues are unique. Your children are unique. And so are many of the solutions.

For the last eight years, I've dedicated a great deal of my life to working with single parents—from focusing the majority of my private practice on single parent families to writing my first book on single parenting (Helping Single Parents with Troubled Kids, NavPress 1991; David C. Cook, 1993) to helping pastors start single-parent support ministries within their churches.

As a result of these efforts and those of countless other persons, there has been a heightened awareness throughout the country to the needs of single-parent families.

As you read this book, please keep one thing in perspective. Some of the healthiest, most well-adjusted children I've met have come from single-parent homes. Conversely, some of the most confused, angry, and misguided children and teens who ever walked into my office were from two-parent homes. Because you are a single parent, don't ever get the misconception that you are destined to encounter trials and struggles.

Empowering Single Parents will take an in-depth look at the issues surrounding single-parent families, including the problems parents stated were most important to them.

Sit down, buckle up, and prepare yourself for what I hope is an enjoyable and informative journey into the real-life world of single parenting—a journey that will help you meet your single parenting challenges head on, armed with that most wonderful asset, knowledge.

Note

1. Single Adult Ministries Journal, no. 89 (January 1992), 4.

· 1 ·

UNDERSTAND YOUR CHILD'S SECRET THOUGHTS ABOUT THE DIVORCE

Connie tore through her closet like someone who had just won the lottery but misplaced the ticket. Even the fake furs flew, as her bed filled with jeans, skirts, business suits from her working days, even a few peasant skirts, and a pair of platform shoes left over from the seventies. *It's got to be here somewhere,* she thought, widening the search area.

Seizing the opportunity, Thief, the family terrier, quickly carted off as many items as he could without getting caught. Finally, Connie found what she was looking for—the royal blue, sequined dress tucked safely away in the corner of the large walk-in closet, forever preserved in plastic and mothballs. She had planned to wear it on their ninth anniversary, but a last minute argument had ruined the occasion. David stormed out (nothing new), and the dress went back in the closet for good. Until now.

You should have wised up right then, dummy, she thought, inspecting the garment. How she loved that dress. It was aqua-blue. A long-sleeved sheath with a sweetheart neckline, padded shoulders, and a forgiving waistline. "Not bad," she nodded approvingly, as she turned in front of the mirror just in time to see Thief slinking off with one of David's expensive European dress shirts. "Stop, Thief," she said, forcing back a smile. "Well, okay, keep the shirt. You might as well take a tie to match, but keep your paws off my stuff, or you're homeless!"

The frenzied hunt had begun shortly after she had restricted her son to his room for talking back. Aaron, thirteen, had taken his parents' separation particularly hard and was becoming more difficult and defiant. She was still thinking about him when she glanced at the kitchen calendar. Scrawled in big, red, ominous letters were the words "15 YEAR HIGH SCHOOL REUNION—SATURDAY!"

"Nice going, lady," she muttered aloud, remembering that she had ordered the tickets about a month before the split. "What other torture can I sign up for this month—bungie jumping? Root canal?"

Connie was doing her best to hold her family—and herself—together. Her sense of humor had helped. How else could she deal with three children; a dog of dubious character; assorted hamsters, turtles, lizards; and a husband who, she reasoned, must have had his fingers crossed when he recited his part of the marriage vows.

During these painful days, Connie sometimes felt like a White House press secretary fielding questions from an openly hostile press —her kids. Every night, after coming home in a complete state of fatigue from her part-time job at the grocery store, she was confronted with a barrage of questions, no-holds-barred zingers, such as "When is Dad coming home, Mommy? Will we see him tomorrow? How come he hasn't called? Why are you so mad at Daddy?"

She often fantasized about answering them truthfully. "Kids, your father is a total jerk. In fact, if you looked up 'jerk' in the dictionary, your dad's picture would be there. Why do you think he hasn't called? He's the prince of jerkdom."

Instead, the answers she actually gave them were full of hope and reassurance. No matter how carefully she crafted her responses, though, they never seemed to satisfy her young, but insightful audience of Kimberly, three, Kelli, nine, and Aaron, thirteen. *Perhaps,* she thought, *it's because I haven't settled on all of the answers myself. After all,* she continued without much conviction, *it's only been two months. Things still might work out with the turtlehead. But first things first—what shoes am I going to wear to this party?*

It was the first time she had indulged herself since the separation. The upcoming reunion, though stressful, was a welcome and badly needed diversion.

Connie had made arrangements with her mother to watch the kids while she was out for the evening. The two had always enjoyed a close relationship. Connie had inherited her mom's good looks and youthful enthusiasm for life. Both were petite, with thick, reddish hair and eyes so turquoise that people often accused them of wearing tinted contacts. Unfortunately, she also received a good dose of her mom's overly passive, people-pleasing side. Which was one reason, she concluded, that she had been afraid to face up to the truth about her husband.

Saturday came much too soon for Connie. She worried about what she was going to say to her old friends. Would Ann be there? How could she tell her about the separation? Would people think she was a failure? *I should have married a guy from another high school,* she lamented to herself. *I should have married another person, period! Come on, get a grip. You're thirty-eight. You won't be the only one in the room with marital problems . . . but what if you are?*

"You look terrific, dear," her mother reassured her. "Where have you been hiding that dress?"

"Don't ask, mom," she laughed, looking over at Thief as if to say 'Keep your trap shut.'"

"It's absolutely perfect for you."

Her little fashion critics offered mixed reviews. "Hey, Mom, how come you're dressed up so funny?" Aaron asked. "Are you going out with Dad?"

"No, honey, I'm not. I'm going to my fifteen-year high school reunion—and I expect you to behave while I'm gone."

"Why?" he shot back. "You don't care about me anyway."

"That's not . . ."

Before she could finish, he ran from her room, out the kitchen door and into the backyard, and darted up the tall evergreen to his awaiting tree house. It was a private place where not even his sisters could reach him.

"We think you're bee-u-ta-ful," said Kelli, who had become quite the little fashion princess in her own right.

"Yeah, so do me," chimed little Kimberly.

She hugged them both and paused to look out the window to make sure that Aaron was okay. "Mom, please be sure he comes down soon. He's been so upset by all of this—nothing I do seems to help anymore."

Aaron was still on her mind as she looked for a parking space at the crowded reunion hall. *Maybe I shouldn't go. I should be with my kids. What kind of mother am I, anyway? Come on, girl, you've gone this far—don't bail out now. Posture. Smile. And don't chew your food with your mouth open.*

The hall was already jammed with people, none of whom she recognized. *That's fine,* she told herself. *Maybe I can just ease out of here without being noticed.* Just as she was beginning to wonder if she had gone to the right reunion, she heard her name being called. Actually, it sounded more like it was being broadcast over the PA system.

"Connie! Connie! Over here. No, over here!" boomed a deep, but familiar voice. She finally saw an outstretched arm waving wildly above the crowd, and then she saw the face—it was Ann. *Dear Ann.* The two had been so close throughout high school. Yet, except for Christmas cards, the friendship had been set aside—like signatures in a yearbook—after their senior year.

She never forgot the touching words Ann had written in her book on the last day of high school: "Forever joined at the hip . . .so don't pork out! Your very bestest friend, Ann."

The two embraced and Ann immediately launched the first wave of questions without pausing for an answer.

"How ya' doing? Where's David? You look great! How many children do you have now? How'd you stay so thin? Where's David?"

"Been better. Gone. Thanks. Three great kids. Stress. History," she fired back, laughing. "You're the same old Ann. Remember when Mr. Rearden limited you to only three questions a week in his history class?"

The two laughed until they were breathless.

"Well, Ann, David and I have split up, separated, for now anyway. I'm not sure what's going to happen. It's pretty scary with three little ones."

"I know . . . believe me, I know," Ann said seriously. "You know, Jack and I got divorced three years ago. I've only got one kid, Megan, a great little girl. Five. We're doing fine now, but it wasn't any fun then. Gotten any counseling yet?"

"No," Connie said, feeling a bit uncomfortable with the subject. "I'm trying to get through this on my own."

"But what about your kids? How are they holding up?"

"Well, Ann, they've had their moments. But they're young, resilient. They'll get over it—won't they?"

"I don't know, Con. Believe me, I'm no expert. At times, it's been pretty rough for me and Megan, and it helped having a third party who could listen to our problems and steer us in the right direction."

The two quickly switched topics to more carefree days.

They laughed some more and made a lunch date for the following week. On the way home, Connie thought about her friend's gentle suggestion to seek outside help. "Well, only if we really have to," she concluded.

CONNIE'S DILEMMA

In the days following the reunion, Connie had become increasingly bitter and openly angry about her situation. She remained resolute, however, in her resistance to the thought Ann had planted. Seeking an outsider to solve family problems was simply not acceptable to her—not for a Christian woman raised in a strong, private, and proudly self-reliant family.

"That's all I need," Connie said under her breath, nervously running her fingers through her newly styled hair. "Some pompous psychologist who will say my troubles began as an infant with a bad encounter with my oatmeal spoon. Next, we'll probably join hands and sing 'We Are the World.' Isn't that what therapy is all about? An hour's worth of happy banter, then my writing a check for seventy-five-bucks? Besides, David would never agree to therapy," she continued, switching gears. "Why should he? He's got it made with his Biffy, or Buffy—whatever her name is!"

She had even had a nightmare in which a psychologist insisted that David's girlfriend and Ann join them in therapy. During the session, the therapist had thrown up his hands and smiled. "You know what, Connie? David here is very fortunate to have found such a lovely young woman . . . obviously in her prime. Just look at her perfect skin, doe eyes, and those long legs. Well, why don't we just wish them good luck. What do you say?"

"Yeah, I agree," Ann had said. "Good luck, Dave and Booby!"

"Ann! Annie! What are you talking about? You're supposed to be my friend!" she had screamed in disbelief. Then she had shrugged. "Oh well, do you think the doctor is single?" She awoke from the dream sobbing in a pool of perspiration.

Connie was consumed with "the other woman" and trapped in a hopeless, destructive mine field of thought. When she wasn't mentally shish-kebabbing Buffy, she was roasting her husband at the stake. "What a total jerk!" she obsessed. "How could he walk away from his family for a drug store ice cream scooper? Where does he take her on dates? Sea World?"

She fantasized what the unlikely pair could possibly have in common, besides good sex. She assumed, sarcastically, that David was probably looking forward to the day when Buffy would be old enough to see a PG-13 movie without her parents.

"Isn't it just like men?" she sighed softly. "I looked like her, once. It's not my fault that giving birth to three children has done a number on my figure. Although I looked pretty good in my blue dress the other night! Plenty of guys were ogling big time. Oh, well, his loss."

She suddenly became aware of Aaron, who had been standing at the open doorway for several minutes. "Oh, hi, honey," she said, her face reddening as she wondered how much of her mindless ramblings her son had heard. "I didn't hear you come in. How long have you been home?"

"Mom, can I ask you something?"

"Sure punkin. Anything," Connie said, taking a deep breath in anticipation on what might be coming.

"I know why Daddy left us," the teenager said in low, somber tones. "He left us because I was having trouble in school."

"No, honey, he didn't . . ."

"Yes he did, Mom!" Aaron insisted, fighting back tears. "Remember how angry he was when he saw my last report card? He said he didn't know what he'd do if my grades didn't improve. They haven't, and I think Dad is so mad at me that he doesn't want to be here anymore. What are we going to do, Mom?"

Connie felt the tears welling up in her eyes too as Aaron looked down at the floor, hands in pockets, shoulders slouched dejectedly.

The two hugged and shared a good cry. It was a bittersweet moment for Connie. On one hand, she thanked God for helping Aaron to finally open up about his secret thoughts. On the other, she realized that she was woefully unprepared to ease his pain.

Ann was right, Connie thought, gently patting Aaron's tears with her sleeve. *We're going to need some professional help through this rough period. I can't go on being angry at the world.*

CONNIE'S CALL

It was one of those particularly draining days for a talk-show therapist, when every call seems to be from somebody really hurting emotionally.

Conducting successful therapy is difficult enough face-to-face in the warmth of your familiar office. It becomes particularly challenging, and downright frustrating at times, when you are attempting to help a faceless, expressionless stranger over the air, and you've only got a few minutes. Some days I feel as though I've made a difference. Other days . . . well, let's just leave it at that.

This particular morning had gotten off to a rocky start. Once again, I managed to dump my Big Gulp on the way to the office.

"Soggy pretzels floating in orange drink—now that's a treat!" I mumbled. "Maybe somebody's trying to tell me to make time for a normal lunch for once—a Big Mac, maybe."

I forced a smile as I walked past Carolina, my receptionist. She quickly assessed the situation. "Spilled your drink all over yourself again, huh?" she said, making no effort to conceal her laughter. "When are you going to learn, Greg?"

I thanked her for the encouraging words and reached into the top drawer of my desk, where I had stashed a large supply of moist towelettes. I was still scrubbing away when Carolina buzzed me. "Greg, there's a women on the line. Her name is Connie. She sounds pretty upset. Should I put her through?"

"Sure, go ahead. No, ask her if she could hold a minute, please."

"Those stains are real boogers to get out, aren't they, doctor?" Carolina said sarcastically, releasing the intercom button without giving me a chance to answer.

Connie sounded like a bright, capable mom who had simply maxed-out her ability to cope. She was terribly worried about her son, Aaron, who apparently was all over the map emotionally. One minute he would be angrily lashing out at her, or his siblings. The next, he would be hiding out in his room, or even up the tree.

"He was such a sweet, happy kid before the separation," Connie said. "What can I do to get him back? Should I just allow him time to adjust, Greg?" she asked, hoping that would solve everything.

"Sometimes, Connie, it's that simple," I told her. "Other times, waiting around for a child to adjust to an emotional trauma by himself can be very destructive. Contrary to what some people believe, God didn't create us to be totally independent. We were meant to be mutually dependent. In other words, we all need supportive, caring people in our lives. It makes us whole."

To illustrate, I suggested that she check out the book of Genesis. In Genesis 3:8–17 we see that God created a wonderful world for Adam. He gave purpose to Adam's life by promoting him to chief grounds keeper in the garden of Eden (we're talking dense shrubbery here, with weeds and no such thing as "weed 'n' feed"). Then, in verse 18, God makes an announcement: "And the Lord God said, 'It isn't good for man to be alone: I will make a companion for him, a helper suited to his needs.'"

"You see, Connie, it's clear that God doesn't recommend we allow Aaron to remain alone with his secret thoughts. Letting him escape into his own world with a knapsack full of anxiety and depression is inappropriate for anyone in crisis, especially a child."

"What can I do?" she asked.

I told her that every child is as unique as the situation itself. There are no sure-fire methods for handling angry and depressed children. We've got to take it step by step. A start would be to sit down with Aaron and try to determine how his personality adapts to stress, such as the shock of a separation.

"Do you think he would be open to speaking with me, Connie?" I asked.

"I'm not sure, Greg," she said. "I'll tell him that I'm seeing you to work some things out and that it might be helpful to me if he came along too. Aaron's always been open about his feelings, but not in regard to the separation. He's only opened up once, and never since. He seems to have shut down inside."

I suggested that Connie come in by herself for the first appointment, so that I could learn more about her son and the overall history of the family. "Kids get a little nervous about sitting through a session when they've become the main topic of conversation."

She agreed to the strategy.

THE CHILDREN'S ZOO

Although every child is unique, following their parents' divorce children usually respond in four basic ways, depending on their personality patterns. And they're all on display at the children's zoo of emotions—but don't feed the animals.

Pattern #1: The Lamb (Isolating Child)
Pattern #2: The Ostrich (Avoidant Child)
Pattern #3: The Bear (Acting-out Child)
Pattern #4: The Porcupine (Agitated and Depressed Child)

You're probably wondering why I've assigned an animal to each of these personality patterns. For starters, I've always found it to be an effective ground-breaking method with children. More important, asking a child to imagine himself as a specific animal helps both the child and me to determine his current emotional mind-set. Even the most forlorn or brooding child will usually play along long enough to pick an animal.

LAMBS:
THE ISOLATING CHILD

The isolating child usually describes himself as a lamb, deer, or some other docile animal that appears wary or frightened of its surroundings. Some kids throw you a curve and choose another critter, such as a turtle. Don't be misled. They're referring to the peaceful, plodding, lettuce-eating reptile—not the sword-wielding Mutant Ninji variety.

For these children, seeking isolation to avoid pain becomes the order of the day. The objective is clear. Stay away from the "Big Bad Wolf," who represents anything or anybody posing a threat to the protective barrier they have worked so hard to fortify.

They flee in terror when they spot a wolf approaching. They may even, as in Aaron's case, hide in a tree. Those branches may be on the uncomfortable side, but it's better than facing the wolves. They can't climb trees, can they?

A child or teen isolates as a form of self-protection. Of course, children don't own exclusive rights to this troublesome behavior. You probably know adults who regularly avoid facing reality by escaping into drugs, alcohol, extramarital affairs, or simply denial. Encouraging our children to become open about and comfortable with their feelings, fears, and insecurities is easier said than done, but if they are able to do this it will give them a leg up on the future.

Be careful not to view your child's isolating behavior as the sole problem. It is only a symptom of a deeper, underlying wound that could evolve into depression if not aggressively treated.

WATCHING CHILDREN WHO ISOLATE

Divorce may have little to do with isolating behavior. There are many events besides a divorce that can trigger this behavior in children and teens. Let's say, for instance, that a child is going through a slightly awkward stage as he enters kindergarten. His munchkin chums delight in pointing out any imperfections, especially the ones they can see—physical traits. They mercilessly tease the child about weight, height, or flapping ears that don't quite fit. Stinging remarks all, and sometimes they bring a child to the point of tears. Some children will say, "Enough," and go on the attack, figuring that the best defense is a good offense. Others will simply disengage, retreating into isolation as a means of emotional self-preservation.

As the child increasingly withdraws, he may opt to play by himself at recess. He might also prefer to work independently in the classroom rather than joining other groups. Later, he may limit himself to one friend at a time, or none at all. Parents, teachers, and others may describe this child as being a loner, but that's not how he began. Stay alert to warning signs and connected to children who isolate after an emotional trauma.

THE OSTRICH:
THE AVOIDANT CHILD

The next stop on our zoo tour is the ostrich habitat (calling it a cage is no longer politically correct).

The avoidant child will probably bristle at the idea of playing our animal association game. His emotional assembly line has become all too efficient at intellectualizing and processing things into tidy either-or packages. He'll snap, "I don't want to play this game! It's stupid!" Since he won't select an animal, we do the picking. "You're an Ostrich." Of course, he hates my choice . . . Oh, well, life's tough and you should have picked first.

The Ostrich is an impressive creature—two hundred pounds of giant, flightless bird with knobby knees and a long neck capped by a tiny head. (Exactly how my son describes his sister.) At first glance, he looks downright silly. Upon closer inspection, however, you begin to see a serious side, as he peers through large, glassy eyes.

During one of our family excursions to the zoo, we happened upon the ostrich compound. One fellow seemed particularly strange. He just stood there staring at me blankly (like my seven-year-old does after I've asked him to clean his room). Emotionless, tilting his head to one side, he seemed to say, "Okay, you called this meeting. Now what?"

The avoidant child and the ostrich have several things in common. Both appear to be serious, stately and calm—almost too cool, though they can clown around at times. Both are skilled at concealing their emotions (at least the ostrich was the day I caught my son hurling peanuts at his beak). They part company in one surprising area, however. The avoidant child will bury his head in the sand (rhetorically speaking) at the first sign of pain. The ostrich won't. That's right: despite its press clippings, when he's in pain the original Big Bird merely flops to the ground in a prone position, neck outstretched. The avoidant child would never chance leaving himself so vulnerable.

LAUGHING IT OFF

The avoidant child or teen often minimizes the seriousness of stressful situations by laughing in the face of pain. These children and teens live their lives "whistling past the graveyard," as the old expression goes—a graveyard filled with emotions. They want people to believe that nothing phases them. When asked how he feels about the "split," the avoidant child might answer glibly, "What's the big deal, I knew Mom and Dad weren't getting along."

His goal? To fool everybody, including Mom and Dad, into believing he is handling the trauma in a mature way. His parents might even brag, "We're so proud of the way he's taken everything that's happened."

It's up to the single parent to help her (or his) children understand that the pain they are feeling is unavoidable. It's not fun, but it is part of the grieving process and needs to be addressed openly. If the process is not addressed openly, the avoidant child will eventually pay the price for burying his emotions. It may take months or even years, but the emotional fallout will end up blanketing every aspect of his life.

Remember, once this child becomes firmly entrenched in his hiding style, it is difficult to pry him loose. It will require an open and honest environment rich with love and support.

THE BEAR:
THE ACTING-OUT CHILD

The acting-out child, like the isolating child, also suffers from a feeling of powerlessness and insecurity over the changes taking place in his family. Unlike the isolating child and the avoidant child, however, this kid never ducks a fight. He springs into battle with the aggressiveness of an gnarled grizzly bear. Instead of powerful claws and sharp fangs, he uses temper tantrums, hurtful comments, or physical acts to gain a sense of control, while effectively using his anger to keep at a safe distance.

His behavior isn't surprising when you consider where his anger and pain likely originated—from watching a typical parental, predivorce pattern. This pattern usually consists of arguing, disengaging, arguing, and then disengaging once again. Kids see that and reason, "Why be subjected to more hurt when you can inflict some of your own?"

When the acting-out child is asked to select an animal with which to identify, he usually chooses a powerful animal such as a bear. Not a happy Yogi Bear, but a big, tattooed, ill-tempered bear with a thorn in its foot. If anyone gets close enough to remove the thorn (his emotional pain), the child attacks him and makes him the lunch of the day.

Sadly, this big, ugly bear secretly yearns for someone to remove the thorn, but his survival instincts take over, and he lashes out at his rescuer.

Moms and dads must hold their ground during these attacks. Lovingly look that nasty old bear straight in the eyes. Tell him you love him and will be there for him. It's difficult, but it works. Once the bear understands your intention—to remove his pain without inflicting more—he will most often allow you access to his secret thoughts without having you for breakfast or retreating into the woods.

THE PORCUPINE:
THE AGITATED AND DEPRESSED CHILD

The agitated (anxious) and depressed child often responds to our animal exercise by saying, "Do we have to?" and insisting that he can't really see himself as an animal anyway. In reality, his resistance to playing along is part of the answer.

To expedite the process, I sometimes say, "I've got just the animal for you."

After a few moments of silence, curiosity gets the better of him and he says, "Okay. What?"

"A porcupine," I answer.

"Why a porcupine?" he protests, fighting back a slight grin.

"Well, porcupines are sort of cute, right? And you're sort of cute, aren't you? But they're also misunderstood little creatures."

"What do you mean, misunderstood?"

I tell him about their chubby little cousins, the beavers, who are popular with everyone. "But who really understands the porcupine? People see those razor sharp quills and back off. But you know what? Porcupines want to be held and cuddled just like all of God's creatures." I conclude by asking if he's ever seen a porcupine in the stuffed animal section of the toy store? Never? "Probably because nobody would buy him." (That usually gets 'em.)

Remember, beneath those angry quills is a warm and cuddly kid who desperately needs love and acceptance. But his ability to inflict emotional pain and intimidate others keeps everyone at arm's length.

In contrast to the ostrich (who hides) and the bear (who attacks) the porcupine's anxiety reaches such a level that he has no choice but to lash out at those closest to him in an attempt to be noticed—to feel alive. Once he has stoked up on attention, regardless of its negative nature, he retreats into the safe confines of his depression. This destructive cycle is repeated when his isolation and fear again become overwhelming, forcing him out of hiding to "stick it" to somebody again. We call this pattern *agitated depression,* a term that describes the child's vacillation between withdrawing and attacking.

In dealing with it, the therapist must first address the child's severe emotional confusion. Not only is he angry, agitated, and anxious, he is also depressed. On one level, he wants and needs to connect with others. On another, he's compelled to run and hide from the help he needs.

The porcupine syndrome takes top honors as the most troublesome and difficult of all trauma-related childhood patterns to correct. With diminished impulse controls, this agitated and depressed child easily engages in self-destructive behavior. This intense condition is technically known as *anger turned inward.* Children and teens who experience suicidal tendencies nearly always display this brand of anger.

Connie, fighting back tears, said somberly, "Aaron fits the fourth pattern, doesn't he?"

"Yes, from what you've told me, he does," I said, before immediately turning to the positive side. "The good news is that you've addressed the situation early. We need to help him learn to understand his secret thoughts and feelings and not be afraid to discuss them."

A PARENT'S RESPONSE TO A CHILD'S GRIEF

How many times have you heard these expressions applied to children in stressful situations?

- Kids are resilient.
- Problems don't affect them the way they do adults.
- Kids bounce back faster because they're younger.
- He'll be back to his old self in no time, just wait and see.

Although there are elements of truth to each of those sweeping statements, they are used more often to rationalize guilt—guilt over feelings of helplessness; guilt over their own selfishness; guilt over not working harder to understand their children's emotions; guilt over their inability to guide their kids through traumatic events because they too are caught up in their own grief.

Fact is, anyone who experiences an emotionally traumatic event, regardless of age, must go through a grieving process. The emotional penalty for avoiding this process is severe. (We'll discuss those penalties in later chapters.)

Fortunately, once a child cracks through denial, he is able to process his grief more quickly and efficiently than an adult. The reason? Adults have had a substantial head start in constructing and reinforcing their defenses systems. It sometimes takes a bulldozer to dig an adult out of denial and force him into the grieving process.

THE POWER OF GRIEF

Whether our grief stems from the loss of a loved one, a financial loss, the loss of a job, or the loss of a parent through divorce, our need to grieve is a natural and powerful God-given response to pain. It enables us to experience the pain fully and move past it, hopefully as a stronger, more compassionate person. Denial only deepens our pain, forestalls the inevitable, and cripples our development as Christians. Still, many children, teens, and adults frequently find ways to short-circuit the grieving process.

Adults may turn to alcohol, overeating, prescription medication, attachment in a compulsive way to church or work, overspending, unhealthy relationships, and even suicide. Children, as we have observed, often turn inward or lash out. Unfortunately, older children and teens often use the same destructive methods for dealing with grief many adults do—not a wise choice. I wonder where they learned those escape routes?

A LEARNED BEHAVIOR

Grief, like nearly every other type of human behavior, is learned through observation. If parents attempt to keep their thoughts, feelings, and emotions concealed from the kids—for whatever reason—how are they supposed to learn how the grieving process works? MTV?

THE STAGES OF CHILDHOOD GRIEF

Try thinking of the stages of childhood grief as stepping stones in a vast garden. The exposed side is reasonably neat and free of debris. A few stray leaves, maybe, but easily swept clean. The bottom side is an entirely different story. It's usually crusted thick with mud and unidentifiable gunk. Think of that gunk as your child's depression—pain and anger he has kept hidden from view. In short, he has failed to begin the grieving process.

Begin by turning over those seemingly perfect stones and taking a closer look. Look for these elements stuck in the gunk:

- Stepping Stone #1: Shock and denial
- Stepping Stone #2: Anger turned outward
- Stepping Stone #3: Plea bargaining (the "if only" stage)
- Stepping Stone #4: Sadness and depression
- Stepping Stone #5: Resolution and forgiveness

STEPPING STONE #1:
SHOCK AND DENIAL

Our need to grieve works much as the instrument panel on the dashboard of the family minivan. When the "Check Oil" light flashes red, we have two options. The first and most logical choice is to pull into the nearest service station and check the oil, right?

The second option involves what most of my patients call "The dreaded 'D' word," which stands for *denial*—probably the most formidable of all defense mechanisms.

The motorist in denial will ignore the oil light completely. After all, what if the car really did need oil? He couldn't face that because it would take so long to stop and find a service station. Or, even better, he might tape a piece of cardboard over the light. "See no evil, hear no evil." In this case, his denial precludes the possibility that there could be a serious problem with his van. "Probably just a defective idiot light," he reasons. We all know the eventual outcome. A little problem that might have required a few bucks, and a couple of quarts of oil, escalates into a blown engine and a nasty bill. Denial doesn't pay!

Many children and teens take their first step toward denial when they notice that their parents are no longer getting along. They've undoubtedly been worried that they might spilt up for some time. Now, those fears are becoming reality. Some children hide their pain better than others, while others check into denial for extended stays. Thankfully, some kids move rapidly through denial and into the grieving process. A child's ability to work through denial is the outcome of the interaction of several elements.

- **The child's personality**

Some children, like adults, are simply better equipped to deal with stress and trauma than others. It seems to be a product of their character or personality.

Kids who deal directly with pressure, rather than retreat into denial, often have a higher tolerance for stress. Most children learn stress management by seeing their parents effectively deal with stress.

• The child's ability and willingness to communicate feelings

Children who have been raised in an open environment, where feelings are freely shared and openly discussed, have a greater ability to communicate their own grief.

A parenting prescription. Even moms and dads who, prior to the divorce, were less than open and honest about their feelings can make adjustments. Once a child sees his parent, or parents, responsibly releasing pent-up feelings, they will feel more comfortable in doing the same. That's why therapy is so effective following divorce. A skilled therapist will elicit those feelings from both parent and child. From there, both the parent and the child can work to reproduce that experience in their daily life outside the therapy office.

• An emotional support system

A child comes into the world in a dependent position. He needs his mom to meet all of his most basic needs—nourishment, love, clean diapers. If, for some reason, mom is unwilling or unable to care for the child, we can expect that he will suffer irreparable emotional damage due to his sense of threatened security.

Most child psychologists agree that the worst time for a child to suffer the loss of his mother is between the ages of birth and twenty-four months. Between those ages the child is totally dependent on the primary care giver for life and emotional support.

All of us, and especially children, are created to share close relationships. Isolation, or the fear of separation and abandonment, is a terrifying experience for a child. Even older children and teens, as well as adults, experience trauma, anxiety, and fear when their parents divorce.

The child may also view his relationship with the remaining parent as somewhat tentative due to his recent loss. In an attempt to safeguard this remaining relationship, the child may go into emotional hiding to avoid dumping his problems on someone he perceives to be unstable, stressed out, or incapable of helping.

A parenting prescription. There are times when a child finally opens up to a parent, only to discover that he has inadvertently tossed gasoline onto the fire. A mother may break into tears when the child makes such statements as "I sure miss Daddy," or, "Why did you and Dad break up, anyway?" If these spontaneous statements are met with anger or make the parent upset, the child might quickly dash back into denial about his feelings.

Some parents are savagely overt in conveying a sense of unapproachability. They react harshly to the child's neediness, instead of seeing his questions as a cry for reassurance and comfort. They view questions as criticism or a reminder of their own anger. "Don't you see that I have my own problems?

Catch yourself before you fall into the reaction trap. This trap is set when your own stress and insecurities drive you into an emotionally vulnerable position. When your child comes to you out of innocent neediness, be careful that you're not emotionally tapped out, unable to give any more. Each time you send your child away without reinforcing his needs, he becomes still needier. He not only leaves emotionally empty-handed, but you feel even worse over your insensitivity and lack of tolerance.

Look for signs of your child's neediness. When he turns to you to replace some of the self-assurance, self-esteem, and security he has lost, give him what he needs. Continually reassure him that he's okay and is still loved. Consistency is an essential element needed by all children, especially those in single-parent families.

STEPPING STONE #2:
ANGER TURNED OUTWARD

The single-parent surveys I conducted revealed some interesting facts about children and teens and their anger throughout the divorce process.

The term *anger turned outward* describes a myriad of actions and emotions. At the less severe end (some single parents might disagree with this categorization) of the anger scale is arguing, swearing, or harsh, angry words directed toward a parent. Acting-out may also take the form of refusing to obey household rules.

The chart below was taken from the single-parent family survey. It documents the most common areas of the anger-turned-outward syndrome. For each category, I have given the percentage of young people who indicated they struggled with that particular problem:

Category	Percentage of Teenagers	Percentage of Children
• Cut school often	78%	12%
• Felt they just hated everyone	66%	62%
• Shoplifted	76%	68%
• Stole from others	66%	41%
• Fighting	61%	18%
• Ran away from home	21%	8%
• Hurt animals	5%	2%
• Wanted to physically hurt others	62%	37%

As you can see, *anger turned outward* includes a wide assortment of behavior. Some of this behavior is relatively moderate in severity, such as cutting school or shoplifting. Other behavior in this category incorporates violence, indicating the desperate thoughts of some children and teens. Remember, these behaviors are generally seen as misguided ways that children and teens vent their angry, hurt feelings.

A parenting prescription. If you come to the understanding that your child may be feeling insecure and out of control, you can more readily understand his impulse to act out in anger. He is unconsciously asking for someone to listen to him and help him put structure back into his scattered world. The structure he is craving has the meaning to him of increased love, attention, security, limits, and boundaries.

Anger turned outward is often a child's way of venting his confusion and pain over a loss. Since many children (including teens and adults) are unable to work through their hurt and angry feelings in appropriate, nonaggressive ways (prayer, conversation, exercise, relationships) they naturally gravitate to inappropriate methods. In addition, all people, and especially children, feel as though they must attach blame somewhere for their painful experiences. Anger is a way of targeting that blame.

To a child, lashing out at others seems like a workable solution, albeit a temporary one. It allows steam to escape from the pressure cooker—just enough to keep it from exploding. In time, though, the pressure will steadily increase until it blows again.

When you begin to notice the pressure building within your child's temperament, try a technique called *empathic listening*. Empathic listening (listening with empathy) is a useful technique to employ with children and teens because it allows pressure to escape gradually.

Be cautious not to confuse empathy with sympathy, which is just feeling sorry for your kids. Empathic listening requires you to identify with, or put yourself in, your child's place in order to understand how he is experiencing his feelings. You may ask questions or make statements. "I sure can understand how upset you might be feeling. I know you were looking forward to visiting your dad this weekend." These types of statements convey your empathy and help to defuse the child's anger.

On the other hand, an irresponsible statement will do harm. "I don't know why you expect your dad to do *anything* he says. I've learned my lesson" may be the truth, but it will only fuel the child's fires of grief and anger.

Empathic listening should be followed directly by closure. In a positive conversation, closure might come in the form of a question: "Would you feel better if you called your dad and asked him to help you understand the change in plans." Or, "I wonder if a letter explaining your feelings might help your dad understand your feelings better in the future."

STEPPING STONE #3:
PLEA BARGAINING (THE "IF ONLY" STAGE)
In this stage of the grieving cycle we often find children trying to bargain with God, and anyone else in authority, for that matter. These are the "if only" feelings. "If only things would be like they were . . ."

In this stage the child has moved from a position of shock and denial to anger over the divorce. Once he sees that his anger has not aided him in effecting change, he decides to appeal to a higher power. The child's secret hope and prayer usually contain the words "If only." "If only my parents get back together, I promise I'll . . ." Or, "If only my dad would visit me more, I promise . . ."

It is not uncommon for children and teens to begin pulling away from God and the church during this stage. Why? Since their "if only" prayers have gone unanswered, God must now view them differently from their Christian friends. Or, perhaps, there isn't any God at all. If there were, the child reasons, why would he have allowed all this to happen? The child becomes so overwhelmed with feelings of hopelessness and despair that he sinks into depression. Not only has he lost his family, as he knew it, but God as well.

A parenting prescription. It is critical that you sit down with your child and walk him through various Scriptures that will help him understand God's will in our lives.

Explain that things we have wished and prayed wouldn't happen, sometimes happen anyway. Let him know that God sees the big picture and has a plan for us all, even though we may not have a clue why these troubles are going on.

It might be of some comfort to your children to point out that Mary, Jesus' own mother, was, for all intents and purposes, a single mom for an extended period of time.

How can we say this? From the time Jesus was twelve years old, we hear no mention of Joseph. In Acts 1:14, following Jesus' ascension into heaven, we read, "They all joined together constantly in prayer, along with the women and Mary the mother of Jesus, and with his brothers." Jesus' earthly family were present along with Mary, but without mention of Joseph. We could make the assumption from this evidence that Mary was indeed a single mom.

Point out to your children that, like Mary, we often encounter hardships along the way. Mary did not lose even an ounce of faith in God, even after witnessing her son's crucifixion. Undoubtedly, Mary had mixed emotions at that time, but she understood that her grief over her loss certainly didn't mean she had lost her good standing with God.

It is also important to help your child understand that God has given each of us the gift of independent thinking and free will. Certainly, He could have reorchestrated the events leading up to the divorce to produce a different outcome, but that would have been tampering. He has chosen to allow us to make our own choices, including the wrong ones. And that's how we learn—from our mistakes.

Help your child to understand that just because he didn't see an immediate answer to his prayer, that doesn't mean God no longer loves him. Pray with your child that both of you will continue to remember that God is sovereign in your lives and that it is His will and timing that we are called to be obedient to, not our own.

Finally, teach your child the message of hope contained in Romans 8:28. "And we know that God causes all things to work together for good to those who love God, to those who are called according to His purpose."

STEPPING STONE #4:
SADNESS AND DEPRESSION

In the grieving cycle, sadness and depression are the result of your child's anger turned inward. First, he denied the divorce. Then he became angry and lashed out at others. His attempt to find someone to intervene on his behalf failed too. Now, coming full circle, he has internalized his feelings. That means he has experienced a full range of emotions, including sadness, fear, grief, anger, depression, anxiety, helplessness, and a sense of vulnerability through his aloneness.

Although this is the most emotionally troublesome part of the grieving cycle, keep in mind your child's emotions, now turned inward, are a necessary part of the natural progression of grieving.

Let's look at the survey results for the most common signs and symptoms of anger turned inward.

Category	Percentage of Teenagers	Percentage of Children
Depression *	35%	35%
Smoked marijuana	69%	38% **
Taken other drugs	43%	18% **
Used alcohol	82%	48%
Had suicidal thoughts	69%	38%
Developed an eating disorder	11%	4%

* These depressions were not merely light feelings of sadness, but critical levels of depression. This will be discussed further in chapter 8.

** Predominantly older children between the ages of eleven and twelve.

A *parenting prescription.* Anger turned inward is often a child's way of erecting barriers to further pain by allowing him to escape inside his depression and emotional isolation.

If you look at the categories above, the common link to each of them is that they produce a numbing (or protective) effect on feelings. Each of them enables the child or teen to avoid dealing with the true source of his anger—which is pain, vulnerability and its accompanying tension.

You don't have to be a rocket scientist to see that prying a child loose from his emotional bondage is going to be easier said than done. Why? Because on the other side of numbness is pain. That's why he chose numbness in the first place.

The secret is in making the intolerable tolerable. That means you need to identify what's causing your child the most emotional pain, and bring it into the light. For instance, if you've noticed that your child is spending an inordinate amount of time secluded in his room since the divorce, it's time to learn what's behind this behavior. In other words, what is the attraction to isolating in his room? You may empathetically say, "I've noticed you've been alone a lot lately. Sometimes I wish I could hide in my room too. Then I realize even though it seems safer, being alone really doesn't make me feel any better. What I wanted was to be closer to you and to others, and I realized I couldn't do it while hiding from everyone. Is this maybe how you've been feeling too?"

Always try to bring your feelings into the conversation, while being cautious not to overwhelm him with deep messages or your own depression. Instead, let him see that you share many of the same feelings that he is experiencing, which makes you qualified and able to comfort him. In times of grief, despair, and depression, we are all looking for someone to understand what we are feeling and to help us feel better.

STEPPING STONE #5:
RESOLUTION AND FORGIVENESS

If I could make one point, and make it stand out in your mind, it would be that your child cannot experience resolution and forgiveness through isolation. Both require the act of reconnecting emotionally with others in order to thrive.

Christians often hear advice from well-intentioned friends to "read the Scriptures to get over pain," or, "pray harder and let go of the sin in your life and you'll feel better." Although there is no denying the fact that God's words are absolutely all we need in life, we must also acknowledge how difficult they are to apply, at times.

Your child needs to feel the Scriptures come to life through your care and comforting. God didn't intend for us to be solitary creatures. From Genesis to Revelation, God makes it obvious that He never intended for us to be alone.

Getting to a place of resolution, followed by forgiveness, requires redirecting your child's way of thinking. In the section that follows are steps you can take to help your child move toward forgiveness.

HELPING YOUR CHILD
MOVE TOWARD FORGIVENESS

LETTING GO OF ANGER

For both adults and children, the opposite of experiencing emotions is denial. Anger, especially for children, is an all-consuming emotion. When anger is present, there is little capacity for anything else, especially forgiveness.

Help your child process his anger by encouraging him to share his innermost hurts and insecurities. Remember, anger is a child's way of protecting himself against future hurts.

UNDERSTANDING THE TRUTH

Might as well face it, part of being a child is feeling omnipotent or all-powerful. That's why, like Aaron, children tend to make the divorce their problem and assume blame even though that concept is incomprehensible.

Help your child to understand his role in your divorce. Be sure he realizes how powerless he is to solve them. Above all, talk to him about change and adaptation in positive terms while reinforcing your love and other consistent aspects of his life.

Although we'll discuss this point in further detail in later chapters, helping your child to understand the truth—that things are going to be different, but okay—is very important. Discuss, in age-appropriate language and detail, the fact that changes are coming. Help him to see that those changes really only affect his external world and that he isn't to blame for your marital problems. Make sure he knows that his internal world (his sense of security, well-being, and your love) won't change at all.

RESISTING BLAME

The act of blaming causes children (and adults) to remain "stuck" in the anger-turned-outward position we discussed earlier. Most people want to attach fault (or blame) to others when things go wrong. It's a natural, yet unproductive, means of trying to deal with stress and problems. Adam blamed Eve, Eve blamed the serpent, and for all we know, the serpent probably blamed his mother.

Help your child to see that life's circumstances can actually be "nobody's fault," so there's no point in blaming.

TAKING PERSONAL RESPONSIBILITY FOR HAPPINESS

Consider communicating a message of taking personal responsibility for happiness to your children. Most children (ages five to ten) can understand the point that ultimately we are all responsible for our own happiness. We can choose to be miserable, doubting, vindictive, and blaming. Or we can choose to be happier, to forgive, and to get on with our lives.

Often, communicating this healthy message of ownership over feelings provides a shot in the arm for someone who is feeling helpless and victimized. "You mean I can choose to feel better?"

THE ANTIDOTE TO FEAR

Throughout Scripture, our reliance on one another is compared with interrelationship in the plant kingdom. When we plant a tree, we nurture and care for it by tending to its special needs. We search for just the right spot to dig the hole: a place with the right amount of sunlight and just enough shade. We worry about frost, fertilizer, and how much water the plant requires to thrive.

Plants left unattended generally wither and in time die. A child needs the same psychological tending to thrive and grow strong. If not, his emotional growth will suffer.

Following a divorce a child's secret thoughts revolve around his fears of abandonment, isolation, and being unloved. With this in mind, it's your responsibility as a single parent to provide him with the antidote for his fears. It's a simple solution, really: a mixture of love, nurturing, and a sense of security.

Paul wrote in Ephesians 4:17 that God created us to be rooted and established in love. Children, like trees, share a basic need to feel a sense of security through attachment. It is this simple antidote to emotional pain that allows both children and adults to tolerate the pain of a sometimes intolerable world.

· 2 ·

DEVELOP A
WELL-BALANCED
SINGLE-PARENTING STYLE

IN SEARCH OF PERFECT PARENTS
(AND OTHER MYTHS)

I should have seen it coming! Connie thought, half laughing, half crying, as she signed the final divorce papers. *I should have known our marriage was in the Dumpster when he agreed to use coupons at the grocery store—double savers, no less. He had always flatly refused in the past, saying he wasn't "comfortable with coupons." Some macho nonsense, like "real men don't eat quiche." He must have been feeling guilty about the "D" Bomb he was about to drop. I should have whipped up some quiche that night.*

By today's tabloid standards the settlement was dull at best. David got a younger woman, a new apartment, a red sports car, and a chance to be "Disneyland Dad" to the kids every other weekend. *He's always been a better hero than father, anyway,* Connie thought. She got the house (leaky roof, shrinking equity, and all), a tuckered-out Taurus wagon, and advice from her attorney: "Get a better paying job." She also received custody of the children, which made her feel like the clear-cut winner in the deal.

Attempting to remain upbeat, she reasoned, *At least David will be staying in town to be near the children. They still need their dad.* Secretly, though, she would have preferred that he relocate a little further away, the planet Mercury, perhaps. *Real hot, no oxygen. Perfect! Let's see if Bambi can have a good-hair day there!*

With the papers signed, stamped, and placed in a preaddressed envelope (at least he could have picked up the postage) Connie walked briskly to the corner mailbox and nervously shoved the packet into the slot. "Good riddance to bad rubbish," she said aloud, eyes locked on the opening to be sure the envelope wouldn't pop out the second she turned her back.

She was filled with mixed emotions. There was the relief of knowing that a rocky, sometimes volatile marriage (one she had worked so hard to save) had finally ended. There was also abject terror at the thought of being a single mom. Connie walked home in a total fog, barely noticing several neighbors who cheerfully greeted her along the way.

She opened the front door and reality struck. *You really did it, Connie,* she told herself. *Stood your ground. Maintained your dignity. Unloaded the bum. Yup, you really did it, all right. Now we're alone. I'm alone.*

"Mommy, Mommy, are you okay? You look scared," said Kelli, throwing her arms around her neck. "Thanks sweetie. How did you know I needed a monumental hug right about now?"

"Hey, where's my hug?" demanded Connie's mom, who was staying at the house for a few days while her daughter made repeated trips to the attorney's office to work out the final settlement. "Dear, I've made arrangements for somebody to come out and take care of this stopped-up drain. I hope you don't mind."

"Mind? Are you kidding, Mom? I don't know what I would have done without you. You're the best. I know you've got a million things to do at home. I'll be fine. I'll call you later. We'll go shopping, or something."

"A shopping date next week will be just fine, thank you. I'll see you later. Bye-bye kids!"

Well, this is it, Connie thought as her mother drove off. *We're really alone now. Time for a family meeting.* "Kelli, Kimberly, Aaron!" she called in her best public address announcer's voice. "Everybody on the couch! I need to talk to you guys. You too, Thief."

The two girls fidgeted, then roughhoused with the frisky terrier while they waited for Aaron. "Where's your brother?" Connie asked the girls. "He's not back up that tree, is he, Kimberly?"

"No Mom, he hasn't gone up there for a long time. I don't know why. Maybe, umm, because of the Vampire bats he says are up there. I looked, but I didn't see any bats, just some little sparrows . . . Maybe he was just trying to scare me."

Just then, Aaron came downstairs. "Can't I even go to the bathroom without being hassled," he said with mock irritation.

"Fine, that's a quorum," Connie declared. "I hereby call this family session to order."

"What's a quorum, Mommy?" Kimberly asked.

"A quorum means that the people I love the most are all in the same room.

"I just wanted you guys to know, well, how much I love you."

"You called us together for that? I'm going back upstairs," Aaron said. "When's dinner, anyway?"

"Well, I guess this meeting is adjourned." Connie laughed. "How about pizza and video games at that place where the big hairy rat hangs out?

There were smiles and high fives all around.

With the kids in bed, and the better part of thirty dollars spent on pizza or plunked into video games, Connie's stomach began to churn. *Maybe it's just the pepperoni—or the thirty bucks!* But she knew better. It was the prospect of going home to officially begin her new life as a single mom.

I wonder if I can handle it? she thought, seriously doubting her parenting ability for the first time. *David may have been a cheat, a liar, and a skunk, but at least he was around to help a little.*

Her stomach was turning somersaults as she began to consider some of the difficulties she would be facing.

How can I possibly go back to work full-time, and still be a good mom?

Will David make his child support payments?

Can I continue making the mortgage payments?

Who's going to make sure that Aaron gets to baseball practice when I have to work late?

Who's going to work with him on his curveball now?

What kind of environment will the kids be exposed to when they're visiting with David? Do I want my children hanging out at a place where my Christian family values are not supported? I don't know Bambi, but how can I trust her? Not after what she did to help break apart my family.

Still seething, Connie sipped her hot tea and wisely decided to call an emotional time-out for the evening. What was it Scarlet O'Hara said in *Gone with the Wind?* "I'll worry about that in the morning."

DEVELOPING YOUR SINGLE-PARENTING STYLE

"Don't worry," I told Connie. "Single parenting is a snap. True, you're going to have to run faster, jump higher, and leap tall buildings in a single bound. And the coyote is going to catch the roadrunner too."

Mission accomplished. She actually laughed.

"Seriously, I know you feel as though the weight of the world is on your shoulders, but please don't make the mistake of many newly single parents—attempting to be all things to your kids. You'll only run yourself into the ground—and possibly into a padded cell in the process. You are only one person. Guess what? You were only one person before the divorce too. Somebody once said that God couldn't be everywhere, so He made mothers. This is an excellent time to strengthen your trust in God, because He truly *is* everywhere."

It was vital for Connie (as it is for all single parents) to understand the importance of developing and defining a consistent, practical, parenting style. For married couples, doing this is mainly a matter of making their individual parenting styles gel as part of a team effort, with one style complementing the other. But when a divorce occurs, the custodial parent becomes the CEO of the family. It is crucial that you maximize your effectiveness by honing your style of parenting.

DON'T LOSE SIGHT OF THE PARENT YOU WERE

Many single moms and dads immediately junk their former parenting styles the second the divorce becomes final. An easy-going, even-tempered parent suddenly turns into a tyrant, controlling the children as though she were a traffic cop at a busy corner. A fire-breather turns into a lamb. Big mistake. Don't overcompensate just because you are now single. Do your best to remain the same wonderful parent you were prior to the divorce. (You weren't that wonderful, you say? Read on, help is on the way.)

RESIST THE TEMPTATION TO BECOME A "FIXER PARENT"

Many newly single parents have an overpowering urge to become a "Fixer Parent." The fixer is usually a hardworking, deeply committed parent who, before the divorce, had his or her parenting act together. Then the split occurs, and seemingly overnight, panic sets in. She (or he) becomes convinced that the family will unravel if everything isn't perfect. She loses confidence in her proven parenting style, searching constantly for any loose threads in the family tapestry. In the end, parents like this wind up driving themselves—and their kids—crazy.

Single moms and dads should strive for a balanced approach to parenting, one that incorporates the successful aspects of their former parenting style while taking into account their new family position. The trick is to find a single-parenting style that suits your personality (the person you are now, not the married person you once were). Any attempt to drastically change your core parenting style or adopt a new parenting style will be like asking a sumo wrestler to try pole vaulting. You will probably fall on your face (or another part of your anatomy). Does that mean there's no wiggle room for improvement? Not to worry: there's plenty of room for improvement in most parenting styles.

Let's begin by visiting two of the most troublesome single-parenting styles and the problems they leave in their wake. Next, we'll introduce you to the star of our story, the Balanced Single Parent. In the final analysis, though, it's up to you to integrate the characteristics of the Balanced Single Parent into your own style.

SINGLE PARENT STYLE #1:
THE OVERLY CONTROLLING SUPERPARENT

The most effective way to drive a wedge between you and your children is to try to become "the sun and the moon" to them. Meet the person I affectionately call the *Overly Controlling Superparent.*

How do seemingly normal moms and dads turn into such a person? To understand the mentality of the Superparent, we must begin with this premise: he or she feels responsible for and guilty about the national debt, world hunger, and the fact that Gilligan never got off the island. But most of all, the Superparent feels guilty for having deprived her kids of a "normal" childhood as a result of the divorce. Her lifelong quest (though unattainable) is to correct that injustice by assuming the role of both parents.

Superparents are convinced that the divorce has damaged their children for life. They imagine switching on the evening news and watching in horror as their little boy negotiates with police from the roof of a high rise. "Isn't that little Bobbie up there? What's he doing with a rifle? What's that sign say? 'Don't shoot, I come from a broken home.'?"

For a Superparent, it's either "my way or the highway." They are notorious for being rigid, demanding, overbearing, and exacting about the iron clad rules and regulations they establish. Since they are now the lone disciplinarians, they feel compelled to lay down twice as many laws for their children to obey.

They also try to compensate for the percentage of love and quality time they feel was lost as a result of the divorce. Even though they're convinced that a single parent can't possibly fill that void, they try anyway. Simply stated, Superparents fail because they try too hard.

Since compensating for intangibles—love, relationship, quality time—is difficult at best, Superparents go to extremes in areas they can influence. They control. They nag. And, as you might expect, they end up alienating their children.

THE SUPERPARENT SELF-TEST

Concerned that you may have a few Superparent traits? Take the following quiz and find out. Try answering the questions the way you think others may see you. If you're really brave, give a copy of the test to someone who knows you well. Ask that person if she (or he) agrees with your answers.

1. I often say no to my kids even though I could just as easily have said yes. TRUE / FALSE

2. I feel as though single-parent family kids need more discipline than other kids. TRUE / FALSE

3. I feel as though I will have to make up for the loss of rules and limits that my spouse used to provide. TRUE / FALSE

4. I don't ever have time for myself because I feel guilty if I don't spend every available moment with my kids. TRUE / FALSE

5. Since the divorce, I have become increasingly weary of not having enough control to keep my kids in line. TRUE / FALSE

6. I feel guilty when I say no to my kids. TRUE / FALSE

7. I am afraid of receiving criticism from my ex and others if I don't keep tight control over the kids. TRUE / FALSE

8. I secretly feel my children will never really have a normal childhood now.   TRUE / FALSE

9. I've noticed a pattern of my children lying to me more often since the divorce.   TRUE / FALSE

10. I sometimes find my children going to my ex with their problems instead of to me.   TRUE / FALSE

11. I sometimes find myself forcing my kids to do what I want through threats or by saying such things as "Because I told you so, that's why."   TRUE / FALSE

12. I find myself reacting to my kids rather than listening and responding.   TRUE / FALSE

13. I feel as though I don't get the respect I deserve from my children.   TRUE / FALSE

14. My children seem somewhat sneaky, or they avoid telling me things that they may be afraid I won't approve of.   TRUE / FALSE

15. If my kids didn't think I'd find out, they'd probably say I'm too strict on them.   TRUE / FALSE

SCORING YOUR TEST

Add up the number of times you answered yes on the quiz and compare that figure to the following interpretations.

Number of Yes Answers   *Interpretation*

4 or fewer   No need for alarm. You are probably not a Superparent.

5–7   You are on the borderline of being a Superparent. You may want to post warning signs that read: "Danger, Controlling Superparent on Duty."

8–10   There is a better than even chance that you are a Superparent. You are probably starting to drive your children crazy with pressure, rules, and control. You may want to begin working on a more balanced single-parenting style before your kids put Kriptonite in your coffee. Read on, and consider using a highlighter.

11 or more   Check your insurance plan for accidental death benefits. You are definitely trying to be a Superparent. In fact, you could probably teach Advanced Superparenthood at the local college.

You may want to hire a food taster (consider your ex) and begin warming-up to the term *family counseling*.

OKAY, SO HOW DO I STOP BEING A SUPERPARENT?

Let's say that you scored a 10 + on the Superparent scale. What now? For starters, your chances of disappearing under mysterious circumstances just jumped 98 percent.

Why not save yourself from a nervous breakdown by identifying the glitches in your parenting style.

Remember, you have the power to serve notice on Mr. or Ms. Superparenting Pants. Yes, you'll be making yourself vulnerable, not only to Kriptonite, but to honesty and sensitivity as well. There are no pills or quick fixes. But the the following five steps should give you a running start in the right direction.

STEP #1:
ACKNOWLEDGE THAT YOU HAVE A PROBLEM
Whether it's shopping 'til you drop, double chocolate sundaes, or being a Superparent, we must first acknowledge (confess to ourselves) that a problem exists. This consciousness-raising process is an important first step in dealing with the problem. The next step is far more difficult.

STEP #2:
CONFESS AND MAKE AMENDS
First John 1:9 promises, "If we confess our sins, he is faithful and just and will forgive us our sins and purify us from all unrighteousness."

Confessing our sins and transgressions is fundamental. It enables us to arrive at a place of forgiveness, reconciliation, and recovery. No, you don't need to call your entire family and confess that you are a Superparent. (They'd just look at you funny and think about having you committed.) It does require, however, that you meet individually with the people who have been affected by your rigid, compensating, and controlling style—your children. Let them know that you have identified a personal problem and are striving to overcome it.

Ephesians 6:4 instructs us not to "provoke [our] children to anger" (NASB; "exasperate," AMP). As an experienced Superparent, it's a safe bet you have picked fights and done your share of child provoking. Confess that to them. Yes, it will be a humbling experience, but stop whimpering. Nobody said being a successful single parent was going to be easy.

STEP #3:
ASK FOR FORGIVENESS
Now that you've bared all, so to speak, ask for forgiveness.

Asking for forgiveness is an emotional prerequisite for recovering from your current problematic parenting style. The fact that you are open enough to ask for forgiveness proves that you are on the road to recovery. Only a short time ago, you would have been thoroughly repulsed by the idea of asking a child for forgiveness. Though divulging any weakness is a scary thought, especially for a Superparent, it is a mandatory hurdle that must be cleared if you are to make headway on becoming a more Balanced Single Parent.

STEP #4:
MAKE A COMMITMENT TO CHANGE
After you've taken the steps to "own" and then reveal your dysfunctional single-parenting style, don't forget to begin making changes. This task isn't like those household chores you've been putting off for months, such as cleaning above the refrigerator. (Have you ever noticed how many items, dating back to the Dead Sea Scrolls, seem to end up on top of the refrigerator?) It's a job of true importance that can't be put off or forgotten when you're half through. Committing to

change is where the rubber meets the road. Once you've crossed that hurdle, and have asked for your children's forgiveness, be prepared to ask for their support as well. You're going to need all the help you can get to keep positive momentum rolling.

Well-balanced parents police their styles. They catch themselves before they slip back into a Superparenting mode. If you catch yourself thinking, *If only my kids would do what I want more often, I wouldn't have to be so controlling,* call a time out. Hear that whistle? That's a parenting referee throwing his hankie and shouting, "Fifteen yards for continuing to control after the play is dead." Anytime the words, "if only," or "you should" leave your lips, you're sneaking back into your controlling ways.

Let your kids know about your commitment to change. You might begin by saying, "I realize now that I've been very strict and rigid with you since the divorce. I was afraid that I couldn't be a good parent by myself, and I've been trying too hard." (Don't stop now while you're on a roll.) "I'm trying to make some changes, and I will probably need your help. When you feel that I'm being unfair, rigid, or controlling, you have my permission to let me know. I promise to discuss the situation with you openly. What do you say?" (They'll probably be too stunned to speak.)

If you're already breaking into a cold sweat over the prospect of asking your children to critique your parenting style, calm down. It doesn't mean you're bound by law to change your mind every time you make a decision or ask them to do something. It does mean, however, that you are communicating a willingness to examine their "read" on things with an open mind.

Again, don't try to make these changes alone. Invite family and friends to be involved in the healing process. They'll probably feel flattered by the respect you've shown in their opinion, and you'll find it easier to keep on track. After all, aren't we all more likely to accomplish our goals when we feel a sense of accountability?

STEP #5:
GET SUPPORT WHILE YOU ARE MAKING PERSONAL CHANGES
We break commitments every day: that closet you promised yourself you'd clean; the women's Bible study you agreed to join; the dentist's appointment you keep putting off because you know you're in store for more than just a cleaning. It's no wonder that making an emotional commitment is just as difficult to keep. Perhaps harder. There are several proven methods for increasing the odds of keeping com-

mitments. While Step Four (accountability) is certainly the first line of defense, other methods may also be helpful.

• Books and tapes

Fortunately, there are a growing number of excellent books and tapes on subjects important to single parents. Remember, though, no one book or tape has all the answers. Keep your eyes and ears open. Read it all. Watch it all. Talk to other single parents about materials that have proven helpful to them. You'll rapidly gain insight as to what to purchase, and what to leave on the bookstore shelf.

• Counseling, support groups, and friends

Many churches are now offering single-parent support groups. Try calling around to some of the larger churches in your area. You'll probably find resources you never dreamed existed. If you are unable to find a support group in your area, consider starting your own through your church.

You may also have friends who are single parents. Get together with them on a weekly basis for mutual support, encouragement, and accountability. A number of books will be helpful. This book is, of course, a resource, and you may also find another book of mine useful: *Helping Single Parents with Troubled Kids* (Elgin, Ill.: David C. Cook, 1993). There are books available that can show you how to start a single-parenting ministry.

There's no shame in seeking professional help with troublesome issues. Some specific problems can be addressed with only one or two visits. Pastoral counseling is also very helpful in working through single-parent family issues.

SINGLE PARENT STYLE #2: THE TOXIC PARENT

A close relative of the Superparent is the Toxic Parent. Both styles are rigid and controlling. In both, one parent is attempting to compensate for the absence of a spouse. The Superparent, however, never imposes his will out of maliciousness. The Toxic Parent does. She (or he) employs anger, resentment, intimidation, and other dirty tricks to manipulate and control his children.

Toxic Parents are easily identifiable by the greenish glow that surrounds them—a glow that originated when they were exposed to the fallout from their once-nuclear family (pun intended). Hazardous waste materials left over from unhappy marriages, ugly separations, and knock-down-drag-out divorces; anger, bitterness, and resentment about being raked over the coals emotionally or financially. Nobody knows what "mood de jour" to expect of these persons. Rest assured, their next victim will be somebody handy—probably a child.

One particularly toxic type of anger is known as *unresolved anger*. Unresolved anger is extremely venomous because it is anger turned outward. Using anger as a defense mechanism to protect themselves from further emotional pain, people with pent-up anger eventually estrange themselves from family and friends.

Another extremely toxic variety of anger is called *transference of anger*. This condition harnesses any leftover anger, rage, hurt, and insecurity to inflict pain on others. For example, it is not uncommon for a single parent to report feeling angry at a child because the child's mannerisms, even physical characteristics, are similar to those of an ex-spouse. Intellectually, the parent experiencing this kind of anger understands the difference between the child and the spouse, but at an unconscious level his mind still registers the association of hurt and anger.

CHARACTERISTICS OF TOXIC PARENTS

It is easier to understand what a Toxic Parent looks like if we take a look at some typical characteristics in chart form. The items in the left column below are emotional or psychological characteristics. Those in the right column are some of the physiological downsides of being a Toxic Parent.

Emotional Characteristics	Physiological Characteristics
• Depression	• Headaches
• Rage	• Elevated blood pressure
• Mood swings	• Nausea or abdominal distress
• Anxiety	• Lower resistance to illness
• Manipulativeness	• Exaggerated PMS symptoms
• Defensiveness	• Heart palpitations and dizziness
• Powerlessness	• Increased risk of heart disease
• Desire for revenge	• Increased risk of stroke
• Intimidation	• Bowel problems
• Immaturity	
• Misdirected anger	

THE TOXIC PARENT SELF-TEST

Do you think you have toxic characteristics? Answer the following questions to find out. Again, as you did for the quiz for Superparents, try to respond to each item as objectively as possible.

1. I sometimes find myself using my kids as leverage against my ex.   TRUE / FALSE

2. I seem to be stuck in the rut of continually thinking about my divorce and the effect it has had on my family.   TRUE / FALSE

3. I often feel very angry at and hurt by my ex.   TRUE / FALSE

4. I don't understand why God allowed this to happen to me.   TRUE / FALSE

5. My children often think I'm mad at them.   TRUE / FALSE

6. I sometimes think of ways I might get back at my ex for hurting me.   TRUE / FALSE

7. I think my ex is trying to win my kids' affection away from me.   TRUE / FALSE

8. My ex and I still argue much of the time about issues that affect both of us and our family.   TRUE / FALSE

9. I have a hard time controlling my temper.   TRUE / FALSE

10. I am often moody and unpredictable.   TRUE / FALSE

11. There is a great deal of anger in my house.   TRUE / FALSE

12. I'm not able to talk with anyone about my anger.   TRUE / FALSE

13. I spend a considerable amount of time wondering how my spouse could have done this to me and the kids.   TRUE / FALSE

14. I secretly feel insecure and a bit angry when my kids show affection toward my ex.   TRUE / FALSE

15. Sometimes I lash out at my kids even though they didn't do anything really wrong. They were just there.   TRUE / FALSE

16. I have a great deal of anger left over that just doesn't go away.   TRUE / FALSE

SCORING YOUR TEST

Add up the number of times you answered yes and refer to the following chart for your score.

Number of Yes Answers	*Interpretation*
3 or fewer	Within the normal range for single parents.
4–6	You are definitely approaching the threshold of being a Toxic Parent. You may want to consider buying your children radioactive suits for their protection.
7–10	Welcome to the toxic wasteland you used to call your living room. You are firmly entrenched in a toxic single-parenting style.
11 or more	Prepare for a nuclear meltdown if you don't begin a more balanced approach to single parenting. Read on, there's hope.

OKAY, SO HOW DO I STOP
BEING A TOXIC PARENT?

Again, as with the case of the Overly Controlling Superparent, making an accurate diagnosis of your parenting style is the first step toward recovery.

Need further motivation? Try this. The biggest obstacle on the way to a healthy single-parenting style is anger.

If you have unresolved feelings of anger, deal with them on a timely basis. Don't wait for a crisis to arise. The most effective way of working through unresolved anger is to talk about your feelings with someone who can empathize with you and who understands what you are going through. That might be a pastor, family counselor, parent, or simply a good friend. Don't let pride keep you from reaching out for help.

Next, consider attending divorce recovery groups or workshops. Most single parents agree that becoming active in a church-sponsored single-parent fellowship group played a vital role in helping them make a successful transition into their new parenting roles.

SINGLE PARENT STYLE #3:
THE ENABLER

The Enabler lives by the motto, "If I do everything perfectly, and don't make any mistakes, my kids will turn out fine." Whether it is an unconscious or conscious decision, Enablers assume responsibility for the divorce. Their relentless mission is to make the world a nicer place for kids, dogs—even ex-spouses. The Enabler allows everyone to go to the head of the attention line, while placing his own needs on hold. Excessive guilt over the divorce, coupled with a driving desire to avoid further anger and unhappiness, force the Enabler into a position of compliant codependence.

Enablers generally start out with the best of intentions—to be nice, caring, loving, single parents. Typically, though, they try too hard to overcome their lack of parental leadership by becoming overly permissive. As a result, important parental limits and boundaries slowly erode.

Many Enablers were dependent on their ex-spouses to provide structure, limits, and consequences for the family. Since the Enabler never was too comfortable with structure in the first place, he thinks his kids will be just fine without it. But in reality, a family without structure is like an army without a general, or a football team without a coach. When there is no one to provide leadership, structure, and the enforcement of consequences, anarchy takes over.

In this weakened state of authority, the Enabler often becomes a pushover for her children. Her equal status on the family organizational chart allows the kids to take advantage of her almost at will.

Some Enablers believe the most effective way to be a good single parent is to be a "best friend" to their children. Still others can't bring themselves to set limits or provide structure. They believe their divorce-scared children have already been through enough, without asking them to behave too. They imagine that spanking, scolding, or meting out any disciplinary consequence for misbehavior will only damage their fragile self-esteem.

My kids will reject me if I'm too strict. That's a crushing, burdensome thought for the Enabler, especially since she is already preoccupied by her own insecurity, loneliness, and guilt over the divorce. She won't do anything that might jeopardize her children's love for her, so she fails to set limits or follow through with consequences.

Many single parents believe that children, especially teenagers, would prefer to have Enabler moms and dads. The truth is Enablers send confusing messages to their children by not providing the guidance, accountability, and structure children crave. The Enabler feels that she must be the consummate diplomat. Negotiation before discipline. If all else fails, pull out the heavy artillery: "Don't make me call your father."

Since the Enabler often abdicates any authority, the patients are free to start running the asylum. It's a simple law of child physics. If you give a kid a free pass to act out, he'll say, "Thank you very much" and do just that. When things deteriorate to a certain point, a call for help usually goes out to dad. That is the last thing the Enabler wants, because it reinforces failure. It also leaves the door wide open for the ex-spouse to get in some digs about her inability to maintain order.

For some reason, the local supermarket seems to attract Enabler parents in droves. A child is pitching a major fit at the check-out line because his parent said no (perhaps for the first time) to Frosted Flakes. For some parents, an intimidating stare would be enough to levitate the child right out of the store. Others would firmly, but gently, hold onto the child's hand until safely within the confines of the family minivan. The Enabler parent will attempt to reason and negotiate with the child by sharing their feelings about the cereal situation. We've all seen what follows. The child gets the Frosted Flakes and immediately goes into a victory dance at the express line. There should be a sign over the cash register: "10 Items or Less. No Victory Dancing."

CHARACTERISTICS OF THE ENABLER

As we did with the Toxic Parent, Let's take a look at the main characteristics of the Enabler.

- Taking on responsibilities of others
- Depression
- Excessive guilt
- Passivity
- Psychosomatic illnesses/ frequent complaints about health
- Fear of being abandoned
- Fatigue
- Money problems
- Boundary/limit setting problems
- Peacekeeping

THE ENABLER SELF-TEST

Do you think you might have Enabler tendencies? Respond to the following statements to find out. As you did on the earlier quizzes, try to respond to each item as objectively as possible.

1. Do you make allowances for your child's poor behavior on the basis that he's been through a lot since the divorce? TRUE / FALSE

2. Do you find that your children obey you less and less since the divorce? TRUE / FALSE

3. Do you ever say, or imply, that you will tell their father if they don't do as they are told? TRUE / FALSE

4. When you say no to your kids do you find yourself feeling guilty or changing your mind later? TRUE / FALSE

5. Do you find yourself quick to apologize and back down from any display of anger toward your kids? TRUE / FALSE

6. Are you quicker to give in to your child's whims, wants, demands, temper tantrums and wishes since the divorce? TRUE / FALSE

7. Do you feel your ex is too strict, harsh, or short-tempered with the kids?   TRUE / FALSE

8. Do you find yourself buying toys or gifts for the kids more often since the divorce?   TRUE / FALSE

9. Do you find it hard to stick to the rules of the house that were established before the divorce?   TRUE / FALSE

10. Do you frequently place your child's wants and wishes ahead of yours or others?   TRUE / FALSE

SCORING YOUR TEST

Add up the number of times you answered yes to the questions and refer to the chart below for the scoring.

Number of Yes Answers	*Interpretation*
2 or less	You are within the normal range of most caring single parents. Even though you may have answered "True" to less than three questions, you are probably able to identify when you are being an Enabler and you are able to adjust in time.
3 - 5	You have one foot on the borderline separating Enablers from other parents and the other foot on a banana peel. You have some backbone, but it turns to Jell-O when you are put to the test. Read on. You should begin working on a more balanced single-parenting approach.
6 or more	No offense, but your backbone is mostly made of marshmallow. It probably makes you nervous to eat seafood because, as a jellyfish, you realize you are in the same family. You may want to consider buying a big, ugly, mean dog to help restore order to your home. Just teasing. Relax. There's help on the way!

If you are like most caring parents, you're probably concerned that you appear to have traits belonging to each of these troublesome parenting styles. Don't be too alarmed. Even well-balanced parents make brief visits to these less attractive styles now and again. However, they spend the vast majority of their time within a balanced parenting framework.

THE WELL-BALANCED SINGLE PARENT

The well-balanced single parent knows when to be firm and when to be flexible. She (or he) has learned how to use an ideal mixture of truth, grace, love, and limits.

Let's look at the basic ingredients that go into the making of a Balanced Single Parent. A Balanced Single Parent is:

- Loving
- Consistent
- Fair
- Supportive

- Forgiving
- Communicative
- Firm

Sounds a little like the Cub Scout Oath, doesn't it? Let's take a closer look.

LOVING

Why do some parents have difficulty saying "I love you" to their children? Strange as it may seem, it's not uncommon for many parents to find it nearly impossible to put their love into language.

This inability to verbalize love often stems from a single parent's subconscious feelings of rejection, anger, isolation, and sadness after a divorce. A single parent may even go through long periods when he or she doesn't feel the least bit loving or giving. The parent is emotionally out to lunch. Unfortunately, the timing couldn't be worse. Not only are the children starving for I-love-yous, so is the parent.

There is another extreme that is nearly as damaging as failing to communicate love: smothering. Smothering occurs when the parent places a higher value on his or her own emotional neediness than the child's. In other words, the parent is giving 150 percent trying to get back 100 percent.

- ## Unconditional loving

At first blush, the concept of unconditional love and acceptance sounds wonderful, but it is confusing for a child or teen who has just experienced his parents' divorce. Divorce destroys the child's idealization that love transcends all problems. He begins to see that love is conditional and fragile. He learns that love is vulnerable to outside influences, such as physical health, attractiveness, infidelity, money, and work problems. It is a rude awakening, one that often produces symptoms of insecurity and low self-esteem in children and teens.

- ## Idealized, or Perfect, Love

Problems arise when a child (or an adult) confuses unconditional love with "idealized" or "perfect love." Perfect love simply doesn't exist among humans. No wonder we have such a difficult time dealing with the concept. It's a reflection of our imperfection.

Perfect love does exist in the Bible, however. First John 4:18 reads: "We need have no fear of someone who loves us perfectly." That perfect love for us eliminates all dread of what the person might do to us. I believe "perfect love" is reserved for the way God feels about His children. He alone is capable of perfect love.

When a solid foundation of unconditional love is established from birth, it allows a child to make his or her way through pain, disappointment, and broken relationships without collapsing under the weight of disappointment. The child emerges whole and intact.

Unconditional love has two distinct properties. The first is acceptance. In Scripture, to live in hell is to live in broken relationship to God. Your child has already witnessed the breaking of relationships and the pain that ensues. Forcing him from the safe confines of your relationship by withholding love and acceptance is the earthly equivalent of a living hell.

Withholding love because your child has failed to measure up to your expectations is a cruel communicator. It's like forcing the child to wear a large sign emblazoned with the words "I'm not loved. I'm not lovable." Children who have had love withheld from them often carry their emotional battle scars into their own parenting, and so pass on that set of wounds to their children.

It is vital that you communicate unconditional love and acceptance to your children. Give them a healthy environment where they can be "just good enough kids," not perfect children. "Just good enough kids" have faults and fail. They make mistakes, get into jams, miss soccer shots, get Cs and Ds on report cards, and get parking tickets, but they never have to worry about not being loved and appreciated.

FORGIVING

If you live in a two-story house, you've probably witnessed the heart-wrenching sight of your child sitting at the top of the stairs, dejectedly poking his head through the rails—tracking your every move. His expression looks like the one on your dog's face when you catch him rooting around in the trash. It can best be described as a "do-you-still-love-me?" look.

With our kids, "the look" appears shortly after we have been pushed to the limits and have sent the little fire starters to their respective rooms (called the penalty box in my house) to consider their transgressions. It's amazing. We parents actually believe our kids will spend the time thinking about what they've done wrong. Sure. I can just see them meditating about their actions. Right, and all kids want second helpings of asparagus too.

Anyway, after a few minutes without toys (or an hour with multiple toys), they assume the stairway position awaiting just one thing from you— forgiveness. After a tough day of breaking things, terrorizing the neighborhood, shaving the neighbor's cat, and thoroughly wreaking havoc, a child needs to know that he's still okay in your book.

Since the divorce, your child is probably confused about the whole concept of forgiveness. *If we are supposed to be forgiving of each other, how come my mom couldn't forgive my dad?* he reasons. *Are there some things that can never be forgiven? Have I done any of them yet?*

The Balanced Single Parent forgives unconditionally, but with eyes wide open. The parent realizes that his or her kids are human, fallible, and fully capable of—even proficient at—making mistakes. A Balanced Parent knows how to address inappropriate behavior without being hurtful or critical and without minimizing or withholding. The child knows he is unconditionally accepted, despite the fact that he sometimes does bad things. His behavior may have been bad, but he's still a good kid. The Balanced Single parent keeps any response to the negative behavior separate from the child's overall feeling of self-esteem.

Sure, he tried to bathe the hamster by dunking him in the toilet. The act was imperfect, but the intent was honorable. As a forgiving parent, your child knows that he can come to you even when he's really messed things up. He knows that when it's all over you will offer forgiveness and guidance, not condemnation and judgment. If your kids can't approach you when they've messed up the small things, how can you expect them to tell you when they're tempted by drugs, alcohol, or sex during their teens?

CONSISTENT

Predictability and consistency are bad traits in a cat burglar, but they are tremendous assets in a single parent. Balanced Single Parents are positively predictable through their consistent track record—something their children need more than ever before. Why? Because, predictability has been lacking in their lives lately. Inconsistent relationship between mom and dad. Inconsistent visitation. Inconsistent spiritual support. These are just a few of the things I hear from children of single-parent families.

In one particular case, I met with a single mom regarding her teenage son, who was having trouble controlling his temper and inappropriate language. He had even physically shoved her several times. I asked her how she responded.

"Well, I made it clear I didn't appreciate it," she said, going on to say that he had been physically abused by his father. "When he did it the next time, I told him I was calling the police, but I didn't," she continued. "The next time he pushed me, I called the police. When they arrived, I decided not to press charges. Then the last time he swore at me and threatened me physically, I tried to slap him, but he pushed me against the wall."

The issue with this mom wasn't so much the type of discipline she imposed, but the "crazy making" inconsistency in the way she responded.

During a recent family outing to Sea World, I saw an example of parental consistency in action, only in this instance it was between man and dolphin. Hours before the main show, I noticed a trainer working with two young dolphins. He was preparing them for the day when they would mature into the first-string performers (a process that can take years). As I watched, a clear pattern developed. Each time one of the dolphins made an honest attempt to follow the trainer's command, he was rewarded with a fish. Not once did the trainer forget to dole out a prize for doing well or making an effort. Sea mammals, like kid mammals, learn best when they are provided with consistent and predictable reinforcement. (A word of caution, however. Most kids don't respond well to sardine incentives.)

In contrast, unpredictable and inconsistent single parents (and dolphin trainers) confuse their children by making them continually guess about the rules and what will happen if they fail to obey them. Children desperately want to meet your expectations, but how can they when they don't know what's expected of them, or if you keep changing the rules?

COMMUNICATIVE

Let's give credit where credit is due. Moms are extraordinary communicators. When provoked, however, they have the amazing ability to punctuate each word with a figurative cuff to the back of the child's head: "Now [smack] I [smack] told [smack] you [smack] . . ." (Dads, don't try this at home—you'll never pull it off.)

Balanced Single Parents are above average communicators, a skill not lost on the business world. In the forties and fifties, many business studies were conducted to assemble a practical, working model for corporate communication skills. The studies showed that for a business to be successful, there had to be an upward flow of communication in addition to the traditional downward flow. In order for workers to feel valued and respected, there had to be a mechanism for their ideas, wants, and complaints to be communicated to their bosses.

Some employers scoffed at the idea, but others immediately began changing. Those who changed their practices realized greater potential from their employees, which translated into higher productivity, greater job satisfaction, less turnover, and less employee sick time.

The concept of upward communication is even more important in single-parent families. It is undeniable that a lack of communication is probably at the core of most divorces. The failure of married couples to communicate needs, wishes, limits, and boundaries can't help but stick in a child's mind. The message the child receives is clear—don't risk touching off an emotional prairie fire, keep your problems to yourself. Kids have an internal "emotional radar" more sensitive to relationship issues than that used in an air traffic control tower to detect the movement of airplanes.

Balanced Single Parents continually communicate their needs, wishes, wants, expectations, and boundaries to their children. This will bring benefits already mentioned but it will also cut down on what is called *triangulating*. Triangulating is a type of dysfunctional communication in which an individual communicates indirectly to another. For instance, rather than speaking directly to his wife, an angry father may ask his daughter to relay messages to her mother for him. We'll talk more about triangulating in later chapters.

The most powerful aspect of good communication skills is found in its "valuing" effect. Making your kids part of the decision-making process will enhance their self-esteem, and give them a sense of responsibility and freedom of expression—even if they don't get their way. Compliance is always easier for children when they feel that they are a part of the decision-making process.

FAIR

One of the secret thoughts of children following divorce is that the *whole thing* isn't fair. It's not fair that they have only one parent at home while other kids have two. It's not fair that they have to move. It's not fair that they will be changing schools, have less money, and have to give up their friends. It's not hard to understand how children develop mild to severe persecution complexes following a divorce.

So even though children (and teens) are capable of overplaying the fairness issue (I've had entire therapy sessions that felt like one long wail—*"That's not fairrrrrr"*—with the final "r" coming out right at the end of the hour), it's critical that the child's vision of fairness be examined, validated, and discussed. A single parent (or a therapist, for that matter) is making a mistake he attempts to convince the child that he didn't get the raw end of the deal—everyone knows he did. It's also critical that fairness issues not be used by the parent to let down discipline standards or to abandon leadership of the family.

For the fair-minded, balanced, single parent, fairness goes hand in hand with firmness and consistency. Being a fair single parent means more than just listening to your child—it means hearing what she's saying and noting the underlying feelings behind the words "That's not fair."

Being a Balanced Parent means hearing your child's side of the story before making hasty decisions. Being fair also means having the ability to change your mind. In contrast, Superparents and Toxic Parents seldom, if ever, hear (or look for) opposing points of view. Even if some mitigating evidence surfaces, they won't change a decision for fear of appearing weak.

The opposite occurs with the Enabler parent. She says yes to almost everything. On those rare occasions with a no emerges, the child knows he can change his parent's mind with little effort, or more precisely, manipulation.

Finally, a fair, well-balanced parent can apologize when he's wrong. Can you imagine how hard it is for Superparents or Toxic Parents to entertain the concept of being wrong and then admit it? Conversely, the Enabler Parent apologizes just to avoid conflict, even when she's right. It is easy to see the negative effect that each dysfunctional style has on a child's sense of what's fair.

FIRM

Firmness is perhaps the most elusive character trait for a parent to possess, but it is a hallmark of the well-balanced parent. That's because firmness lies somewhere between truth and grace, right there in the middle of love and limits.

Again, the cereal aisle of the supermarket is the best place in the world to study child psychology. Eighty percent of all begging, moaning, complaining, and pleading occurs in this one aisle. And don't think cereal companies haven't analyzed this very subject. Notice how they position all the surgary, kids' stuff at a four-year-old's eye-level. The easiest way to spot a parenting problem is by watching the reaction of parents when the begging begins. Begging escalates, depending on the situation. Children often begin with the simple yet effective "*Paaallleeezzzeee.*" If that doesn't work, they take a stab at manipulation: "I'm not going to be your friend anymore." Or they may go straight for the jugular: "I want to go live with daddy!" Others turn to crying, screaming, and the ever-popular holding of breath. My personal favorite: You're at the checkout line and you suddenly notice that your child has stopped lobbying for goodies. Odd. Then you realize your little jewel has hidden four candy bars beneath the bananas and coffee. Busted. "Hey, that's not *Faaaiiirrrrr!*"

As well-developed as a child's manipulative skills may be, the Balanced Single Parent quickly, firmly, and appropriately confronts any unacceptable behavior. The Bible teaches us that ignoring problems only leads to more problems. As Matthew 18:15 says, "If your brother (child in this case) sins against you, go and show him his fault, just between the two of you. If he listens to you, you have won your brother over." The same holds true for parents. Ignoring your children's problems and manipulations will only make confronting a similar behavior, or a more severe one, more difficult down the road.

SUPPORTIVE

Life is full of consequences. One of the glaring differences between the Toxic Parent, the Enabling Parent, and the Balanced Single Parent is seen in the quality and quantity of support. When a child messes up in the Toxic Parent's home, he is likely to hear the all too familiar chants of "I told you so."

In the Enabler's house, the child is seldom allowed to be in a position where failure is even a possibility. In the event failure does happen, the Enabler rationalizes it away or takes full responsibility.

In the Balanced Single Parent's home, failures are understood and used as measuring devices to be learned from.

A FINAL PERSPECTIVE ON
THE FOUR SINGLE-PARENTING STYLES

Whether you have identified yourself as an Superparent, a Toxic Parent, an Enabler Parent, or a Balanced Parent, there is one central theme in this chapter—that you must strive to become more balanced in your parenting style. It won't happen overnight, so be patient with your child and yourself.

Achieving and maintaining a balanced single-parenting style is at least an eighteen-year job. The real payoff will come when you see your child growing up to be a loving, responsible, well-balanced person with healthy self-esteem. Remember, the dream of every parent is to live long enough to become a burden to his children. It's no different in single parent families.

Above all, don't be too hard on yourself. Just do your best, and you'll be fine. Remember, whenever you feel yourself reaching the end of your rope, reach up, tie a knot and hold on—help is on the way.

·3·

DEVELOP LIMITS AND BOUNDARIES, THE ANTIDOTES TO CHAOS

Aaron struggled valiantly, seemingly undeterred by long bouts of coughing, wheezing, and occasional gasps for air.

"Don't be a complete wuss," chided his new friend, Kevin. "Just one more puff. That's it! Now, slowly let it out."

About to dispose of the badly mauled cigarette, he finally managed to take a complete drag without gagging. His eyes crossed as he tracked the thin wisps of smoke that filtered from his nose and out the car window. "All right!" he blurted with pride, and a new sense of adultness.

"Look at those waves, dude," hooted Kevin, as they pulled into the state beach parking lot. "We've practically got the whole place to ourselves. What do you say now, boy? Beats sitting in fourth period, right? Hey, grab my towel and CD player from the backseat, will ya. Oh, and there's a fresh pack of smokes in the glove box."

The pair had slipped off campus just after homeroom attendance, but their departure hadn't gone unnoticed. A swimming coach had spotted the teenagers driving off together and had reported them to the vice principal.

Aaron, an above-average student who had never cut a class in his life, was already experiencing major guilt pangs over the great escape. He was also worried about forging his father's signature to the absence slip the next day.

Kevin, on the other hand, bore no such burden. The product of an alcoholic family and divorced parents, he had become a consummate liar and all-around problem causer. Worse, he had recently passed his driver's test, which meant he could now export his irresponsible behavior outside the city limits.

The two unlikely friends lay out for a while, wandered over to the pier, watched old men fishing, smoked a few cigarettes, and even struck up a conversation with a couple of "older women"—meaning cute girls in their twenties. It took some time, but Aaron was beginning to push aside his guilt and paranoia and was beginning to relax in his newfound freedom.

"So, what do you think?" Kevin beamed. "I bet we can pull off another beach trip next week, or sooner. Who knows, maybe those girls will be here again. Anyway, a couple of guys and me are going up to the mall. Marty's gonna bring a couple of 'sixers'. Want to join us?"

Aaron hesitated for a second and inhaled the last drag of his cigarette before answering. "Why not? Dad's always busy with his new girlfriend. And Mom's always worrying about something—the girls, work, bills . . . whatever. Besides, I'm old enough to do what I want. I'm the man of the house now."

Still, he figured, why push his luck, and quickly suggested that they get going so he wouldn't have to answer any "stupid questions for coming home late."

Aaron changed back into his school clothes and carefully stashed his towel, trunks, and sandals into a gym bag. Kevin just laughed as he returned from the rest room, saying "My mom won't give me any grief about where I've been. I could walk into the house wearing flippers, a lobster stuck to my face, and smoking a joint and she'd probably never notice."

"You're lucky, I guess," Aaron said. "I've always had a bunch of rules to follow. But lately, since my folk's divorce, it hasn't been too bad. I can pretty much do what I want too."

On the way back, though, Aaron kept staring at his watch, wishing he could get home faster. When they finally arrived on his block, the antsy teen jumped out of the car before it had come to a complete stop. "See ya at the mall, dude," he yelled, rushing through the front door and up the stairs before anybody could say anything.

Safely locked inside the bathroom, he brushed his teeth with uncharacteristic fervor to rid himself of any telltale odor. Good hygiene had its value after all, he had to admit, before showering off the ocean's salty residue. As he was drying off, he glanced at the mirror. "Oh, no! How am I going to explain this!" He grabbed a washcloth and began scrubbing his face for all he was worth, but the bright shade of crimson wouldn't budge—he was sunburned.

Panicky, he hatched a story. "I know! That's it! I went on a field trip to a farm with the 4-H Club. Mom will buy it, and Dad's not around to nail me."

Feeling pretty good about his alibi, he came downstairs just in time for dinner. Mom and Gram were busily opening all kinds of boxes, heating up soup, and dispensing huge mountains of dried noodles from the local Chinese take-out.

"Mommy, do we have to use these big toothpicks," said Kelli, pointing at the wooden chopsticks.

"No, dear, a fork will be just fine," Gram said.

"Look, Kelli," demonstrated her sister, "all you have to do is stab your food with one stick. Of course, it doesn't work too well on rice."

Aaron kept his head down in hopes that nobody would notice his red face. It didn't work.

"Oh, dear, look at Aaron," announced Gram. "Connie, do you tell your kids to use 15 if they're going to be out in the sun over long periods?"

"Of course I do, Mom," Connie snapped. "Aaron, how did you get so burned?"

Everybody stopped eating and waited for his answer.

"Oh, well, we had a field trip today," he mumbled. "I guess I forgot to tell you. Sorry. We went to the farm. It was real hot."

Connie's mom rolled her eyes in disbelief, but her daughter decided to let it slide. It had been a rough day at the office. *Besides,* she thought, *Aaron has never really lied to me before, and he has been through an awful lot lately.*

Aaron downed his food in record time—even with chopsticks—before excusing himself. "Mom, is it okay if I go to the mall with my friend Kevin?"

"All right, but be home no later than nine. Who's Kevin?"

But Aaron was out the door.

A few minutes later the phone rang. "It's for you, Mommy," said Kimberly. "It's Aaron's school."

"Is this Mrs. Perry, Aaron's mother?" the caller asked politely.

"Yes. Please, call me Connie," she nervously responded. "Is anything wrong?"

"Yes, I'm afraid there is. My name is Jim Coubiack. I'm the Dean at Maple Combined School. I've got to inform you that Aaron cut all of his classes today. He and a friend left campus after attendance was taken. I don't know where they went. I wanted you to know that we're going to give your son detention every day after school next week. His friend Kevin will be suspended, again. Connie, could you please talk with Aaron and then tell him to see me tomorrow? He's never had any problems before, and I want to make sure this won't happen again."

"Yes, Mr. Coubiack, I will."

"Is Aaron in trouble?" Kimberly asked sadly.

"Well, we're not going out for ice cream when he get's home, Kimmy," said Connie.

It was well after 10:30 when Aaron finally returned home. Reeking of cigarettes and beer, he opened the door as quietly as he could, but Connie was waiting.

"Aaron, we need to talk."

"I don't want to talk!" he screamed. "I'm old enough to go out without you questioning my every move."

She suddenly realized that she was in over her head. "Okay, go up to bed. We'll deal with this in the morning."

What am I going to do? she anguished. *David was always the disciplinarian. How in the world am I going to cope with a fifteen-year-old who's smoking and drinking?*

THE SLIPPERY SLIDE
AWAY FROM BOUNDARIES

You're worn out and stressed. Your own anxiety and pain has made you feel emotionally shut down. During the dog days of divorce—when you're often the least emotionally available and capable—your kids need you the most. That's when your love tanks are on empty, and theirs need to be filled up.

Now, like the line in the song goes, you're supposed to pick yourself up, dust yourself off, and start all over again. Sounds easier in a Broadway musical, doesn't it? This is a time when everyone, kids and parents alike, becomes emotionally challenged. The status quo is out the window. During these periods of emotional chaos brought about by change it is easy to forget about a major aspect of single parenting—maintaining limits and boundaries.

If science can put a man on the moon, and place pop-up timers inside a turkey, why can't someone invent something to tell parents when their children need more limits? Maybe those turkey brainstormers could come up with a pop-up kit for kids—a timer in their belly button to warn their parents when they need more attention.

Seriously, we all know there's no accurate way of measuring our children's need for limits. It's up to the primary parent to keep a finger on their child's emotional pulse—not an easy task.

You're ahead of the game, though, if you already understand the importance of setting and maintaining limits and boundaries during the transitional weeks and months following a divorce. That's news to you? Don't worry, we're going to identify the areas where boundaries are essential. Next, we're going to give you the single-parenting tools you need to get the job done.

DINOSAURS, BOUNDARIES, AND OTHER EXTINCT THINGS

As we've been discussing (and as you're probably already know), setting boundaries, rules, and limits can be a major problem for the newly single parent.

If we were to start digging for dinosaur bones, for example, we would need some idea of our quarry. If not, we might spend weeks uncovering the perfectly preserved remains of an old sprinkler system when we're looking for Stegosaurus eggs.

Are boundaries nearing extinction in your household? Then it's time to clearly define just what you're after: a set of practical boundaries and limits that will work in your new single-parent household. Fine. Get out your shovels. We'll show you where to start digging.

BOUNDARIES 101 AND THE SINGLE PARENT

A BIBLICAL PERSPECTIVE ON BOUNDARIES

Are boundaries and limits biblical? The answer is a resounding yes. The Bible is filled with references to God's boundaries and limits for mankind. For an early example of God's limits, open your Bible to the book of Genesis. Adam and Eve's Bible was a fast read back then, wasn't it? "Don't eat the forbidden fruit!" Easy, right? Well, you know how the story goes. God left no doubt that all real limits and boundaries come with consequences. If not, they are merely suggestions.

God's boundaries and limits for our lives were never more apparent or rigid than when He said, "Thou shalt not." How much respect would we have had for the Ten Commandments if they had been called the "Ten Suggestions"? Fact is, they could have been called the "Ten Absolute Limits and Boundaries," limits and boundaries closed to negotiation, interpretation, or mediation. But Moses would have gotten a hernia carrying all that down the mountain. God's firm, but fair, set of boundaries and limits are designed with our interests at heart.

THE CHARACTERISTICS OF BOUNDARIES

But God, our own single parent, does leave some room for flexibility in His handling of the boundaries He has set up. An excellent example of this flexibility is recorded in Genesis 18–19. God has finally run out of patience with the wayward people of Sodom. The city was filled with robbers, muggers, rapists, and prostitutes. It was thoroughly immoral. Just as God was about to destroy the city, which had slipped well beyond His boundaries for human behavior, Abraham intervened on the city's behalf.

Talk about nerve! How many of us would have asked God to reconsider His judgment of so wicked a city at that late juncture? If it were up to me, I would have said, "Okay God, if You want to destroy Sodom, it's Your call. I'm outta here. You're the boss."

Here's how Abraham handled the crisis.

> Abraham approached [God] and said: "Will you sweep away the righteous with the wicked? What if there are fifty righteous people within the city? Will you really sweep it away and not spare the place for the sake of the fifty righteous people who are in it? Far be it from you to do such a thing—to kill the righteous with the wicked, treating the righteous and the wicked alike. Far be it from you! Will not the Judge of all the earth do right?" (Genesis 18:23–25)

God must have been amused by Abraham's simple, yet effective, psychological approach, but He appears to appreciate the logic and compassion behind the challenge: "If I find fifty righteous people in the city of Sodom, I will spare the whole place for their sake" (v. 26). Abraham's sense of satisfaction must have been short-lived when he realized how difficult it might be to find fifty righteous people in Sodom. Hoping his luck wouldn't run out, he continued to negotiate with God: "Now that I have been so bold as to speak to the Lord, though I am nothing but dust and ashes, what if the number of righteous is five less than fifty? Will you destroy the whole city because of five people?" (vv. 27–28).

God again accepts Abraham's line of reasoning and eventually reduces the number to ten righteous people. In doing so, God demonstrates flexibility toward His children. Does this mean that we should always be flexible with our single-parenting boundaries? No, certainly not. Doing so would communicate the wrong message to our children—that our limits are merely suggestions. It does, however, allow us the freedom to reconsider our boundaries when conditions change. Try not to lose sight of the fact that even firm, righteous boundaries can change with the circumstance.

As in the case of God's dealing with Abraham over the city of Sodom, how many of us allow our children to negotiate the boundaries we have already put into place? Assuming that none of us is perfect, shouldn't we be open to the possibility of being wrong? At the very least, shouldn't we be willing to give consideration to other points of view, even those of our children? How can we presume to be the last word when our Lord, who is perfect, alters His own boundaries when the time is right? (By the way, Sodom was blown to bits, but Abraham's nephew, Lot, and Lot's wife and two daughters were guided from the city by angels before it was destroyed.)

WHAT FALLS WITHIN
YOUR PERSONAL BOUNDARIES?

As a single parent, it is possible (if not probable) that you are up to your eyebrows in redefining personal boundaries based on your new separateness. It's important to realize that *your* boundaries (how *you* define *yourself*) are exactly that—*your* boundaries. They should no longer be enmeshed, clouded, or subject to the influence of others, including your ex-spouse.

As a single parent, it is critical that you define what falls within your own limits. If you don't do that first, you can't help your children understand and set boundaries for themselves. Here are the parameters of personal boundaries.

WHO YOU ARE—WHAT YOU ARE NOT

You've changed. You're a single parent. It's time to define your new role and the personal boundaries you bring to the job. Why? Because you are now a whole as well as a half. Let me explain. When you've got the kids, you are essentially operating in the autonomous role of a single parent. There is, however, always the other parent to consider. You and the kids remain part of a more loosely defined two-parent system. It's up to you to clearly define that system.

Part of your redefining yourself as a single mom (or dad) is realizing that part of setting proper boundaries has to do with understanding your limitations. As we've discussed, you can't be everything to your kids. You never could. Realize that you can't be both parents, only the best mom or dad you can be, which is more than enough.

YOUR FEELINGS

"For the past _____ years, I've put my feelings aside for the sake of the family." Does this describe you? Have you ever given yourself permission to have feelings? Or have they been on a permanent vacation? Now is the time to dust off your feelings, and experience again what makes you feel happy.

A word of caution. Some single parents immediately go to the other extreme. They become a "me first" person. Certainly, your feelings fall within your personal boundaries. Indeed, many newly single parents find that having their own feelings—rather than being manipulated to feel a certain way—is an exciting and challenging new freedom.

Your anger falls within the boundaries of feelings. At some point, however, you must choose whether to continue being angry or to work through it.

YOUR BELIEFS

As you redefine yourself you must deal with your belief system, which is at the center of who you are. Taking control of your belief system is merely taking ownership of what was already yours. Religious beliefs, political beliefs, parenting beliefs, social beliefs—they all fall within your own personal boundaries.

As the primary care-giver to your children, your belief system will play a significant role in helping your children develop their own belief systems.

YOUR BEHAVIOR

Your behavior should reflect your choices, not how others would like you to behave.

Fact. If you were in a challenged marriage, your spouse may have demanded that you curb your freedom of action. As a result, you may have begun to change your behavior to please others. That would be especially likely if your spouse was controlling or domineering.

Begin to assert your personal boundary characteristics by redefining your behavior. Remember to keep your priorities in order as you work through this important step, which includes your behavior toward:

- God
- Your children
- Yourself

Any shuffling of these priorities will certainly produce complications somewhere in your life.

YOUR CHOICES

Your choices include the ones you make for yourself and the ones you make your children.

Freedom of choice (or free will) isn't just a constitutional right, it's a God-given right. Unfortunately, many people unwittingly try to usurp God's authority through controlling, demanding, and insensitive actions. We all know people like that. It is even possible you were married to one.

Now that you have won your freedom, define and defend it. If you and your family's choices are still being manipulated and controlled by others, get your personal boundaries in for a tune-up—fast.

YOUR VALUES

Your values are housed within your boundaries. They are based on what is important to you as a Christian parent.

You may recall that Joshua made a value decision for himself and his family in Joshua 24:15. "But as for me and my household, we will serve the Lord." You have the right—indeed, the strong encouragement from God—to make that same value judgment for your children.

You also are charged with the task of deciding values you want to instill in your children. Talk about responsibility. All newly single parents should take a few minutes to read 2 Corinthians 5:17. This Scripture teaches us to see ourselves as "new creatures" in Christ. We are no longer bound in the old, but free to make new decisions. It speaks to us of making a fresh start through Jesus.

Keep this in mind and you'll stay on track.

YOUR LIMITS

What are your limits and boundaries? It's up to you. As a single parent, it is important for you to begin defining your personal boundaries by the limits you set.

You may be one of many persons whose parents never encouraged you to grasp this responsibility. You may also have been married to a spouse who was more than happy to assume this role in your life. But now you free (and responsible) to define your limits based on your own belief system.

Defining your limits means saying no to people who abuse or take advantage of you. Make a conscious decision to stop enabling others to act irresponsibly or selfishly at your expense.

Understand that we all have blind spots in the way we see ourselves, and relate to others. Seek God's counsel and the counsel of friends and others who will help you define healthy limits.

YOUR DESIRES

Newly divorced parents often come to the realization that their needs went unnoticed or were discounted by an overly controlling spouse. Those needs may have been in cold storage for years, but they never vanished. Reexamine your life's desires and go after them. Maybe you always wanted to be a nurse, teacher, doctor, or whatever. You hold the key now.

YOUR NEEDS

Here comes a shocker, so brace yourself. You are responsible for meeting your needs—nobody else.

Your most basic need, like everyone else's, is to feel loved, bonded, and attached to God and others. And in case you didn't get it the first time, meeting those needs is *your* responsibility.

You may have sought love and acceptance through somebody else. Guess what? You gave away too much. You may also have given up your interest in having your own needs met because you were focusing all your attention and energy on meeting the needs of others. One of the hardest things for Christians to understand is that it is not selfish or unchristian to have needs and to try to have them met. The problem arises when you give away a sacred possession, your identity, to a person who cannot handle it and should never have had it in the first place.

Take the time to prayerfully consider your needs before sitting down to make a list. I think you will see that only two beings are capable of helping you meet your needs: God and you.

As a single parent, it is important that you take full ownership of your boundary system. If we allow our boundaries to be molded or manipulated, undermined, or stolen from us by others (such as a controlling ex-spouse, our parents, well-intended friends, or a strong-willed child), we will loose sight of ourselves. Without a sense of self, we will become human jellyfish who simply drift along with the current. We will become slaves to the needs, wishes, desires, whims, and control of others.

PLAYING THE VICTIM

At all costs avoid playing the role of victim. It places you in a subordinate, one-down position. You may play the victim well, but you will lose all sense of responsibility and personal power in the process. If you are wondering if you might already have assumed the victim's role, monitor your conversations for words such as, "I can't", or, "He won't let me." Whenever your responses begin with the word "but" and end with "I don't think I should," you're probably a victim.

RESPONDING VS. REACTING

If you're catching on to the power of limits in your life, it's important to be clear about the difference between reacting and responding. Briefly (we'll go into greater detail in later chapters) reacting is the act of tapping into your emotional self. Losing your cool. Blowing your stack. Your mouth is in overdrive while your brain is in park.

Responding, on the other hand, allows the thought process to become fully involved. Bottom line? Remember Dr. C's rule number 135. "Think before you talk. It takes far less time to plan what you will say than it takes to retract what you just said." I should sell that one to a fortune cookie company.

STICK-TO-ITIVENESS

"Let us run with perseverance the race marked out for us. Let us fix our eyes on Jesus" (Hebrews 12:1).

Parenthood is like running a marathon that takes eighteen years to complete. Stay on track by clearly defining your own personal course. Once you do, keep others from impeding your progress. One day you'll shake hands with an independent, well-integrated young adult who benefited from your parenting skills. You will have crossed the finish line.

HONESTY IS THE ONLY POLICY

As the Bible points out, honesty can bond a relationship (Ephesians 4:15.) Being able to speak the truth in love to others strengthens your position because it identifies you as an honest person. Keep in mind, the opposite of a truth is not a lie. It is denial.

A CHILD'S NEED FOR STRUCTURE

For children, the first important limit they learned might well have been the sense of touch. When your one-year-old reached for the candle on his birthday cake, you said, "No, no. Hot!" He pulled his hand back. It was a boundary imposed to protect your child. Since it seemed like a sensible limit, he eventually adopted it as his own, especially after being burned once or twice. He learned that getting too close to a lighted candle wasn't exactly a Kodak moment.

Let's say, however, that you are a single parent whose limits and boundaries were never defined before or after the divorce. In fact, your ex stomped on all your flimsy personal boundaries all the time. Guess what? Your children have picked up the same rotten habit. Notice how they take advantage of your good nature? Even your parents tell you what to do, how to raise your kids, and how to budget your finances. Everyone takes advantage of your inability to say no.

It might be agreeing to bake eighteen dozen cookies for the church charity auction on eight hour's notice. It might be letting your husband have the kids on Christmas, Thanksgiving, Easter, and their birthdays. If establishing and maintaining boundaries are a problem in your life, you will find yourself in a weakened position when it comes to identifying your own single-parenting style.

As we saw in Genesis and in the Ten Commandments, introducing limits and boundaries to your children is a responsibility that God has given to you. You must first, however, get a handle on your own limits and boundaries. Doing so will give you the personal control to shepherd your children in the direction of setting their own.

DISRUPTING THE LAWS OF BOUNDARIES

Do you recall those irritating little brain twisters we were punished with in grade school? Nonsense such as, "If two airplanes, one white and the other blue, left California bound for New York, and one left at 9:00 and the other at 9:05, and one airplane went north, and the other south, which arrived first?" Who cares? I'd sit there rubbing my forehead with the eraser from my pencil, hoping the answer would magically pop into my mind. "Let's see, the plane that didn't have engine problems and had to make an emergency stop in Arizona. Right?"

Who cares which plane arrived first. That's why God made travel agents. Ask me about something important, teacher. How about the combined batting average of the 1962 Los Angeles Dodgers after two outs? Now that's math.

Boundaries should be practical, or your kids will constantly be nodding off. Don't waste your time flexing the rules and regulations muscles just because you can. There's barely enough time to drive home the important stuff.

And speaking of time wasters, let's take a look at some of the typical single parent mind-sets that quickly lead us down the path to the boundary outhouse.

MIND-SET #1:
"IT WASN'T MY JOB IN THE FIRST PLACE."

Single parents often forget about the family rules that worked so well prior to the divorce. Perhaps those rules were set and enforced by the ex. The kids look around—no enforcer parent. Do you think they'll remind you about the old rule of going to bed by 9:30? Not a chance. It's the substitute teacher syndrome. You know, "When the cat's away, the kids will play." "The primary enforcer is gone, so let's party." Adults aren't much better. Ever notice how lunch hours expand when the boss is on a business trip?

It's critical to adapt and adjust to changes in your family system. Simply because the other spouse was more comfortable in setting and enforcing limits doesn't give you permission to neglect this essential element of parenting. Setting and maintaining boundaries must be viewed as an investment in your child's future, and your own peace of mind.

MIND-SET #2:
"I'LL GET TO IT LATER."

The second most common way that the boundary setting gets sidelined is the single parent's belief that there are more serious subjects at hand—such as food and shelter. Not that those aren't important, but they can't supersede the task of setting limits and boundaries.

It's true, there is a daunting grocery list of priority issues on the single parent's plate, including the groceries. Unfortunately, the children wind up losing, since they miss out on the emotional structure and sense of security that comes with consistent limitations.

MIND-SET #3:
"I'M JUST TOO TIRED."

As you're aware by now, setting and maintaining boundaries take considerably more effort than allowing your children to run rampant through the house. Take vitamins, jog, have an espresso, maybe a double, but find the energy to keep your boundaries intact.

Newly single parents often follow the path of least resistance, a path marked by over-indulgence, enabling, and denial. Remember, it's the road least traveled—the one with consistent limits —that will help you and your children arrive functionally, happily, and safely at your final destination: a place of happiness, wholeness, and purpose.

MIND-SET #4:
"HAVEN'T THEY GONE THROUGH ENOUGH ALREADY?"

Many parents consciously (and unconsciously) avoid placing limits and boundaries on their children because they want to protect them from further conflict. After all, they reason, haven't their children gone through enough? In a sense, parents who do this may be over-compensating or resisting conflict due to what we call *transference*. Transference is the unconscious transferring of one's own feelings into somebody else's mind-set, in this case, a child's. In other words, you are feeling a certain way, so you expect your children to feel the same way.

These single moms and dads become peacekeepers. They let their kids get away with murder, or at least away with things they never would have permitted predivorce. Things such as letting their kids eat ice cream before dinner, while seated on the living room couch. Or letting them stay up until 10:00 P.M. when bedtime used to be 8:30. Or giving in to whining that before would have received an immediate "Knock it off!"

All in the spirit of giving them "a little more time to adjust," these parents allow their children to become self-centered, irresponsible, and disrespectful. These parents figure, Why heap more pressure on the kids in the form of additional structure, limits, and boundaries?

This line of logic, though understandable, is very destructive. The more freedom a child is given, the less happy and increasingly confused he becomes. Kids have a heightened craving for limits and boundaries during and after a divorce. Structure connects them to family, helps them organize their thoughts and feelings, and supplies them with a sense of security. If a parent cuts back, suddenly scrubs rules, and ends discipline, the child will feel cut off, adrift, and unsure of her- or himself.

MIND-SET #5:
"I'M NOT AROUND ENOUGH TO DEAL WITH BOUNDARIES."
Here's a common boundary-setting myth: A parent must be present constantly to enforce the boundaries. False. Although it is true that compliance is related to the frequency of reinforcement, it is not totally dependent on it. Here are the essential ingredients for establishing and maintaining fair and consistent boundaries.

Boundary Treats
(serves 1)

2 cups of Fairness	2 cups of Firmness
2 cups of Communication	2 cups of Consistency
10 lbs. of Love	

(For best results, pour ingredients over your kid's head daily. You get the idea.)

Equal parts of each ingredient are required for establishing and maintaining boundaries, with the exception of love. More love is required because it is the key ingredient. If it is not present in a sufficient amount, the recipe will be a disaster.

DIVORCE, KIDS, AND BOUNDARY CONFUSION

They won't show up on the final divorce settlement, but family discipline often gets divided up right along with the minivan, big screen TV, and silverware. Hardly a generous gesture, the other parent may have left you with all of the boundary-enforcing duties. Thanks a lot. Even if you are skilled in boundary setting and maintenance, it's a whole different ball game now that you are essentially playing a two-person sport alone.

HOW DO KIDS FEEL ABOUT BOUNDARIES?
We've taken a look at how single parents view boundaries, but how about kids? Here are some common thoughts of boundary-starved kids.

THE "I-DIDN'T-DO-IT" CHILD

"The sun was in my eyes!" "I didn't hear the teacher!" "I didn't do it. He did it!" Don't you just love the excuses your kids come up with? My favorite is when I come home, see a giant mess in the middle of the room, and ask, "Whose stuff is this?" Now logic dictates that a pile of toys probably belongs to one of my children, since my wife doesn't often play with toys while she's home alone. I love how instinctively both kids will deny the mess at the same time and then stare at it in silence. I know they're both hoping I'll eventually tire of the inquisition and simply go away. Maybe they figure, "He's old, let's wait him out."

As a policeman, I marveled at the multitude of innovative excuses people would come up with for traffic violations. What they didn't know was that I had an unwritten rule. Anybody I pulled over who said, "You're absolutely right, officer. I ran that stop sign back there," got off scot-free. I refused to write traffic tickets for people who took full responsibility for their actions. Why? Because a ticket would serve no further purpose. They were already honest and knew of their mistake. What good would a reminder do?

The moral of this story is that few people, let alone children, will step up to the plate and own their share of responsibility for a problem.

This is especially true of children following a divorce. Remember, they've seen plenty of blame tossed back and forth, like a hot potato, between mom and dad. A child's chronic blaming is a sure sign of an underdeveloped or nonexistent boundary system.

It's important that a child learn to take responsibility for his or her actions. Be sure your children understand that you don't expect perfection from them. Let them know that nobody's perfect, even you. It's very possible they are resisting taking responsibility because of underlying insecurities stemming from the divorce. Remember, kids are black-and-white thinkers. Consider what they witnessed during the divorce. Did you take responsibility for your share of the split? Or were you constantly laying blame? Your modeling an acceptance of responsibility for your own problems will free them to accept more responsibility.

THE HELPLESS CHILD

After a divorce many children become overly dependent on one parent (or both) to make all decisions. Fear and insecurity often send them into a needy position and dependence on others. This child is a classic codependent in the making. Remember, codependents feel unlovable and unworthy of independent thinking.

You are going to have to target your child's self-esteem and independence through boundary exploration. Encourage him to make independent decisions. Even if you don't always agree with his decision, praise him for taking action anyway. Allow him to assume more responsibility in his life, but be careful not to push him away too hard. Doing so may cause more insecurity if the decision-making consequences are too negative.

THE OVERINDULGED CHILD

The overindulging single parent can create a Grand Canyon full of problems for himself. This type of parent simply gives too much of everything. Too many toys. Too much freedom. Even too much love. Too much self.

Here's an aerial view. Let's say this particular child visits his dad every other weekend. Dad goes all out. Disneyland, ball games, fairs, movies, you name it. Whenever the child says, "Know what, Dad, I sure could use another game cartridge for my Nintendo," it's off to the mall. The child harnesses his own insecurities by manipulating dad's guilt—not a bad second prize, is it?

Mom may also be consumed with guilt. She sees dad racking-up the old bonus points and becomes jealous. And Junior, being a master manipulator, fuels the fire by making statements to mom such as, "I like going to Dad's. He's fun to be with." If she is unaware of the scam, she may unconsciously relent and begin trying to do more for the child.

This dysfunctional system often gives birth to a tremendously needy little monster who thrives on a steady diet of gratification in the form of attention and "stuff." The baby beast continues to grow in power and influence until he either outgrows his cage (the family), or the zoo keepers decide to limit his power by reducing his daily feedings of gratification.

THE DEPRESSED CHILD

Divorce can lead to loss of identity in a child, which had been established and then continually reinforced through his role in his family. With change comes insecurity, anxiety, confusion, depression, and blurred boundaries.

Because they are entirely dependent on others to meet their emotional needs, depressed children wonder, "Am I still loved? Who will take care of my needs now?" Depression jumps in when their insecurity takes over.

Help your children to determine the things that fall within their personal boundaries. Work with them in defining their personal sense of self. That will help them become more independent and less reliant on you and others in order to feel good.

THE FORGETFUL CHILD

The forgetful child is a close relative of the dependent child. Raised without personal boundaries and limits, these children are often emotionally disorganized. Their disorganization may show up in the form of helplessness, timidity, or tentativeness. It's a tough symptom to identify, though, since many children have some of these characteristics anyway.

Warning signs become easier to spot in older children and teenagers. For example, you may notice a problem in their completing household chores. They may lack the personal discipline to sit at the kitchen table and do their homework without help or constant reminders. They may forget their school books or lunch money and then call home for you to rescue them. They may arrive at the little league field without their gloves. Finally, you may begin to wonder if they have any neurons firing in their little heads at all.

The forgetful child may be unconsciously saying, "I need to feel more connected to you." Instead of coming right out with it and verbalizing those needs, he communicates this message by appearing disorganized, dysfunctional, or helpless.

This type of behavior can be overcome by giving the child more responsibility for things that fall within his personal boundaries. As with the dependent child, bailing him out or gratifying and taking over his boundaries will cause further dependence and disorganization.

Sit down with your child and try to interpret the wheres and whys of his dependence or forgetfulness. Help him to see that these symptoms are likely due to fears and insecurities stemming from the divorce. Then work with your child to help him realize that taking more personal control doesn't mean he will wind up being hurt or abandoned again. Teach him the principle that taking healthy responsibility translates into increased security.

THE PASSIVE-AGGRESSIVE CHILD

Face the facts. Divorce creates anger, resentment, and potential hostility in everybody—even kids. Following divorce, many children unconsciously feel their personal boundaries have been repossessed. They're looking for someone to take the blame. Guess who's standing there with big, red targets on their backs?

The children may resent one or both parents for causing their problems. They may also resent people in authority—teachers, coaches, bosses, God—since they represent authority, and it was people in authority who caused their hurt in the first place.

At the heart of this resentment is repressed anger for not being strong enough to establish their own limits and boundaries. They hide this weakness by displaying passive-aggressive behavior. They may announce, "I'll do it," despite having no intention of following through. It's an act of subtle defiance that can't be verbalized out of fear and insecurity.

The parable of the two sons in Matthew 21:28–31 aptly depicts this problem. Jesus talks about a father who asked his two sons to help out in the vineyard. The first son says, "I will not," but later changes his mind and goes to work. The second son says, "I will, sir," but goes off to the mall, or wherever teenagers hung out in those days. The second son exhibited a passive-aggressiveness, probably aimed at the father's authority, by telling him he would comply with his wishes to avoid a possible confrontation. Sound familiar?

THE DEFEATIST CHILD

"Why should I chance doing it myself," says the defeatist child, "when you're going to find fault and do it over anyway?" Newly single parents sometimes become impossible-to-please perfectionists in an effort to remain in control. One day their children just throw in the towel. They figure enough is enough. They become irresponsible, helpless kids who continually blame others for their problems. After all, they won't ever measure up, so why not go for the gusto?

Teachers refer to these kids as classic underachievers. They tell the parent, "He has a good mind, but he just doesn't apply himself." If this sounds like your child, check your management skills. Have you turned into a control freak by trespassing over his personal boundaries? If so, your child could be in for a lifetime of underachieving.

THE OPPORTUNISTIC CHILD

Meet the opportunistic child, otherwise known as the manipulator. After you've caught him dead-to-rights, clearly in violation of one of your boundaries, he says in his best Schwarzenegger imitation, "I'll be back," as he slowly marches toward his room.

The opportunistic child comes in all shapes, sizes, ages, and sexes—both of them. He's the one who tells the substitute teacher, "No ma'am, we never have homework on Tuesdays," and then later tells you, "I did my homework on the bus." Remember, the apple doesn't fall far from the tree.

Kids aren't shy about using the substitute teacher routine against a parent unfamiliar with his new parenting role. Beat them to the punch. Admit that things might be a little unorganized for a while. Communicate that you are requesting (not demanding or expecting) their full cooperation. Get set. They are going to test you anyway. Call their attention to the manipulation every time and then calmly meet the challenges. It's normal for kids to test limits. It's in their job description.

STEPPING STONES TO BETTER BOUNDARIES

Personal boundaries encompass everything we are and all we would like to become: what we like and don't like, what our dreams are about, our prejudices and our tolerances, our joys and our sorrows, our passions and our ambivalencies. Above all, our boundaries tell the world who we are and what we stand for. Can we wish or encourage any less for our children?

As single parents, if we can't make our boundaries and consequences understood, how can we expect anyone, much less our kids, to honor them? As you've probably told your ex many times, "I'm not a mind reader. How am I supposed to know if you don't tell me?" The same holds true with your kids. It's our responsibility, as the adult in the relationship, to communicate boundaries.

STEPPING STONE #1:
MODELING LIMITS AND BOUNDARIES
The most effective way of communicating boundaries, as with most behavior, is to model them for your children. For instance, if your child has become a follower—totally dependent on you and on others—double-check your boundaries. If people don't respect your boundaries, or you trounce all over everybody else's, why should your child act any differently?

Nobody is born with the inherent ability to set and maintain boundaries in his life. It's simply not a trait we inherit the way we do Aunt Edna's sense of humor or mom's weird toes. Your ability to set and maintain boundaries stems from a complex combination of things.

• Your Personality Type

To an extent, the personality type that God gave you when you came into the world plays a role in your ability to set and maintain boundaries.

Nobody, however, is born with a personality type that makes boundaries impossible. Boundaries simply seem to be easier for people with stronger, more aggressive personalities than for those who are more sensitive, passive, dependent, or compliant.

• Your Observations

Environment or genetics? It's always a lively topic for debate as to which plays the predominant role in deciding an individual's personality. Why can't we just argue about politics and religion like other people?

Simply stated, if you were raised in a home where your parents modeled healthy limits, you are considerably better prepared to apply boundaries in your life.

• Your Emerging Boundaries

As you matured, you were either allowed to experience greater ownership of your life through setting your own boundaries, or you were discouraged from doing so. In other words, did your parents allow you to take more responsibility for defining and policing yourself, or did they maintain control over your boundaries and discourage your independence until you finally left home?

• A Battle of Wills

Unfortunately, we sometimes place ourselves in relationships where we have chosen to give up our boundaries. Maybe we just got tired of fighting over boundary issues and decided it was easier to give in.

This most often occurs when we marry someone with a stronger will than ours. In relationships such as these, boundaries seem to erode over time.

IN SEARCH OF
THE ELUSIVE BOUNDARY

"Don't hold back. Give it to me straight, doc. Am I *boundary challenged?*" Building better boundaries is covered in countless books.

If you are interested in doing more work in this area, may I suggest a book titled *Boundaries* (Grand Rapids: Zondervan, 1992), written by two colleagues of mine at the Minirth-Meier Clinic West, Dr. John Townsend and Dr. Henry Cloud.

Whenever a person begins to lay down boundaries, others are likely to take exception. Why shouldn't they? They've had their way so long, why should they celebrate your newly found limit-setting ability?

STEPPING STONE #1:
START WITH "BABY BOUNDARIES"
I suggest you begin by setting "baby boundaries." If your ex asks if he can make the child support payment a couple of weeks late because he's scheduled a vacation and you're hesitant to demand the whole two weeks, try saying, "I'm really not in agreement with two weeks. What about one week late?"

Are you ready for a monster boundary? How about if your ex is always tardy in getting the kids back after visitations? When you ask him nicely to adhere to the policy, he discounts your feelings and then does whatever he wants to do. Flexing your newly developed boundary muscles, you might tell him, "The terms of our settlement state the children are to be home by 6:00 P.M. If you are unable to return them to me on time, then the whole issue of visitation is in question. What is it going to take for you to understand how seriously I see this problem?"

Setting baby boundaries serves two purposes. First, it allows those around you to adjust to your new limit-setting style. Second, it helps you to flex and develop your "no" muscle.

STEPPING STONE #2:
MAKE SURE YOUR BOUNDARIES ARE CLEAR
Before you can expect compliance with your boundaries, be sure your messages are being received clearly. Like a supervisor assigning new responsibilities at work, it is mandatory for you to clearly define the new job duties and responsibilities before you can expect your employees to perform.

Whether it is with your kids, your ex, or others, make sure you are stating your needs and expectations up-front, clearly. Doing so greatly improves their ability to succeed in complying with your boundaries.

STEPPING STONE #3:
MAKE SURE YOUR BOUNDARIES ARE FAIR

Remember, sometimes we can ask too much of ourselves, our children, and others. A boundary that isn't fair is a boundary destined to be tested.

Take, for example, a parent who really lays down the law about dating. No dates until she's eighteen. Is that a fair boundary? Probably not, by most standards. Is that boundary going to be tested by the teenager? Undoubtedly.

STEPPING STONE #4:
COMMUNICATE THE REASONS BEHIND YOUR BOUNDARIES

You might have the most reasoned, well-intentioned boundary in the world, but if you fail to communicate the reasons for it, the meaning is lost. Your children will be more accepting and respectful of your boundaries if they don't see them as arbitrary, punitive, or a flexing of your parental muscles. You'll only strengthen your position as a well-balanced parent by explaining your boundaries first.

STEPPING STONE #5:
EXAMINE THE MOTIVATIONS
BEHIND THE BOUNDARIES YOU ESTABLISH

Boundaries should be defensive, not offensive. Don't use them as a cover to punish. Before you set a boundary, read the label. Examine its contents for purity. If you are setting a given boundary out of spite, to punish, or to bolster your position, let it go. Remember, there are laws about truth in advertising.

STEPPING STONE #6:
ASK FOR COMPLIANCE

Why wait for a problem to occur when it comes to your boundaries? Try a little preventive maintenance by asking for compliance instead of demanding it. That will help your children feel involved rather than forcing them to look for ways to go over, under, or around you. Ask for compliance as soon as you set a boundary.

STEPPING STONE #7:
MAKE BOUNDARIES REALISTIC

Some people expect the impossible from their boundaries. You know, like two small children sitting quietly for an hour while you try on dresses at the department store. Be realistic. Give your children a fighting chance to obey your limits and boundaries.

STEPPING STONE #8:
ESTABLISH CONSEQUENCES IN ADVANCE
When you establish consequences, be sure they are consistent with the severity of the broken rule. For example, would you restrict your kid to his room for the weekend for snatching an extra cookie after you said no more? Consequences serve as reminders or motivators for your child to make good decisions. They are meant to teach.

STEPPING STONE #9:
COMMIT TO CONSISTENCY
Remember how we defined good single parenting as being somewhat predictable? This goes double for setting, maintaining, and responding to your children's personal boundaries. Simply put, what's right today has to be okay next month. What wasn't still isn't.

These stepping stones mark the path that single parents should follow when establishing positive and consistent rules and boundaries for children. Venturing from them usually means wading hip deep in mud. These steps are equally effective whether you are just starting out as a single parent, or are a veteran at the job looking for new techniques.

THE LETTER OF THE LAW

You are not a Christian *single parent,* you are a Christian *parent.* As such, you are responsible for your children's well-being, for keeping them safe, and for training them "in the way they should go," as the book of Proverbs puts it.

Ephesians 6:1–2 reads: "Children obey your parents. . . . Honor your father and mother." Passages such as that can be truly inspirational, but they should be kept in context. Parents often slam head-on into child-rearing problems when they interpret Scripture from a black-and-white, absolutist perspective. The Bible often gets put back on the shelf before mom or dad reads the rest of the passage: "Fathers (moms too), do not exasperate your children; instead, bring them up in the training and instruction of the Lord" (Ephesians 6:4).

We've already witnessed God's ability to be in complete control while parenting us with a mixture of love and limits. If nothing else, remember that love plus limits equal something very special to our children. It adds up to security, acceptance, and the ability to be more self-reliant. If we are forgiving and set reasonable, clear, and consistent rules, our children will develop a sense of security in themselves.

BOUNDARIES THROUGH CONTROL

When a parent employs Gestapo tactics—fear, manipulation, and intimidation—to keep his children under tight security like prisoners of war, he may win "the battle of the wills," but rest assured, he will lose the war. If your children are afraid of losing your love because they haven't remained behind your barbed-wire boundaries, then fear might well give way to resentment and emotional distancing. Don't be surprised when your kid finally tunnels out from under those rigid boundaries, making good his escape from your life.

PARENTING WITH ALL LOVE AND GRACE

Parenting with love and grace. It has a certain ring, doesn't it? It sounds like a perfectly civilized approach to parenting—a "Christian" way of doing things. Unfortunately, in the final analysis, it just doesn't work. God knew immediately it wouldn't work for Him, and it won't work for us either.

For starters, a child views all grace as a pizza party with enough video game tokens to last him until he's twenty-two. And why not? He has passively been given permission to do as he likes without knowledge of consequences for his actions.

Life is good! His enabler parent has allowed him to become self-centered, irresponsible, and disrespectful—what more could a kid ask for? Again, it is a proven fact that children prefer limits and structure to ultimate freedom. Problem is, they're usually not mature enough (of course) to realize it.

PARENTING WITH ALL RULES AND LAWS

On the other hand (usually the back of the hand), a controlling, all-limits type of single parent has all the sensitivity of a hungry sumo wrestler. We were introduced to this parenting style (along with others), in chapter 2: The Superparent.

Such a parent has enough rules, limits, conditions, clauses and fine print to wallpaper the Astrodome. "You want my love? You better earn it, Mister. Get down and give me fifty push-ups! . . . I can't hear youuuu!"

A kid raised by a Superparent should seek representation, be-cause it takes a court order to get any grace. These children jump through hoops in hopes of earning even a few shreds of love and respect. After they tire of jumping through hoops, they jump ship.

UNDERSTANDING
THE DREADED TWO-LETTER WORD:
THE DISOBEDIENT NOES

Nearly all parents seem to remember that their child's first words were either "Mama" or "Dada." It just depends on who's doing the remembering. The truth is, the word no probably sprang from his lips long before Dada or Mama. Sorry. In fact, I was six-years-old before I realized my name wasn't "No, Greg!"

Our children actually possess two distinct types of noes, disobe-dient noes and responsible noes.

A disobedient no is a cinch to spot. Unlike many of those gray areas in parenting that leave you mumbling to yourself, a disobedient no comes gift-wrapped in neon colors.

If you ask your teenager to be home by 9:00 P.M. and he counters with "No, I already told the guys I'm hanging with my friends 'till ten or so," you could file this one under the "disobedient no" file. When you tell your six-year-old, "No cookies before din-ner," and you catch him with Oreo residue all over his mouth, bingo, another disobedient—albeit nonverbal—no.

Now that you've identified the problem, what's next? A disobe-dient no should never be ignored or taken lightly. I'm not suggesting that you implement a "Use a no, go to jail" policy, but there should be appropriate consequences attached when your parental boundaries have definitely been crossed. Disobedient noes should receive imme-diate correction.

TERRITORIAL NOES

A territorial no is a completely different creature. If you own a woman's clothing store, for example, you're the owner, the proprie-tor. It's your territory. You have the right to fill your racks with the apparel you have personally selected. You also have the right to re-fuse service (or to say no) for appropriate reasons. Children too have an inherent right to responsible, or territorial, noes. Saying no or yes at the right time is an important part of formulating and guarding one's boundary systems. When a child's personal boundaries are arbitrarily struck down by the parent or others, a slough of problems can develop.

EMPOWERING KIDS

The urge for all parents, single or otherwise, to paint their children into their own personal boundaries is tempting, but should be resisted. When you empower your children with a full compliment of personal noes, they are free to begin expressing their own boundaries and limits. If your children are forbidden to say no to things that fall within their proprietary limits, how can you expect them to say no to drugs, alcohol, premarital sex, or other inappropriate behaviors? When a child's right to his personal no is honored at home, his need to act out with disobedient noes is greatly reduced.

ARE THERE CONSEQUENCES
TO A TERRITORIAL NO?

It may be easier to win the lottery than to achieve a family consensus about dinner out. One child lobbies for hamburgers, while the other has mounted a major write-in campaign for pizza. A basic truth remains: they will never agree on the same thing at the same time. I think it's a kid's union thing.

The votes are counted, and the family arrives at the pizza place (the dog's signature was deemed valid) and orders the "Ultimate Classic Cheese Experience." As you are dishing out the slices while grumbling about the lack of cheese, the kid who you swear was left on your doorstep by aliens declares, "No, I don't want to eat here. I don't want pizza. I want tacos."

"That's okay, son. You don't have to eat here," you say calmly. "If you're hungry later, there may be a few pieces of cold, picked-over pizza left." The boy suddenly reassesses his position and snaps up a hot slice. He found out that there were consequences to his personal no, so he acted in his best interest. In other words it is true he had a right to say no, "I choose not to eat pizza." However, boundaries come factory-equipped with consequences. In this case, the consequence was beginning to look like cold pizza.

The same scenario with a boundary-less (or enabling) parent looks quite different. You can see how the parent's boundaries can determine an entirely different outcome. When the boy says no to the pizza, his pushover mom quickly rushes next door to the taco place and brings back a deluxe taco. Big mistake. By giving in to his desire for a taco, his mom ignored and actually encouraged his desire to say no. He was stripped of any chance to take responsibility for his actions—to experience the consequences that go along with certain boundaries.

IN CONCLUSION

Did you ever stop to notice that boundaries wouldn't be at all necessary if only we lived in a world where nobody took advantage of us, a world where we were all compelled to reach the high standards, morals, and principles that God asks us to attain? As we have seen, that worked with mixed reviews in the first book of the Bible, and it still does today. Hence, the need to set and maintain boundaries.

Building boundaries is like beginning a regiment of exercise. When you start out, you'll find yourself becoming stiff and sore. As the stiffness wears off, your muscles begin to strengthen, and before you know it, what used to seem like an impossibility has now become a routine.

·4·

CULTIVATE THE FINE ART OF SINGLE-PARENT COMMUNICATION

Coping with her anger was challenging enough, without having to worry about forgiving the guy too. *Forgiveness? Fat chance!* Connie thought, trying to remember something that Jesus had told the apostles.

She finally found her Bible buried under a bunch of old phone books and a stack of *Reader's Digests*. *I think it's in Luke something or other.* She ran her finger down the page until she came to Luke 17:3–4. *Here it is!* "If your brother sins, rebuke him, and if he repents, forgive him." *What is this stuff? It says here I'm supposed to forgive him as many as seven times in a day if he's been repentant. You've got to be kidding!*

"Lord, please. Do you understand who I'm dealing with here?" she said, looking upward, her eyes shut tightly. "This is a guy without a remorseful bone in his body. He only feels remorse when he gets caught the second or third time. Then he's Mr. Remorseful. He's never hinted that he was sorry for anything other than the fact that he was caught. Why should I forgive him? And about this 'seven times in a day' thing, God . . . He wronged us more than that on a good day."

"Ummm," she whispered, hoping God wasn't still listening. "Yeah, that's it. I'll just forgive him. That's what I'll do. I'll forgive the tiny, little pinhead on the fifth Sunday of every month. The 29th of February. The 12th of never."

Connie had grown weary of weighing her words with the kids. She was tired of being evenhanded about the split and speaking in respectful, even positive terms about their dad.

Kimberly was having bad dreams almost nightly. Kelli was embarrassed and ashamed. She's was afraid that her friends at her private Christian school would find out about the divorce and begin treating her differently. And Aaron, who originally handled the pressure of the divorce by scampering up his tree, smoking cigarettes, or cutting school, now seemed to be dealing with his feelings fairly well.

The way Connie saw it, the divorce was a done deal. Visitation rights had been arranged. Child support had been hammered out. Why should she continue to prop up dad with the kids? Why should she shoulder half the blame? It was time the children knew the truth, she decided.

For Connie, the final straw had come when Kelli returned home—unruly as usual—after a weekend stay with her father. "Hi, Mom," she bubbled. "I had the greatest time at Dad's. We went skating, bowling, and saw two movies. One was that movie where the guy—what's his name? Arnold something-or-other—goes around blowing everybody away. It was totally radical the way they made people's heads blow up! And guess what? I got to stay up as late as I wanted one night when Dad had a giant party. And Mom, Dad's new girlfriend, you'd really like her—she's really cute and nice. She even showed me how to style my hair differently and use lipstick and eye shadow. Do you like it? Next time I visit, she said she'll take me shopping and get me some nicer clothes."

That was it. She could handle Aaron blaming her for the divorce. But this? Her very own daughter calling the girlfriend cute? Not in her home. No way. Off came the gloves.

"Listen, Kelli," she vented, "I'm glad you had a nice time. But you're almost ten. You're old enough to understand what I'm going to say."

"Understand what, Mom?" Kelli answered, not really listening as she admired her new look in the mirror.

"You're father is the ultra dirt bag of the nineties. I did everything I could to make him happy. I worked my tail off to be a good wife, and how did he respond? By trading me in for a younger, thinner, 'cuter' model. I'm sick of doing all of the work around here. I'm sick of being the bad guy—the one who says no. I'm sick of paying the bills and struggling to keep our family together while your father mugs for the camera and says 'Come on kids, we're going to Disneyland!'

"He's not the one who carts you all over town and manages to hold down a full-time job. I am!

"He's not the one who makes sure you get to Brownies, soccer practice, piano, and baton twirling lessons. I am!

"He's not the one who helps two of you with your schoolwork. I am!

"He's not the one who has to assign chores and then keep on you because you aren't doing them. I am!

"He's not the one who gets everybody dressed up every Sunday and then takes you to church. I am!

"He's not the one who cleans your dirty clothes, or takes care of you when you're sick, or comforts you when you've had a nightmare. I am!"

Fortunately, she again caught herself a split-second before she could unleash the tirade of her dreams. Instead, she simply said to Kelli when she arrived home, gushing about her visit, "I'm glad you had a good time, dear. Yes, I like your new hair style. Now, take off the lipstick and get cleaned up for dinner."

It's only a matter of time, Connie thought, looking like a cartoon character with steam whistling out of her ears, *before I really cut loose and tell the kids just exactly how I feel about dear old dad. I'm going to stop being Little Mary Sunshine and start being Atilla the Hun. Won't that be special?*

At the very least, she would have something to talk about tomorrow in therapy, she reasoned.

HOW MUCH DO YOUR KIDS NEED TO KNOW?

Connie took her usual place on the couch, wrapping her arms tightly around one of the large, overstuffed pillows. "So, Connie, catch me up with what's been happening with you and the kids this week. Aaron still staying away from his tree house?"

She didn't even hear my last comment but asked instead, "What do I tell the kids about their father? Sometimes I just want to tell them the truth. That he traded us all in for a part-time aerobics instructor with an IQ the same as her bra size—before the surgery. I'm just so angry and frustrated, Doc. It makes me want to hurt David back, but I know it will only hurt the kids."

Connie had obviously hit the wall in terms of her own frustration and anger and her quandary about what to tell the children about the divorce. First, I assured her that her feelings were understandable at this stage. Then I asked again for an update about what had been going on with the family.

"Last I heard, Kelli was going to spend the weekend over at her dad's. How'd that go, Connie? Did you sit down with her and talk about what she might expect before she left for her visit?"

"That's my problem. I froze with Kelli." I didn't prepare her for anything, especially the girlfriend sleeping over—she's so little and infatuated with her daddy. But I did tell Aaron pretty much the truth because he's older and could handle it better. I told him his dad is confused about his life, and that he was doing things differently these days. Things that I certainly don't approve of. Like sex prior to marriage. I ended up just telling him that we hadn't been getting along for the past couple of years, so he left us."

She paused for a minute. "I probably shouldn't have said this, but I also told him that when men get older, they go through a middle-aged craziness and sometimes think they need a girlfriend and a sports car to feel younger again. What do you think?" Connie asked, slouching on the couch in expectation of my response. "I shot myself in the foot, didn't I?"

"Well, there certainly are some things that are better left unsaid," I said, "but I think you're aware of that. Let's talk about setting some communication boundaries as they relate to what kids need to know. And then let's get some bandages for that foot."

We both laughed.

There are three major areas you should examine before deciding what, or how much, your kids need to know about the divorce. The first involves age-appropriateness. The second revolves around your mood. And the third examines parental motivation.

AGE-APPROPRIATENESS OF THE MESSAGE
Before you "spill your guts" about the divorce, first consider the ages of your children. This is true during all stages of the divorce process—whether it's before, during, or long after the fact.

In Connie's case, Aaron, thirteen, was old enough to hear certain truths that would be inappropriate for Kelli, ten, and very inappropriate for Kimberly, age four.

Kids have a right and a need to know some of the circumstances regarding the divorce. They don't need to know all of the gory details.

Most children under ten don't need to know much more than the basics. Those include the facts you need to include in what I call "the first talk." The first talk is the roughest. It means breaking the bad news—mom and dad aren't going to be living together any more. Here's a possible way to begin.

"Moms and dads fall in love, get married, and have children. Sometimes, though, their feelings for one another change. When that happens, it's usually time for moms and dads to get some help with their marriage. Most of the time, it works. If it doesn't, then moms and dads sometimes separate. Just as we have separated. It doesn't mean we no longer care for each other. It just means that it's easier to stay friends when we're not living together."

"We're still a family, but instead of living together in one house, Dad (or Mom) now lives in another house. That doesn't change how much we love and care for you."

Make sure your children know that divorce is something that happens between married people only. For all practical purposes it doesn't occur between parent and child.

Even after you've had "the talk," don't expect your children to stop asking questions. As they mature, or hear things from their friends, they'll want to know more about the particulars surrounding the divorce—which is precisely why you don't want to begin lying or shading the truth under the guise of "it's for their own good." As the years go by and they continue to show an interest in that period in your lives, feel free to give them additional facts, while remaining mindful of age-appropriateness. If they catch you in half-truths, they will always doubt your credibility.

Older children or teens may ask more insightful questions, such as "Why does Dad have a girlfriend?" or, "What was the real reason you left Dad?" Be as direct as possible, while avoiding the punishing details. No child wants (or needs) to know that his mother or father has moral, ethical, or character problems. It serves no constructive purpose.

STOP, LOOK, AND LISTEN

Before you utter a single word about the divorce to your children "Stop, Look, and Listen" before crossing the street to this subject.

We learned in grade school the danger of not following this adage before venturing off the sidewalk. We might get run over by a Mack truck, right? The same holds true for venturing from the safe sidewalk of silence into the heavy traffic of oncoming emotions. So before you talk to your kids about sensitive issues, follow these steps.

Stop. Stop and allow your mind to catch up with your emotions or mood. To put it bluntly, don't put your mouth in drive while your brain is in park.

Look. Look within yourself before you speak to your children about the divorce. If what you see is honest, pure, and honorable, proceed. If not, and you see yourself becoming punishing or manipulative, call a "time out" until you are able to regain perspective.

Listen. Pay close attention to what your children are saying, asking, and feeling about the divorce. Try to determine how it may have affected them. Remember that all of us, especially children, initially focus on our own well-being, security, and future following a divorce.

EXAMINE YOUR MOTIVES

Respond to your children's need for and right to information, but don't allow yourself to get caught up in your own agenda of anger, sarcasm, or vindictiveness.

Punishing your ex by communicating harmful or hurtful messages to your children will *always* blow up in your face. You may feel better briefly, but these hurtful messages will come back to haunt you later.

COMMUNICATION LAND MINES IN SINGLE-PARENT FAMILIES

Over the years, I've come to refer to any commonly repeated mistake in communication as a "land mine." Why? Because the expression best describes the emotional force of the way we react to sensitive issues.

Following a divorce, communication land mines are detonated regularly in the interchange between you and your children, between you and your ex, and between you and anybody who's invading your private turf—your boundaries.

When it comes to communication land mines, nobody is out of harm's way, not even the family dog.

Haven't you ever gotten up to get a cup of coffee, only to find your favorite donut missing? You immediately scream at the dog, who sits there—frozen—like a deer caught in your headlights. As you're reading the mutt his constitutional rights, you hear the sound of muffled snickers from down the hall—the unmistakable sound created when a six-year-old tries to laugh with an entire jelly donut stuffed into his mouth. *Kaaa boom!* Communication land mine.

"Sorry, Spottie. Here, have a few donut holes. A little something to ease my guilt. And have a nice day."

COMMUNICATION LAND MINE #1:
REACTING VS. RESPONDING

Face it. There's often enough emotional toxic waste after a divorce to mutate an entire civilization of Ninja Turtles. Things may appear to be going smoothly, and boom! Somebody says the wrong thing in the wrong way. You immediately go into a "terminator mode" and proceed to annihilate the guilty party with a barrage of slams and insults. A passive individual would respond to the same situation by withdrawing, sulking, becoming defensive, or isolating. Regardless of your personality type, you're still reacting rather than responding.

When we stumble over communication land mines, it's typically because we've allowed our emotions to govern our actions. To put it just one more way (I promise), your brain is on vacation and your mouth is home alone. You're reacting instead of responding. Let's examine the differences between the two.

Reacting is an emotional form of communicating, whereas responding allows the thought process to become fully involved. It's important that all parents, and especially single parents, be alert to the following warning signs before reacting emotionally:

- Does your face feel flushed?
- Have your listening skills shut down?
- Do you feel yourself becoming defensive?
- Are you already thinking of punishment or consequences?
- Are you getting angrier by the second?

There's no easy way of avoiding a reaction-charged land mine. If you feel yourself about ready to explode, I suggest the following steps:

- Force yourself to stop or call a time-out.
- Listen and ask clarifying questions.
- Take a few deep breaths.
- Get a second opinion if necessary.
- Try your best to deal with the situation using love and logic instead of emotions and reactions.

COMMUNICATION LAND MINE #2:
DISCOUNTING FEELINGS

"When I go shopping with Dad he lets me choose whatever clothes I want," your child says, home from a weekend visit. "If he wants to spoil you, that's his business," Mom reacts. "Just look at that awful combination. You're just like you father. Neither one of you has any taste in clothing."

Discounting or minimizing a child's feelings is one of the most destructive communication land mines you can touch off. He's already experiencing enough insecurity from the dramatic changes in the family. It's cruel to compound those insecurities and anxieties by minimizing his feelings. Discounting feelings are usually followed closely by an explosion—and a ringing sensation in your ears.

Remember that children and teens have a right to their thoughts, feelings, and opinions. Sure they may be silly, pointless, and irrational, but they are still valid. Before you minimize, consider these questions.

1. Ask yourself if your child seems to be more emotionally charged-up in this matter than you would normally expect.

2. When it comes to communication matters regarding your ex, bear in mind this is already an emotionally invested area for all concerned.

3. Ask clarifying questions: "Help me understand how you are feeling," or, "I don't think I'm seeing your side of this issue. Can you help me out?" These questions will help you get a clearer picture of the emotionally charged issues beneath the surface.

4. Be cautious of the main discounting phrases:
   - "Don't feel that way."
   - "I can't believe you're acting like this."
   - "Why are you making such a big deal out of this?"
   - "How come your brother (sister) isn't making this such a big deal?"

5. Validate your child's feelings by making statements such as, "You certainly have a right to feel the way you do," or, "I don't really understand what you are feeling, but I respect your right to feel that way."

Let your kids know that you respect and honor their feelings. God gave children feelings, but nowhere does He give parents the authority to revoke them. Even if we don't agree with or understand them, remember that feelings are never right or wrong—they just are. Your child's feelings are part of his personal possessions and boundaries. They must be respected.

COMMUNICATION LAND MINE #3: NAGGING

Most children and teens, if promised amnesty, would say that their parents are professional nags. Many feel the nagging intensified during and after the divorce. As we mentioned earlier in this book, nagging is often a parent's way of overcompensating in an effort to maintain discipline.

What exactly is nagging? The *American Heritage Dictionary* (Houghton Mifflin Company, Boston 1991) defines it as annoying "by constant scolding, complaining, or urging." Fine. That's you. Now how to stop?

Do the following conversations sound familiar?

Mom:	"How many times do I have to remind you to pick up your room?"
Child thinks:	"Well, that was number 1,346 this week alone, and I was sort of hoping it would be the last for a while."
Mom:	"I'd stop nagging you if only you would put your clothes away."
Child thinks:	"I'd probably do better at putting my clothes away if you'd quit nagging me so much."

Nagging is a lowly, and largely ineffective, form of communication. Parents start nagging when they feel as though they're not being taken seriously by their children. It can become a vicious circle. Does the nagging cause a child to disregard parental boundaries, or did this disregard lead to the nagging in the first place? Either way, it's a loser.

Kids learn how to "pick their spots" to avoid Mr. or Ms. nag— especially if they want something. They've learned from experience that they can get away with anything—at least twice—if they can catch you with your defenses down, when you're distracted on the telephone, if you're in a great mood after winning the lottery, or if you're having a good hair day.

Poll a million kids on the subject, and roughly 1.2 million will say that their parents are world-class nag-aholics. Wouldn't we be surprised if our kids compared nagging notes with their chums at school? I can see them gathered round the lunch tables swapping can-you-top-this stories. It might go something like this:

"Guess what? I got my mom to yell at me eight times for kicking the ball inside the house," says one kid proudly.

"Break any windows?" asks another buddy. "No? Bummer, dude."

"That's nothing," shoots back another. "I got my mom to tell me eleven times to pick up my room—and then she picked it up for me. Don't I get bonus points for that?"

High fives are shared all around.

Which one of the two following models for communicating house rules do you fall under?

The Nagging Single Parent

Child	You
He breaks a rule.	You tell him he broke a rule.
He breaks the same rule again.	You tell him he did it again.
He breaks the rule a third time.	You tell him he did it again and ask him what's wrong with his head.
He stares at you, wondering, really waiting for an answer.	You get tired of staring and go away.

He goes back to terrorizing.	You walk away, shaking your head, and go back into denial because you've lost the little bit of control you once had.

The Non-nagging Single Parent

Child	You
He breaks a rule.	You let him know the rule was broken and ask for his future cooperation.
He breaks the same rule again.	You tell him you won't be nagging him about it any longer and you discuss the consequences if he chooses to break the rule again.
He wonders if you've been abducted by space aliens who left a fake mom in your place.	You show him your driver's license to prove to him you're still his mom.
He takes a chance and breaks the rule again.	You remind him of the rule and enforce the consequences as discussed.
He releases control.	You are in control.

Bottom line: You don't have to be a nag if you are:

- Consistent.
- Firm but fair.
- Able to follow through. If you say it, mean it. If you don't intend to do it, don't say it.

COMMUNICATION LAND MINE #4: FORGETTING TO CATCH YOUR KIDS DOING SOMETHING RIGHT

Children from single-parent family homes can evolve a mind-set crammed with negative messages. *Mom failed Dad. Dad failed Mom. Mom and Dad failed together. My family failed. I'm a failure.*

A simple, yet effective, way of keeping your child's view of himself in proper perspective is to give him twice as many positive messages as negative ones.

Be patient, you may have to wait a while before you catch your kids doing something positive. But when they do, strike up the band, break into a verse of "Hallelujah Chorus," and let them hear about it.

COMMUNICATION LAND MINE #5:
"I-DON'T-HAVE-TIME-
FOR-YOU-RIGHT-NOW" MESSAGES

"No, not tonight, honey. Mommy's working late." Or, "I'll help you later after I finish the housework."

"Spare time" is a distant memory for the single parent. And quality time has just made the endangered species list. When you do have a few free minutes to spend with your kids, you're probably too exhausted to be much fun.

On the other hand, if you drop whatever you're doing every time your children beckon, you'll go crazy, and you won't get anything accomplished.

The secret is in setting boundaries around your outside interests. Work, recreation, church events, dating: they all need to be prioritized and compartmentalized into time slots. This is a fancy way of saying "Don't spend all of your time doing important things, when essential things—such as spending time with your children—are still on the list."

Think of it this way. Your kids were exposed to a potentially lethal dose of neediness, and you have the antidote. All that's required of you is time, energy, and your ability to communicate love.

Again, your children didn't ask you guys to get married, have a baby, and split up. Don't indulge yourself in a nonstop guilt trip, but do your best not to let your children pay too big a price for your divorce.

We'll take a closer look at quality time versus quantity time in a later chapter.

COMMUNICATION LAND MINE #6:
PRESSURE-PACKED COMMUNICATIONS

Pressure-packed communications come in all shapes and sizes. Here are some of the more common ones:

- Asking the children who they want to live with following the divorce
- Asking the children how they feel about visiting the other parent
- Grilling the children on how the visit went
- Putting pressure on the children to choose one parent over another

Always try to put yourself in your child's place before you communicate with him about divorce issues. What may seem like a simple, nonthreatening message to you may be heard as just the opposite by the child.

COMMUNICATION LAND MINE #7:
OVERCOMPENSATING POSITIVE MESSAGES
Here's one you won't believe. You can actually overdose your kids on encouragement and positive messages. How is this possible when, as parents, all we seem to hear about is positive reinforcement? Simple. The answer is found in the law of saturation. If all you do is tell your children how wonderful they are and how well they do things, eventually your message will become a broken record. Once that happens, the value they place on positive reinforcement from you takes on the significance of an old shoe.

Instead, teach your children the value of a positive, yet accurate, self-image. That will require honesty on your part so that when the child really does something well, the recognition carries greater value. That doesn't mean that positive, reinforcing messages are no longer a part of his minimum daily requirement. It just means he needs to hear an honest mixture of the good and sometimes the not-so-good.

COMMUNICATING THROUGH DENIAL

Denial is the most powerful drug known to mankind. A child's denial is even strong enough to manufacture and maintain the belief that mom and dad will get back together. Unfortunately, denial only deepens the pain, forestalls the inevitable, and cripples a child's development.

Why do children and teens continue to cling to this false hope? Simply put, denial is a defense mechanism, or wall, that the mind erects to protect it from the truth. In this case, a very painful truth. Breaking out of denial requires mom and dad to find and administer the denial antidote to the child. Fortunately, the antidote is readily available in unlimited quantities and is kept in every household. This antidote is simply the truth spoken in love.

Children and teens in denial stand out in a crowd. Here's how to spot them. They're the kids talking about mom and dad getting back together. They may manipulate one or both parents, trying to get them back together. They often become inconsolable, even violent, if a parent, relative, or friend tells them that this can't be done. They often haul denial around long past the postdivorce period. They may resist accepting a stepparent or any dating because it flies in the face of their fantasy.

Helping a child or teen to disclose his personal feelings is the most effective of way undoing denial. Single parents might try the following approach with a younger child.

"You know, Son, I want to share a secret thought that I've been having about your father and me." (Note: any sentence that includes the term *secret* will immediately grab most children's attention.) "After your father and I separated, I was very sad. I hoped he would come home and things would be just like they were before. Do you know what I mean? Now I realize that he's happy with his new life, and I'm happy being here with you in our life. I've accepted that he isn't going to be coming home. So, it's up to us to decide to be happy. There's really no reason why we can't be . . . is there?"

This approach penetrates the denial fortress by normalizing any secret thoughts. It also shows your child that you share some of his same anxieties. Better still, you're living proof that he can be happy again. It may take as few as one or two chats, or as many as dozens of such conversations before your child begins to recognize the situation for what it is—tolerable.

TALKING THROUGH POSTDIVORCE FEELINGS

Divorce in a family sometimes resembles the proverbial elephant in the living room. You've heard the story. Everybody knows there's an elephant standing in the middle of the room, but nobody wants to acknowledge its presence for fear the elephant would become that person's responsibility.

As in the story of the elephant, some parents choose to avoid or neglect noticing many of the characteristics common to children and teens of divorce.

Let's take a closer look at some of those characteristics and the methods you can use in communicating about them.

UNRESOLVED ANGER

Unresolved anger during and following a divorce generally revolves around feelings of frustration, mistrust, victimization, and blaming. When anger goes unresolved, rest assured, it will negatively affect all present and future relationships.

Unresolved anger eventually turns into anxiety and/or depression. These children and teens have feelings of hopelessness, helplessness, fear, agitation, and isolation.

Your kids, however, haven't cornered the market on unresolved anger. Sure, they're fully capable of producing their own toxic waste dump of unresolved anger, but some of it may be spilling over from you or your ex.

A child or teen's characteristic expression of unresolved anger often includes:

- temper tantrums
- disregard or disobeying
- saying/doing hurtful things
- oversleeping
- quitting activities

- disrespect
- acting out
- dishonesty
- school problems
- suppressed appetite

These characteristics usually occur during the first year following a divorce. If symptoms are evident, immediately begin opening up lines of communication. Most children and teens will dig in their heels at first, but don't let that bother you. We've already learned how denial works. Be patient. Keep initiating dialog and sharing your own feelings about the divorce.

A word of caution: Don't let your child's feelings go for more than a few weeks without looking into them. Don't hesitate to talk to your child's school counselor, pastor, or mental health worker if his symptoms persist even after you have been successful in getting him to open up.

SEPARATION ANXIETY

Separation anxiety is a child's fear of being separated from the remaining parent, or both parents.

Separation anxieties can be identified by the following behavioral patterns:.

- increased dependency on you
- increased susceptibility to illness
- calling you from school
- faking illness (psychosomatic illness)
- clinging to you physically and emotionally (following you around or being at your heels constantly)
- tearfulness when leaving you or when leaving the house
- wanting to sleep in your room or in your bed
- regressive behaviors (e.g., bed wetting, thumb sucking)

I often counsel parents to *gratify* (or understand and tolerate) these behaviors—but with one condition, that they make the child aware of them and help him to talk about his feelings. For instance, if your ten-year-old suddenly wants to sleep in your room following a visit to dad's, go ahead and let her. What's the real harm? But take the opportunity to initiate a dialog about her feelings and motivation for sleeping with you. For instance, saying, "I think I understand your wanting to sleep with me tonight. You know, honey, if it were I coming home after staying at a strange house for a few days, I'd probably feel kind of awkward and scared too. Is that what you've been feeling? Would it make you feel more secure to sleep with me for *a night or two* until you get readjusted to being home with me?"

Some psychologists feel you have to immediately "nip this activity in the bud." My feeling is that a single parent should take every opportunity to keep all forms of communication alive. Who cares whether or not you played into, or gratified, your daughter's need for closeness. In the final analysis, it allowed you to become closer and develop a better understanding of what makes her tick emotionally.

INSECURITIES

Just as your child may be experiencing moments of deep insecurity, so are you. Examine those feelings for a moment. They probably include worries about finances, living conditions, whether or how much you'll have to work, your new standard of living. Some people might say that these considerations are too worldly, but in fact they are important matters and worries about them are completely normal.

Remember, after a divorce a child's insecurities are rooted in very personal—often selfish—concerns. The child may wonder, "Will I be able to keep my drum set if we move into an apartment?" "Does this mean my allowance will be cut in half?" Some parents fail to understand that beneath the material concerns are deep emotional insecurities.

It would be highly unusual, even impossible, to believe a child or teen could pass through his parent's divorce without having at least moderate feelings of insecurity. It is your responsibility to uncover and help your child process those insecurities.

Some symptoms of insecurity may include:

- sleeplessness
- tearfulness
- depression
- helplessness
- phobias

- separation anxiety
- clinging on to you
- isolation
- aggressive behavior
- avoidance

Phobias include fears of various types (fear of the dark, fear of leaving the house, fear of abandonment). Avoidance includes not wishing to participate in activities that take him away from the primary care-giver or refusing to visit (or resisting visiting) mom or dad out of a fear of losing one or both.

You could make a case for the view that any type of postdivorce behavior that is out of the ordinary for your child can be chalked-up to insecurities. If you address them as such, you are moving in the right direction.

REGRESSION

Regression is an interesting aspect of human dynamics, especially in children following divorce. Like many of the other characteristics we've been discussing, regression is part of the mind's defense, or coping mechanism, in the face of uncomfortable change. Regression usually occurs in younger children (ages two through ten), but it is not uncommon for latency age (preadolescence) children to regress after divorce.

The regression itself is usually temporary in nature. It is possible, however, for the parent's response to exacerbate the child's underlying fears and insecurities to the crisis point.

Here are some common signs of regression in children.

- thumb sucking
- baby talk
- neediness
- returning to old objects, such as dolls, teddy bears, or blankets
- bed wetting, even when previously stopped for months or years
- acting dependent when previously more independent
- going back to patterns of childhood

When any of these signs show up on your doorstep, be cautious not to slam the door of overreaction. Instead, invite them in as opportunities to learn more about your child's secret feelings and as a chance for the two of you to grow closer.

TRANSFERENCE

Passive feelings of pain or anger are often passed around in single parent homes like a bowl of popcorn. A child transfers his anger from the person most responsible for his pain to someone else—usually the other parent. And usually the mom since she's the closest target. (Isn't that special?)

When this occurs, do your best not to react defensively. Instead, recognize that the child is feeling angry, hurt, and scared. He's desperate to find a place to dump those feelings. Unfortunately, you hold the keys to the recycling center. Help your child to identify his bad feelings by helping him to verbalize them. In most cases, it's advisable to discuss the child's problems with the other parent. (Here the hope is that your ex will be open to what's in the child's best interests.)

Help your child see that his transference is a case of mistaken identity. Explain to him that what he's really mad at is the situation his life is in—a condition he had no control over. Allow him, through open dialog, to understand that transferring his hurt and anger from one parent to another (or the situation to the parent) will solve nothing.

Transference of anger can also work in the opposite direction. Remember, we most often attack and hurt the ones closest to us. Be cautious that you don't take your own anger and frustration out on your kids for the very reason they chose you. You're there!

OVERRESPONSIBILITY

Do you really want to know what infuriates me even more than blacked-out local baseball games on cable TV? A newly single parent who tells her child, "You are the man of the house now." Or, "Take care of your mother." *Please*, bite your tongue, and catch yourself before laying this burden on your children.

Parents who lay inappropriate responsibilities on a child commuicate a potentially damaging message: that he is no longer a child. Acting his age isn't good enough anymore. Now he's expected to "take it like a man." In a sense, sending such a message is one way parents deal with their own stress and guilt. If the child acts unnaturally mature, he is less likely to appear hurt, which enables the parent to feel better by escaping guilty feelings or his own sense of hurt.

COMMUNICATION FAILURES

During the separation and divorce process, there is often a total breakdown in communication between parents and children. When that happens, kids frequently start feeling responsible for everything—including the divorce—and stop talking.

They stop talking because they've learned to associate open communication with anger or an eventual big hurt. Any idea where they might have seen this behavior modeled? I encourage parents to shelter their children from as much of the public divorce stuff as possible. Children just don't need to hear it all. All they're really interested in is the headline that applies to them: "How is this going to change my life?"

Some other examples of communication breakdown are the following:

- Both parents assuming that communication is okay and that the child is doing just fine
- One or both parents getting caught up in his own emotional pain and sense of loss, causing them to lose sight of their child's needs

- Parents having the misbelief that the child does not need to know or does not care about anything that is happening around him
- Parents assuming that the child is not old enough to understand or deal with any of the changes going on around him
- One parent falsely assuming that the child has been kept informed by the other parent
- Parents interpreting a lack of questions as an indication of the child's lack of interest in or feelings about the situation when it is really a sign of fear
- One or both parents placing the child in the middle by talking to him about the other parent

REJECTION

A young married couple approached me one evening after a seminar I had given on single parenting. The husband sheepishly asked, "Can you settle a debate between my wife and me?" Recognizing this as a set-up question, I reluctantly agreed.

"My wife thinks that my father's leaving my mom when I was four has something to do with me being emotionally needy. I keep telling her I hardly even knew my father, so how could it have mattered?"

"I sure hope you haven't put any money on this psychological wager," I said, smiling.

After his wife had finished saying "I told you so," I said that God's plan was, and is, for a child to have a mother and a father. Period.

We can debate the relative merits of what are the best and worst ages for a parent to separate from a child, but in the final analysis, no matter when the separation occurs, the child experiences a sense of abandonment, loss, and rejection. If allowed to remain unprocessed, those feelings may indeed accompany the child into adulthood and infiltrate his relationships. Being overly needy as an adult (although we are all needy people) could certainly be explained as the mind's way of protecting itself from further relationship rejection.

Shame and embarrassment are two other feelings that may accompany a child's thinking following divorce. Let's take a brief look at each.

SHAME AND EMBARRASSMENT

Feelings of shame and embarrassment may be seen in many different ways in children of divorce. Some may exaggerate or lie to cover their insecurities, whereas others may find it difficult to make eye contact with adults, choosing to look at the ground instead. Whatever the case may be, shame and embarrassment are often at the foundation of this behavior.

In postdivorce studies, children may talk about being "different" now. As foreign as it may seem, they report feeling ashamed or that they are different because their family failed. They feel an urge to avoid situations and relationships where attention may be called to their family status and in turn bring about more shame or embarrassment.

It is a parent's responsibility to help the child integrate those unconscious feelings so that they are processed into the conscious mind—to bring them into the light, so to speak. Once they can be identified and labeled, they can be worked through. This working-through process is exactly that, a process. It is not a matter of telling a child, "You shouldn't feel embarrassed or shameful about the divorce," and expect the matter to be resolved. Remember, yeast is to bread what time is to process. The crucial ingredient in processing is always time. Bringing problem feelings into the light of day where they are experienced in the safety of close relationships, over a period of time, will heal these bad feelings.

Children from single-parent families may subconsciously feel that they are damaged goods. They begin to define themselves differently as their world is shaken. They no longer view themselves as part of a normal world. They feel different, tainted, and often unacceptable to their old peer group.

They may also have a hard time understanding how God could have allowed this to happen to them in light of how Christians talk about divorce.

At these times, parents should remember that children are black-and-white thinkers. Their emotional assembly lines are highly efficient at processing everything into tidy either/or packages. Things are either right or wrong, black or white. Gray doesn't exist on their color chart. They are certain about one thing—they'll never be normal or happy again—unless, of course, mom and dad get back together. Are you beginning to see how a child might try to manipulate events to accomplish that goal?

It is impossible to address all the different communication needs kids require during and after a divorce. To do so would fill volumes and then some—and most of the communication needs don't even fit established patterns. They are as individual as you and your child. The best we can hope to do in the context of practicality is to lay a foundation of what children need to hear during and after a divorce.

"Everything's going to be okay." "We'll be fine." And "You'll be fine." Those are the single most important messages kids need to hear during times of stress, such as a divorce. That brief, but powerful, message speaks directly to a child's sense of security. Don't pass up the opportunity of delivering that message whenever you have a chance.

Again, don't be afraid to ask your children how they've been feeling since the divorce. Do they feel any different? Are they worried about changing schools? Are they afraid they might have to give up their dog when mom moves into an apartment? Let them talk about how they will miss their friends, or their fear that that the kids in their youth group might make fun of them. Listen emphatically as they describe the pain of not being able to see dad anytime they want, or their concern over the fact that their allowance is going to be cut, since money is tight. These are just a few of the common fears voiced by children and teens following divorce. Some of them seem immensely important, some of them ridiculously trivial. Nonetheless, they are sources of anxiety to your children. They should never be discounted or overlooked.

Your task is to communicate that things will turn out okay and to refrain from turning into a Superparent whose goal is to fix all of their problems. If you try the latter you will set yourself up for failure, and you and your children up for more disappointment.

You may also find it helpful to remind your children that some one-half of their friends have been, or currently are part of either single parent-families or stepfamilies. That means that they are really not as isolated and different as they may feel.

You may want to talk to other single parents with children in the same general age group as your own. A contemporary who has been down the divorce road before can reinforce for your child from first-hand experience that things will, indeed, be okay.

When dealing with your children, remain positive. Do your best to communicate hope, possibility, and a bright outlook for the future—even when things might not look all that rosy.

· 5 ·

MAKE THE MOST
OF QUALITY TIME

Linda was fulfilled and happy to be a stay-at-home mom. She understood the importance of being there for her child during those first critical months and years. As time passed, however, she was beginning to experience resentment. By the fourth year, she felt totally estranged from her lifestyle. She felt trapped. Stuck at home watching Oprah, Geraldo, Sally, and the rest of her friends while the world went by. Stuck in a relationship she had outgrown. Linda's best friend, Gail, thought she was crazy. As a single mom, she would have traded places anytime to be able to stay home and share quality time with her children instead of punching a clock every morning at 8:30.

"What have you been doing?" Gail asked incredulously. "Breathing in too many exhaust fumes on those morning jogs of yours? Do you know how may women would kill to have your life . . . not to mention your husband? I mean, he's nice looking, he's a great dad, he's got a steady—"

"Job?" Linda interrupted. "He delivers bread and hamburger buns for a living. Don't get me wrong, Gail, I have nothing against that. But he has no dreams for the future. No ambitions about advancing in a career. He's content doing exactly what he's been doing until he's old enough to retire.

"I've come to the realization that if we continue like we are, we'll be poor for the rest of our lives," she continued. "Have you seen my checkbook lately? Hey, have you seen my car? It's held together with duct tape and coat hangers.

"Kenny wants another child. We could never afford it. Our budget is just stretched too tightly, and I'm tired of living this lifestyle—if you can call it a style!"

"Well, Linda, if life is so miserable, why don't you do something about it?" Gail smiled. "You've always wanted to go on to college one day. Why don't you do it?"

Kenny, as always, was supportive, though he couldn't understand why simply being a mother wasn't enough for his wife. After all, he was perfectly content with his delivery job for the bakery. They had a nice apartment. A great kid. Things were fine as far as he was concerned. But if Linda wanted to go to college, they'd scrape the money together somehow.

As the months dragged on, Linda became increasingly unhappy. Her college studies were exhilarating and only confirmed her fears that she wasn't cut out to be the traditional housewife. At least not with Kenny. She needed more out of life. Worse yet, she began to realize that her marriage had been a mistake. "Why did I get married right out of high school and then get pregnant on my honeymoon?" she lamented. She tried to visualize herself with Kenny in ten years, and the thought was terrifying.

Finally, she knew she had to be honest with Kenny. It wasn't fair to him. He was a nice guy, but she had fallen out of love and was bored out of her mind.

Leaving, unfortunately, would mean moving back with mom and dad—not a pleasant thought. But she could think of no other options.

Kenny took the news rather well, as if he had seen it coming. The two agreed to a trial separation. Devon would live with her, and Linda's parents agreed to take care of their grandchild while she attended classes on a full-time basis.

After a few days back with mom and dad she remembered some of the reasons why she was so anxious to bolt from home in the first place. Her parents were constantly squabbling over the silliest of things. They also did their best to control her every move. *Maybe that's why I liked Kenny so much. He hated to argue,* she thought. One thing was for sure, she couldn't remain at home too much longer and retain any degree of sanity. She took a night job in the hopes of earning enough money to afford her own place in a few months.

Between school, work, and study time, there was almost zero time to be with her son. When she was home, she was too tired. Not only that, her parents were pressuring her to get back together with Ken. That kind of support she could live without.

Making matters worse, Devon was becoming more disobedient. He was acting out and throwing tantrums whenever he didn't get his way, in spite of the fact he nearly always got his way.

"I'm beginning to lose it," she admitted to Gail over the phone.

"I'm beginning to think I should go ahead and let Devon live with his father. You know, the only quality time he gets these days is when he's with his dad. He's terrific with him.

"I've really made a mess of things, haven't I? Now on top of everything else, I feel like a rotten mother.

"I know I'm not doing what's best for Devon and he's got to be my number one concern, but there's so little time. If I give up school, I'd have more time, but I'd give up my dream and goal for our future."

THE QUALITY-TIME DILEMMA

Linda's dilemma—how to create quality time with her son— isn't unique to single-parent families. All parents grapple with issues of time and attention. However, parenting problems often become magnified for the single mom or dad. Let's face it, if there aren't enough hours in the day for a married couple (I can vouch for that), how's a single parent going to manage? Minor issues become major. Inconveniences become burdens. Child care, work, laundry, shopping, cleaning, late payments—finding affordable, but safe housing— it all takes time and energy, both of which are usually on "back order" for the single parent.

Even well-balanced parents, once confident in their predivorce parenting prowess, can find themselves shaken by severe doubts. They feel like an athlete who has lost a step. A singer who no longer hits the high notes. How can one person do the job of two?

SINGLE PARENTING ISN'T
NECESSARILY SOLO PARENTING

Newly single parents, completely immersed in a torrent of conflicting emotions following the divorce, often view their role in a distorted way. They see themselves as solo parents— a person who is truly parenting alone. For whatever reason, the spouse is totally out of the picture. No visitation. No support. Nothing.

If there is an ex taking an active interest in the family, consider yourself lucky. You're not alone at the parenting helm. You're not a solo parent. Worldly thinking—protectionism, ego, revenge—can cause some divorced parents to assume the role of a solo parent. Solo parents, or parents playing the part, often isolate and protect themselves and their children from the outside world. But don't try to protect your child from quality time, even if it does come from your ex spouse.

The faster that anger, resentment, and bitterness can be placed on the curb for the trash collectors, the better. Remember, as painful as it may be, your ex is still the father of your child. And your child probably doesn't feel the same way you do about dad. If he does share your rancor, help him to overcome it. In cases where the father has moved hundreds of miles away (shame on him), that doesn't decrease the child's need to spend quality time with dad. It just makes travel plans more difficult.

If compelling evidence surfaces that your children would be living in an unfit or unsafe environment with the ex spouse, then all bets are off. Refer the case to an attorney.

Single-parent families seem to run the smoothest when both parents work cooperatively to focus attention on spending as much quality time as possible with the child.

WHAT EXACTLY IS QUALITY TIME?

The best way for me to define "quality time" is to show what it means to my son and daughter.

My daughter loves to play with Barbies, whereas my son is devoted to Nintendo games.

There's no point in sugar-coating this one. Like most dads, I dislike Barbie dolls. They have no socially redeeming value other than the considerable enjoyment they provide my daughter. Did I say "dislike"? I meant to say, "I hate Barbies!" (There—I feel better now.)

I hate the fact that Barbie has five thousand outfits, and my daughter wants every one of them. I hate knowing that Barbie drives a Corvette and I a Datsun. And I hate all her little plastic accessories and plastic friends, especially Ken—he's got a Corvette too.

But I love the action Nintendo games offer. For me, it's baseball, football, and hockey rolled into one. Best of all, my son loves Nintendo too. You're probably not surprised to learn that my daughter hates Nintendo. My son, of course, hates Barbie. Don't you wish everything in life were that clear?

Here's my quality-time dilemma. If I never play Barbie with my daughter, but only Nintendo with my son, what message am I sending to my daughter? I'm discounting her feelings and needs by discounting the things she likes to do. Worse, I'm telling her that her interests are less important than those of my son. (I have this recurring nightmare: that Nintendo will introduce a Barbie game and I'll end up with an aversion to Nintendo as well.)

My job is to slice quality time as evenly as possible between my kids. If that means playing Barbie, I'll have to play Barbie—even if that means racing her little red Corvette across the carpet while fighting back an almost uncontrollable urge to crash it into a wall. "Sorry, Honey. Barbie had an awful accident. I'm afraid she's in the hospital for the rest of the week for tests, and Mr. Goodwrench says it will take at least a month to get the Corvette running again. Too bad, kiddo."

I must confess: my daughter and I have different rules for quality time spent with her and her Barbies.

My Barbie Rules

1. There must be absolutely no chance of being discovered by a friend, relative, or even the meter reader.
2. The doors must be locked, dead-bolted, and all shades drawn.
3. If someone should penetrate this defense, they must be silenced. Bribery is acceptable.

Her Barbie Rules

1. I must get down at carpet level and play Barbie the way she likes to play.
2. I must be Ken and only Ken. (Trust me, I've attempted being G.I. Joe, who has just been hired by Barbie's parents to protect her from guys, but no dice. She won't buy it.)
3. I must always marry Barbie. And I must hum the wedding song as the handsome plastic couple strolls down the aisle.
4. I may not use excuses to get out of marrying Barbie, such as saying that Ken is too tired from his bachelor party or that he has an ingrown toenail or that the wedding is postponed until after the football games. After the wedding I'm free to play Nintendo.

THE INGREDIENTS
OF QUALITY TIME

INGREDIENT #1:
MUCH TIME EQUALS QUALITY TIME

Where do you draw the line on quality time? How much is enough? How much is too much? The good news is you never have to worry about your children overdosing on quality time. You can, however, seriously underestimate their daily requirements for quality time. Try this simple formula for calculating quality time: fifteen minutes of quality time is worth at least on hour of quantity time.

What's the difference between quality time and quantity time? All the difference in the world. Quantity time activities are time-killers—watching TV, reading the newspaper at the dinner table. These are passive activities. You're physically with your children, but you're mentally and emotionally in anther time zone. Quality time, on the other hand, requires an active interaction between parent and child.

A child's *minimum* daily requirement of quality time, in my opinion, is between fifteen and thirty minutes. This may sound like a snap, but single parents are painfully aware of how difficult it can be to scrounge up an extra fifteen minutes in a day—let alone thirty. Something simply has to go. Or does it? Perhaps the answer is to read them a story instead of making that phone call. It will wait until they are asleep, won't it? How about playing thirty minutes of Monopoly, a game you can pick-up right where you left off the following evening, instead of watching the first episode of a two-week mini series? Or what about letting them plan and then help you prepare dinner rather than go out to a fast-food restaurant? If the message you are receiving is that quality time and parenting by remote control are not conducive, you're getting it.

What happens when you've compounded your quality time problem by having more than one child? Can you even hope to spend enough time to satisfy the needs of two or more kids? The answer is yes . . . and no. And I'm not even running for elected office. Here's the scoop. Shared quality time is better than alone quantity time any day of the week. That's not to say that quality time can't successfully be shared with multiple siblings. It can, but do your best to carve out quality moments with one child at a time.

INGREDIENT #2:
QUALITY TIME IS NEVER WHAT YOU WANT

Don't be offended. But you're probably not the best judge of what quality time means to your children. The fact is, you'll probably come up with an activity that went out of style months ago. I remember asking my daughter if she wanted to go out and play with her collection of "My Little Ponies." She was incensed and appalled. "I don't play with my little ponies anymore, Dad. My little ponies are for babies!" Well! Excuse me for breathing!

The best way to learn what kinds of quality-time activities your children would enjoy is to simply watch them play or ask them what they like to do. But be prepared for the three most popular words among children between the ages of four and twenty-four: "I don't know."

INGREDIENT #3:
QUALITY TIME DOESN'T HAVE TO COST A PENNY

When I speak to single-parent groups on the subject of quality time, this comment is usually made, "But we don't have the kind of money it takes to go around doing things all the time." Precisely the point. The best quality time activities are usually free of charge. Here's a brief list to illustrate my point.

- Visiting museums
- Playing sports
- Visiting the library
- Board games
- Arts 'n crafts

- Going fishing
- Bicycle riding
- Going to the beach
- Window shopping
- Exercising

- Feeding the ducks
- Reading stories
- Outdoor concerts
- Going for a walk
- Sewing

As you can see, the list is endless, and you can't beat the price.

Author's insights: Experience tells me that about 20 percent of you are already coming up with excuses why the activities on this list wouldn't work in your single family. If you are part of this 20 percent, ask yourself: Why am I being so negative about something as positive as spending quality time with my child?

INGREDIENT #4:
TOYS, CREATIVITY, AND THE "GIMMIES"

The gimmies are thoughts, feelings, and greedy little wishes verbalized when your kids want something. It usually starts off with "Paleeaaassseee," before escalating to a "That's not fair!" The gimmies, like a metal detector passed over a chunk of iron, become loudest when your children are within a hundred feet of any toy aisle. The gimmie alarm also sounds when your young child is bored or has just watched three hours of toy commercials. Or, for a teenager, after he has just spotted the latest jeans fad. There ought to be a sign around their little necks that reads, "Please don't feed the Gimmies."

Toys are among the most efficient quality-time killers known to man. Some toys are capable of isolating children physically and emotionally. Others are so boring they simply stagnate their minds. But take heart, I've stumbled upon a simple formula for beating the gimmies: arts and crafts. If this is old news to you, just skim the next few lines.

One morning, after my son busted a vase with his new split-fingered fast ball, we went shopping for hot glue sticks. (What ever happened to Elmer's Glue-All or that horrible white paste we ate as children?) We decided to check out the neighborhood hobby shop.

To my surprise, our little glue-stick excursion also introduced my kids to the world of arts and crafts. They were fascinated by the many art projects on display—from wooden airplane kits to "puff paint" T-shirts. They were anxious to try them all. We soon began spending more time in the balsa wood aisle at the crafts store than we did in the Batman aisle of the toy store. A perfect swap if ever there was one.

Now when I see the gimmies approaching at breakneck speed, I cut them off at the pass by whipping over to the craft store for some modeling clay, glider kits, puff paints—whatever is new. These projects are not only inexpensive, but they create tremendous opportunity for quality time. Be sure, though, that your kids keep the hot glue gun away from the family dog. It's really tough on his fur.

INGREDIENT #5:
MAKING DATES WITH YOUR KIDS (ALONE TIME)
Alone time is an important part of spending quality time with your kids. My advice is to make a date with your child once a month. Once the date is set, be sure you keep it. I believe that quality time needs to be scheduled or it will get lost in our never-ending list of "things to do."

Ideally, attempt to set aside a minimum of two hours of individual date time with your child each month. If you have more than one child, you'll probably need to rotate one child per month. That's all right. Don't get frustrated.

These dates should center around your child's favorite activities. Visiting the zoo, a trip to the carnival, almost anything that is "really special" to your child and will be remembered for a long time.

INGREDIENT #6:
MAKING A QUALITY-TIME COMMITMENT

I know a single mom who hasn't missed a week of scheduled quality time with her teenagers in over four years. Must be a single mom who has the luxury of not having to work full-time, right? Wrong. She enjoys the relationships she has established with her children, who are continually strengthened and reinforced by the quality time she spends with them. She also understands the investment she is making in their futures. *If you're thinking, How can I afford to make that kind of time commitment each and every week?* you really can't afford not to!

I was curious to know how she had accomplished this enviable record for keeping quality-time commitments. "There are some weeks when it's pretty difficult and I have to be a little creative," she said. "After dropping my son off at soccer practice, I might take my daughter to the coffee shop where we can share some time. My son is another story. Since he's so busy at school with various sports, I might make a breakfast or lunch date with him for the weekend, or I might meet him at school and go out for lunch. The amazing part about our quality time is that, even if it's only an hour a week, it makes a difference. It's an investment in their futures."

The litmus test of quality time comes after the fact: Will your kids remember those golden moments tomorrow, next week, or—in many cases—the rest of their lives? How many quality times do you remember from your childhood?

INGREDIENT #7:
SPONTANEITY AND QUALITY TIME

If you're saying, "I'm not the spontaneous type," then you should learn how to be. Kids love it. Not only that, spontaneous people, especially parents, are the most fun to be around.

I have found one way to be especially effective in combining spontaneity and quality time is to occasionally have quality time at night. As a therapist, I naturally must keep late business hours, as that's when most people tend to make appointments. Sometimes, I get home as late as 9:00 or 10:00 P.M. Once in a while, one of my kids will awaken and greet me at the front door. I admit it. I've been known to take one or both of them out for a late-night ice cream sundae a time or two. You might be thinking, *How can you, a therapist, do this when they will be so tired when it's time to get up for school the next morning?* I asked myself that same question until I realized that in ten years, they'll never remember how tired they were that next morning. They will likely, however, remember sneaking out for a once-in-a-while-at-night ice cream with daddy.

The point? Spontaneity is a wonderful gift to give your kids. After all, they have it and you did too. Back before you stopped having so much fun in life.

INGREDIENT #8:
STARTING A QUALITY-TIME PROGRAM
When is the best age to begin spending quality time with your children? How about today? But don't feel like you've missed the boat if you haven't considered quality time until now. Quality time can begin at any age with tremendous results.

If you are interested in beginning a quality-time program with your children or teenagers, I suggest the following:

- Let them know you are interested in spending more quality time with them. (You enjoy spending time with them and see this time as an opportunity for the two of you to get closer.)
- Explain your ideas and ask them what they think of spending more quality time with you.
- Ask them what types of things they would enjoy doing during your quality time together.
- Let them know that you want to consider and respect their quality-time wants and wishes as well.
- Post a family calendar with quality time blocked out each week. When scheduling time to be with your children, ask them if they are free on that particular day. Ask what they might like to do while you're together. This will help them to feel more personally invested in the success of your quality time together.

INGREDIENT #9:
LITTLE THINGS MEAN A LOT
Don't overlook those seemingly insignificant little things that mean so much to our children. For example, both our kids love to draw.

Naturally, these art projects are often presented to us as gifts. This is a tremendous opportunity for a quality moment—don't let it slip away. Make an appropriately big deal out of their special projects. If you only glance at it quickly and say "That's nice, dear," or, "Hey, I didn't know bananas had legs," you're sending a minimizing message.

I'm not saying you need to hustle out and have every finger painting and plaster hand cast professionally mounted, bronzed, framed, and hung with museum lighting. I'm saying you need to give the creation a sufficient amount of praise. We all know how sensitive artists can be, so provide the little Picasso with a place of honor for his work—the refrigerator will do nicely. Ask questions, such as, "How did you come up with the idea for this wonderful art work?" or, "I love the way you use all those different colors. May I have this one?"

After one critically acclaimed artistic triumph after another, your kids might be thinking to themselves, "Why limit our exhibits to the kitchen? Work this good should be shared with the entire world—or at least our friends at the office. The same principle also applies to older children and teenagers. When they are obviously proud of a particular artistic offering or other achievement, sit up and take notice.

A single mom once scheduled a therapy session for her son in hopes I could determine why he had become so defiant of late. He proudly told me about his favorite class at school. Art. When I asked him if he was gifted in this area, he mentioned that he recently sculpted a series of clay pots all of which received rave reviews from his teacher. "Does your mom realize your artistic talent as a potter?" I asked sincerely. The following week, he brought in four recent projects along with a hand-made coffee mug for me. The ice was broken and a therapeutic bond was formed on the basis of my appreciation and praise for his efforts. Sounds simple, doesn't it? It really is.

INGREDIENT #10:
WE'RE HAVING QUALITY TIME
AND YOU'RE GONNA LIKE IT!

You can lead a child to water, but you can't make him wash his hands. And you can't force your child to have the time of his life every time you are together.

Quality time should be considerate. It's important to respect your kids' free time and the activities they enjoy, especially with other children. Begin with an understanding that most older children, and especially teenagers, would rather spend dull, lousy, wasted hours with their friends than ten quality minutes with a parent. Actually, many parents would rather have root canal (on a good tooth) than struggle for topics of conversation with a teenager. If you are forcing your children to conform to your concept of quality time, you're just about guaranteed of ensuring quality-time failure.

INGREDIENT #11:
QUALITY TIME COMMUNICATION TAKES EFFORT
There's nothing worse than scheduling quality time and then the two of you sit around staring at the dirt for an hour.

"So how's school?"

"Okay, I guess."

"Doing okay in math?"

"Okay, I guess."

I strongly suggest parents plan several topics of conversation well in advance of their quality-time outing. For instance, ask yourself what your kid is really interested in, and then think of five or more questions pertaining to that interest. And don't make them questions that can be answered by one or two words. You know as well as I do, the two most overused words in your child's vocabulary are "uh huh."

After you have one set of questions in mind, select a second topic of conversation and come up with five more questions. It may seem like a lot of work to go through just to spend time with your kid, but don't underestimate its value. If quality-time conversation is experienced as laborious by both of you, I guarantee you'll both avoid it the next time.

SCREAMING HORMONES, QUALITY TIME, AND TEENS

Those of you with teenagers might be thinking, *Right. My teenager doesn't even publicly acknowledge that I'm alive. He doesn't want to go on family outings. He doesn't want to be seen at church in my company. He even ducks down in the car should we pass somebody he knows. How can I get him to start spending quality time with me?*

As your children mature, they will enter a difficult stage of development between the ages of twelve and fourteen—you know, that period in a youngster's life when his parents become increasingly stupid and he becomes more difficult. In developmental terms, you can compare some of his behavior to a stage he went through at around twenty-four-months of age. It was called separation and individuation back then—what do you know, but it's beginning to surface again.

Remember when, at around twenty-four months of age, your child embarked on a real power trip? He discovered the word no and began to define and express his own personality. He also began to pull away from you for the first time and realized he was his own person, not an extension of mom.

Many developmental experts agree that somewhere around puberty, teenagers go through a second phase of separation and individuation, similar to the one they went through around two. During this phase, they will probably put as much distance as they possibly can between you and the house. Take heart. You're not alone.

When starting a quality-time program with your teenager, expect resistance. Be open to discussion. You're going to have to sell the concept. Follow the steps described in the quality-time program and ask if they would agree to give it a thirty-day trial period. (Teenagers find it easier to accept uncomfortable things if they think they're not going to last forever.)

If you know what activities your teen would enjoy doing, talk to him about it. If you're not sure what he's into, ask. Your quality-time date might include a trip to the compact disc store with the promise of buying him a new release, if that's within your budget. Sure, this is a shameless way of bribing him to spend time with you, but if it gets the ball rolling, so be it. Anything to help him see that spending quality time with his mom or dad doesn't have to feel like a chore.

A QUALITY-TIME WAKE-UP CALL

One day I was swimming with my son, who was three at the time. Suddenly, my pager went off from atop a pile of towels on a nearby chair. Before I could pull myself from the pool, my son leaped out (arm floaties, sea horse ring and all), snatched the pager, and hurled it into the pool—the deep end no less. We could hear a faint gurgling sound as it slowly sank to the bottom. I quickly looked to my son for an explanation. His arms raised high over his head, palms up, and shoulders back, "All gone," he said with a wide grin.

As I was pondering his fate (perhaps walking the plank, uh, diving board) another beeper began sounding in my head. All at once it came to me—I was getting a bit out of balance in the quality-time department. My family time had been interrupted several times that week with calls from patients who needed me as well, but a three-year-old has a hard time understanding the needs of others. My son had made an executive decision—no pager, no interruptions. It was cutting into his quality time and he'd about had enough.

Most children can travel only so far on a full tank of attention. Don't wait until the needle reads empty. Keep topping off their tanks with as much quality time as you can. Remember, kids are attention guzzlers. If they have to worry when the next fill-up is going to come, they will be continually insecure and needy. Keep their little tanks full, and you'll notice improved mileage figures. The more secure they feel with your love and attention, the longer they can go between fill-ups and the more comfortable they will be with themselves.

I'm happy to report that my son no longer flings my pagers when he needs attention—that's what sisters are for. There are many other ways in which children will let you know when they have a need for additional quality time with you. Here are a few flares your kid might shoot into the air the next time he needs more of you:

- Acting-out (temper tantrums, creating disturbances)
- Being disrespectful
- Being clingy; hanging all over you while you're busy
- Hounding you to do something with him
- Isolating or sulking to get attention
- Becoming more dependent on you

Just because your child seems to be quietly going about his business, don't become paranoid that he's up to something. He's probably been getting enough quality time and attention, that's all. Good for you.

INNOVATIONS IN QUALITY TIME

I wish I could take credit for the idea I'm about to share, but the truth is, I learned of it from a group of single parents from Canada, and who knows where they learned it.

This group of single parents all belonged to the same large Christian church in a province near Ontario. One day, one of the single moms was talking to another single mom at church. They found that both of them had children close to the same age and that they lived only about five minutes from each other. The second mom expressed her frustration at not being able to find suitable child care since moving to her new neighborhood. Being able to identify with her problem, the first mom suggested they might consider helping each other out. From that point, they began an informal system of watching each other's child whenever one of the moms needed a sitter.

Soon, a third single mom from the church joined the two moms and began sharing in the child-care time as well. Word somehow reached two other single moms, who also joined. Now there were five single moms who lived within fifteen minutes of each other. They found they were united in two major areas. First, they were single parents and knew of each other's special needs. Second, they knew the value of needing some time away from their children to take care of themselves.

The original two moms, realizing the wonderful benefits they shared by being able to count on their group of friends for support, fellowship, and baby-sitting, decided to share their success with other single moms and dads within the church.

Within six months from the original conversation, the "Breakfast Club," as it came to be known, included some twenty-five single moms and dads.

This wonderful little idea had grown into a major success and now required additional attention.

One of the original moms started an informal newsletter sent to the other single parents once a month. She outlined the need for some organization among the group. They held elections and appointed a group chairperson and a treasurer. They went on to create a record-keeping system of services received and services rendered so as to keep the program as fair as possible. They also asked each parent for a five-dollar-per-month donation that would pay for a party at the end of the month for all the single parents and their children.

The single parents who participated in the program felt it was a complete success. It allowed them to feel safe and secure with the families they entrusted their children to while allowing them to get out more often to enjoy some quality time of their own.

LOCATING OTHER CHILD CARE RESOURCES

I learned from another group of single parents that, they too, found a viable solution to the baby-sitting dilemma.

With the help of the high school and college groups from their church, they started a baby-sitting program. Each weekend evening, these groups provided baby sitting for the kids of single parents. The staffing ratio varied depending on the number of kids who were signed up in advance. Best of all, the church subsidized the baby-sitting costs, which allowed the single parent to pay only $1.00 per hour.

The single parents reported this program was highly successful.

THE HUMAN BEING ASPECTS OF QUALITY TIME

To really understand the concept of fulfilling your child's undeniable need for quality time, you must first understand the difference between *human beings* and *human doings.*

Human beings are relational creatures. They are continually mindful of the emotional closeness derived from spending quality time with their children. They cherish the opportunity to share quality time by seizing the moment to make it as positive an experience as possible.

On the other hand, human doings folk barely scratch the surface of important matters—such as relationships with their children. They believe in form over substance. Talk over action. They are terrific at checking-off visitation days on their calendars without paying much attention to the quality of those days.

·6·

SKILLFULLY MANEUVER THROUGH POSTDIVORCE ISSUES

"So, how's X-ray tech school going?" asked Gail over lunch. "By the way, if X-rays are so safe, why do the techs cover you with a humongous lead apron, tell you not to move, and then sprint into a tiny room resembling a fallout shelter where they grin at you behind twelve inches of glass? I've always wanted to ask, 'If it's so safe, why not stay in the same time zone?'" They both laughed. "So, how is school going, Linda?"

"Are you kidding, Gail? It's wonderful. I feel like a kid again. I love my classes. I've got great instructors, and and I don't have raging acne this time! Seriously, it's great being around people who are making something out of their lives. People going places.

"After I graduate, in about a year, I'll be able to support Devon and me. We've got it all planned," she said, waving her turkey sandwich. "After I get my first few paychecks, we're going to buy a new car and move into a bigger apartment. We might even go to Disneyland, stay in a nice hotel, and just have fun. I hope our room will have one of those cute compact fridges completely stocked with junk food. We'll eat eight dollar jars of peanuts and drink three dollar sodas. It's going to be a blast!"

"By the way," Gail asked. "Where is Devon? Seems like I haven't seen him in weeks. Where's he been—dad's?"

Linda sighed. "Yeah, he's wanted to spend more time at Kenny's apartment. It's got me worried."

"What do you mean 'worried'? Kenny has always been great with Dev. What's going on?"

Linda took a bite from her sandwich and thought for a second, "It's not that there's a problem, really. It's just that when Devon comes home from his weekend visits, he acts differently. It's hard to explain . . . more disrespectful."

Linda described how Devon once asked her, " 'How come you think you're so perfect, Mom?' When I asked him where he got such an idea, he said he got it from his dad. Apparently, Kenny has told him that I'm terribly confused these days. Can you believe that, Gail?

"And if that wasn't enough, Devon told me that Kenny has a new girlfriend who sleeps over. And one night, he says he heard them in the bedroom. Gail, what should I do? I can't just sit around and let Kenny pollute my son's mind."

Gail smiled slyly. "Well, why don't we get him a segment on 'America's Most Wanted'?"

"I'm serious, Gail! When I expressed my concerns with his new lifestyle, he went ballistic. He actually lost it right there at Buns 'n Suds. He said that I didn't have any business telling him how to live his life or act around his son. And if I didn't like it, I could lump it."

"So, who's the girl at the slumber party?" Gail asked, her curiosity thoroughly piqued.

"Who cares! I don't care if he dates the entire squad of the Dallas Cowboy Cheerleaders, but not when Devon's there. It's no example to be setting, and I told him so," Linda said, her face turning beet-red with rage. "I also said no sleepovers when Devon was visiting."

"Yeah, you've become a real attack mom, haven't you?" Gail joked. "But truthfully, I'm proud of you for being so assertive."

"Well, the important thing is that I took charge when it came to dealing with my son. Of course, Kenny didn't like it.

"For one thing, Gail, he said he'd fight me for custody. He threatened to stop paying child support and alimony altogether if I told him how to act around Devon. He knows I'd have to to drop out of X-ray school and go back to work full-time. Whatta doll, huh?"

"Divorce can do that to people, honey," Gail consoled. "In fact, don't you remember when Jim and I fought about those sick, pornographic magazines he left scattered about his place when Mark was visiting? Next thing I know, Mark is stashing them under his mattress and in the dirty clothes hamper. Pretty appropriate, come to think of it.

"When I confronted Jim about the pornography, he threatened to move out of state with Mark. Finally, Mark got fed up with his dad's lifestyle and decided he didn't want to visit anymore. Greatest day of my life, kiddo. You see, divorce changes people. And it can get really ugly for the first few months—even years—after the divorce."

"I just don't get it, Gail. In spite of our divorce and a few paperwork hassles, everything seemed to be going well between us—at least as well as could be expected. We were civil, even friendly. Remember, we even tried dating a couple of times just to see if it was really over. Why is Kenny being so difficult now? He's so different than he was. Should I talk to his parents?"

"Sure, go ahead. Then you can try clicking your little, ruby slippers together and beat it back to Kansas. Face the facts. It's called 'divorce wars.' I should know. I'm a veteran.

"Did you honestly expect Kenny to just accept both the separation and divorce and go peacefully into the night? Remember, he's living in a one-room apartment eating day-old bread left over from his deliveries, while you're hitting him up for child support, plus alimony. You're finishing your college education, and you're going to have a job that pays three times what he makes. You think he's going to be a happy camper? I don't think so.

"I'm not saying you're wrong and he's right, but get a grip on reality. You declared war. He took the first hits, and now he's returning fire. Get ready to duck!"

THE QUICK FIX

What people need is a fast-acting, over-the-counter magic capsule capable of curing the side effects of divorce. There would be an immediate outbreak of harmonious visitation schedules, an epidemic of hassle-free child support, and a full recovery to a happy life.

Seriously, if divorce has touched your life during the past year, or if you're still suffering from the long-lingering effects of a divorce, then you would benefit from crisis management.

How do we swim through the shark-infested waters of divorce without being eaten alive by anger and frustration? He's mad because she won't let him have the kids this weekend. She's mad because he's two child-support checks late. He's frustrated because she wants the kids on Christmas and Thanksgiving. She's frustrated because he lets the kids stay up past midnight watching MTV.

Let's look at some of the major challenges parents face when working through the slippery postdivorce period. Better bring your shark stun sticks along, just in case.

FORGIVE AND FORGET . . . GET LOST!

"How blessed is he whose transgression is forgiven, whose sin is covered" (Psalm 32:1).

At some point, you knew I was going to drop the original "F" word into your recovery repertoire. Why is forgiveness so important? Because it allows single parents—indeed, all of us—to jettison anger and get on with our lives.

Forgiveness has always been a key issue and a major struggle for mankind since the Garden. Adam's grudge against Eve. Eve's grudge against the snake. If there were any way of knowing, we'd probably find that the snake was ticked-off at somebody too.

In order to define forgiveness, we must first understand the concept of personal choice. When we talk about holding grudges and withholding forgiveness, we are really talking about moving from a loss of control to full ownership over the choices we make.

While preparing this chapter, I remembered a conversation I had with a collegue, Dr. Paul Meier, on a flight from Seattle to Southern California. Both of us sat quietly in our seats making notes on separate manuscripts we were preparing.

Our conversation turned to the subject of forgiveness, and we began to discuss *Happiness Is a Choice: Overcoming Depression* (Grand Rapids: Baker, 1978), a book Dr. Meier and Frank Minirth co-authored. That book makes the case that everything in life involves decisions, or choices. Do we choose to be happy or sad? Do we choose to follow Christ, or do we choose to fall away? Do we choose to be overweight, or do we choose to regain control? Do we choose to cling to our grudges and unforgiveness, or do we choose to release them?

When we are unforgiving, our lives flow unchecked into several troublesome tributaries.

AVOIDING, RETREATING, AND ISOLATING

Withholding forgiveness from those who have sinned against us only pushes us further from the truth and into self-protective hiding places. When we're an active participant in life, we engage others in relationships. In doing so, we're constantly running the risk of being exposed to hurtful people or painful situations. But people who duck pain by hiding usually wind up facing an even deeper hurt, the pain of loneliness or isolation. Many people who fail to come to grips with the painful issues of divorce stow themselves neatly away for safe-keeping. For example, they may avoid friends, fearing they might take sides or treat them differently. They might avoid church, or find a new one, fearing they will be looked upon as less than perfect.

These people are avoiding the very same people and places that made them the happiest: caring people with the ability to pull them from the burning building of fear and anger to the safety of truth and grace.

BLANE ✓

The impulse to lay blame at the feet of others can stop forgiveness dead in its tracks. It allows us to skirt responsibility for our own problems. We're more interested in our neighbor's messy kitchen than we are about our own.

In cases of divorce, blame is often directed at an ex-spouse. In Linda's case, the target was a husband without aspirations. Often, blaming doesn't end with the ex. It's just the beginning. We might blame the girlfriend or boyfriend for busting up the marriage. We might blame an employer who made a spouse work too many hours or take too many business trips. We might blame a spouse's obsession with golf, tennis, or softball.

Whenever you find yourself pointing the finger of blame, look in the mirror. There—*now* you're pointing in the right direction.

ANGER ✓

Of all the natural enemies of forgiveness (and there are plenty) anger tops the list.

I've never met a person who has gone through a divorce, even an amicable, mutually agreed-upon divorce, who didn't experience at least some anger, or at the very least, severe disappointment over the loss of a dream.

Anger encompasses the full range of feelings, from mild disappointment to an intense disgust, even hatred, for your ex and how the divorce has changed your family's life.

Anger turned outward alienates and distances you from others. Anger turned inward leads to a slow, painful, emotional death.

REVENGE ✓

Anger's first cousin is revenge. Anger can live without revenge, but revenge is powerless without anger. Anger is the engine that drives revenge. No anger, no point in seeking revenge. Some people emerge from divorce with vivid fantasies of revenge that may last a lifetime. Their ex was able to pick up the pieces, but they remain weighted down in an unforgiving, revengeful state of mind. In the end, seeking revenge backfires, causing the individual to feel powerlessness and depressed over the amount of time he or she spent thinking about getting even.

FEAR

Although fear approaches from the opposite direction, it also prevents us from reaching true forgiveness. Fear strikes at the core of our "fight or flight" nature. It can lead us to lash out in anger or retreat into submission, passiveness, or avoidance.

What fans the fires of fear into a three-alarm blaze? The list is too long for one chapter (or book, for that matter). However, one of the most striking differences between effective and ineffective single parents is their relative ability to contain fear.

DENIAL

There's no mystery why denial is a stumbling block to forgiveness. After all, if a person already knows how much he was wronged in the marriage, why spend any energy thinking about forgiveness? As we've noted earlier, denial is the most powerful drug known to man.

A VICTIM MENTALITY AND SELF-PITY

As strange as it may sound, some people actually benefit by withholding forgiveness. This concept has to do with what is called *secondary gain*. Secondary gain usually refers to a positive side effect deriving from what would otherwise be a painful situation.

For instance, in refusing to forgive, an individual ensures his own victim status. The victim views divorce as the latest in a long line of crushing blows. *Isn't this just typical of my life?* he thinks. Or, *I'll never be happy anyway.*

The act of forgiveness would allow him to see himself from a different perspective, one that gives him power over his own life. But he unconsciously figures, *Who needs that kind of pressure and responsibility?*

SADISTIC TENDENCIES

The term *lording forgiveness* describes how a sadistic person views forgiveness. A sadistic person revels in his power and control over others. He gets a kick out of making people squirm over what mask he'll be wearing next. Will it be a mask that is compassionate and forgiving, or will it be one that's mean and sadistic? People like this gain emotional strength by punishing others through keeping them off balance and fearful.

A husband asks his ex-wife for forgiveness. Instead of working honestly toward a place of forgiveness, she merely teases him with the possibility. She actually has no intention of granting forgiveness. She wants only to manipulate him into trying harder and feeling worse.

Some sadistic people look at forgiveness as permission to sin again. A wife discovers her husband has had an affair. He asks for forgiveness, and eventually she fully forgives him. A sadistic individual would see her forgiveness as providing a clean slate to cheat again. Many divorced couples are living inside this emotional torture chamber.

GOD'S WORD ON FORGIVENESS

What does God have to say about forgiveness? Here is just a sampling from God's "highlights reel" on the subject.

The Scriptures are alive with God's truth about forgiveness. In Genesis 50:17, Joseph was emotionally and physically abused by his brothers. Even his life had been placed in jeopardy. Joseph could have turned against his brothers in bitterness. God had another plan in mind. He tells Joseph, "I want you to forgive your brothers the sins and the wrongs they committed in treating you so badly."

How many of us would have been strong enough in our faith to let bygones be bygones? "I know, I know . . . you guys wanted me dead, but that's no reason why we can't be friends?" God tells Joseph to forgive, and he does. He was a man of great faith.

In Ephesians 4:31–32, the apostle Paul writes, "Let all bitterness, wrath, anger, clamor and evil speaking be put away from you with all malice. And be kind to one another, tenderhearted, forgiving one another, just as God in Christ forgave you."

Perhaps the best illustration of forgiveness in Scripture can be seen in Luke 7:47. Look at the way Jesus deals with the arrogant legalist, Simon the Pharisee, when he says: "He who has been forgiven little, loves little."

Our willingness to forgive is linked to an awareness of how many times we could use a little forgiveness ourselves. It also reveals how desperately we depend on God's forgiveness in our own lives. Without God's grace and forgiveness, we would be one sorry group of people come the Day of Judgment (2 Corinthians 5:10).

Forgiveness often becomes confused, or clouded, by an assortment of selfish emotions. Don't lose sight of why God gave us the power of forgiveness.

DISTORTIONS OF FORGIVENESS

Here are some distortions of forgiveness.

DISTORTION #1:
"I THINK I'LL FORGIVE TODAY"
Some people think they can switch forgiveness on and off like a light. It's not that simple. Only after you've made a thoughtful decision to enter the loop of forgiveness will the process actually begin.

DISTORTION #2:
"OKAY, BUT I'M DOING THIS FOR YOU"
Some people treat forgiveness as a gift to be given to a deserving individual—if the circumstances warrant it, of course. Talk about distortion. True, the act of forgiving is often mutually beneficial, but its primary purpose in our lives is to free the forgiver of an unhealthy mind-set.

Forgiveness doesn't release the sinner from the natural consequences of the sin, but it does allow him to escape the shackles of his own anger and resentment.

DISTORTION #3:
"FORGIVE AND FORGET"
Forgiving doesn't really have a connection with forgetting unless you choose to combine the two. Forgetting isn't advisable, since it closes our eyes to the truth, leaving us even more vulnerable to further pain.

For a scriptural foundation for the concept of forgiving yet not necessarily forgetting, I like to refer to Matthew 10:16, where we are admonished to be as shrewd as snakes and as innocent as doves in our human relationships.

Here's a more worldly example. Let's say you stopped by the automatic teller machine of your local bank at midnight. As you were on your way back to your car, two thugs sprang from behind the bushes and took your money. Forgiveness for the two men is certainly possible, but would you really want to forget the lesson you learned about not withdrawing money from ATMs at night?

DISTORTION #4:
"FORGIVENESS MEANS MAKING-UP"
Guess where this distortion comes from? Remember when you were a child and you got into a fight with your little friend? Do you remember mom or dad telling you to say you're sorry and then go out and play? It is in our childhoods that we first learn the distortion that we have to make up and go outside and play with people after we forgive them. That is simply not the case.

Forgiveness can be done by letter. It can be done by telephone. It can be done as the last words you ever utter to that person. It can even be done after that person is dead. You don't need to be face-to-face with the person you are forgiving, although many would assert that's probably healthier.

If you remember that forgiving is for your own benefit, then you'll be in a much better position to release your anger and resentment and get on with your life after divorce.

DISTORTION #5:
"I FORGAVE YOU THE FIRST TIME!
NOW GO AWAY"
Sometimes we don't get things done quite right the first time. Just look at your kids if you think that's not true. That's why there are erasers, white-out, and the "delete" key on computers.

You were sure you had forgiven. Then, suddenly, you are angry again. Does that mean you didn't complete the forgiveness process or that something has happened between you and the other person to reopen old wounds? There are no quotas on the number of times you can forgive. In fact, you may recall Jesus' admonition to Peter in Matthew 18:21 when Peter asked, "Lord, how many times shall I forgive my brother when he sins against me? Up to seven times?" Jesus answered, "I tell you, not seven times, but seventy times seven."

What is the application of this Scripture? I take it as saying that we are to forgive as often as it is requested or is necessary.

HOW DO I BEGIN FORGIVING?

If all this makes sense to you, you might be wondering how to take the first step in the forgiveness process. Here are the basics.

ABANDON DENIAL
Before you can forgive, you must first acknowledge that you have

been sinned against or have received an emotional injury. Many of us stop at this intersection for a number of reasons, including anger, anxiety, or withdrawing. It's safe to say, though, that all of your reasons had to do with self-protection.

Leaving denial enables you to identify your injury and better understand the origin of its pain. If you bought a major fixer-upper, your first order of business was to inventory what needed to be done to make the house fully livable. If you were in denial about your abode's true condition, you would just move in, oblivious to the broken windows and missing stairs. Eventually your denial would lead to further deterioration until the house crumbled around you.

Begin examining the areas of your life that need fixing up.

UNDERSTAND YOUR EMOTIONS

If you're mad, be mad. If you're are hurt, be hurt. We create problems in our lives when we deny our emotions or don't understand our feelings.

After divorce, the response of single parents often falls into two main categories: anger and righteous indignation.

A good scriptural depiction of righteous indignation is in Matthew 21:12. That passage is the account of the time Jesus went to the temple and knocked over the money changers' tables and stalls. He said, "It is written . . . 'My house will be called a house of prayer,' but you have turned it into a 'den of thieves.'"

Jesus was righteously indignant. What was going on in the temple was a violation of God's holiness. His indignation was prompted by sinful behavior; it was not simply an emotional expression of anger.

Let's take a look at divorce and how two different people can work through anger and righteous indignation.

Anger	Righteous Indignation
We are wronged or sinned against.	We are wronged or sinned against.
Sins are identified.	Sins are identified.
Fear enters.	Fear enters.
Anger takes over.	Anger is met with an action plan.

| Steps are taken to protect, isolate/or harbor anger. | Steps are taken to forgive, such as reconcile and resolve. |

Anger continues.

It is clear in this model that righteous indignation involves a process of reconciliation and restoration, whereas anger involves only emotion.

CONNECT, DON'T ISOLATE

Whenever we withdraw and isolate from others in order to conceal our pain, we are doing the opposite of what God asks. James 5:16 instructs us to confess our sins to each other and pray for each other so that we may be healed. Nowhere, to my knowledge, does God ask us to retreat into isolation when we are feeling lonely, hurt, and frustrated. Instead, he calls us to connect with Him and with others within the body for strength, consolation, and counsel.

Whenever we embark on a mission of forgiveness, it is better to bring company along—someone such as Gail, Linda's friend, who understands you and has your best interests at heart. It is also helpful to include someone who is walking down the same road you are and who has a similar destination in mind.

A colleague of mine at the Minirth-Meier Clinic West, Dr. John Townsend, has an outstanding perspective of the forgiveness process. He says that forgiveness and grief cannot take place inside a vacuum. It can't take place in isolation. It requires the love and support of others. Dr. Townsend calls these people "safe people." We all need safe people in our world to help us deal with those who are not-so-safe.

In a later chapter we'll talk more about where you can connect with people who are safe.

FULLY GRIEVE OVER YOUR LOSSES

Working toward a place of forgiveness means facing our pain and processing our anger over broken dreams, such as a failed marriage. That enables us to move out of our emotional numbness and into the grieving process.

Grieving is a cleansing process God has designed for us. When we experience the loss of a spouse through divorce, a little bit of us dies too. Grieving is the process of experiencing the hurt and identifying and working through our losses. Put another way, the grieving process allows us to take our negative, toxic feelings and neutralize them by bringing them into the sunshine.

In the Beatitudes, the concept is described in the following way: "Blessed are they that mourn for they will be comforted" (Matthew 5:4). There's nothing in there about, "Blessed are those who live in denial," or, "Blessed are those who remain angry and seek revenge against their ex-spouse."

In postdivorce counseling sessions, I always admonish patients to "reach inside and experience your pain." Some may think this advice is on the callous and sadistic side. Actually, it's the only realistic and viable way to proceed.

The sooner you experience your pain and understand why it feels so rotten, the faster you can begin the healing process. When you bury your grief inside anger or obsessive behavior (chemical dependencies, spending, gambling, sex) you are merely postponing the inevitable and increasing your chance of repeating history.

Matthew 5:4 and Psalm 6:6 clearly illustrate God's plan for us during times of pain. The process God prescribes includes becoming connected with our pain and grieving over our losses within the loving boundaries of our relationship with Him and the body of Christ.

OPT FOR RESPONSIBILITY, NOT BLAME

I firmly believe that it takes far more time and energy to blame somebody for a problem than it does to just fix it.

For example, if you were abused as a child, whose fault was that? Certainly not yours. If you were married to a man who destroyed the marriage by cheating, whose fault was that? Arguably, not yours —right? However, when the question is "Whose responsibility is it that life be as good as it can be now?" the answer is that it is your responsibility. That's right, *yours!* If you shirk the responsibility for controlling what falls within your control, then you are giving into your anger, choosing to live your life muddled in blame.

FORGIVING OTHERS, FORGIVING OURSELVES

For Christians, the subject of forgiveness is about as black and white as any you'll come across. We are all called upon by God to forgive those who have sinned against us. You have many choices in life, but forgiveness isn't one of them. It may help to keep Luke 7:47 handy as you delve into the meaning of forgiveness. Jesus tells us that those with a large capacity for loving receive more forgiveness, more often. Certainly, the opposite is true of people who don't love as much. The connection is clear. Love and forgiveness go hand in hand.

Scripture also draws a parallel between the desire to be forgiven and our capacity to forgive. Jesus used the parable of the man who owed the king millions of dollars (Matthew 18:23). When the man couldn't pay the king what he owed him, he begged that his debt be forgiven. The king agreed.

Here's the kicker. That same guy, who you'd think would be counting his lucky stars, turns around and refuses to wipe the slate clean for somebody owing him a few bucks. Not only that, he has the guy thrown in jail. When the king hears of this injustice, he has the first man jailed, where he pays dearly for his sins.

None of us has the right to stand before the judgment seat of Christ (2 Corinthians 5:10) and ask God for forgiveness when we are actively avoiding forgiving or are engaged in lording forgiveness of another person. No question, forgiveness isn't an easy process—it's just the right thing to do.

LETTING THE BAIT FLOAT BY

If you had to picture yourself as a fish, what fish would it be? A graceful black fin marlin leaping majestically into the salty mist, or a mackerel whose main interest in life is to avoid becoming part of the food chain?

When addressing parenting groups, whether they be composed of two-parent families or of single-parent families, I often begin with this question: "How many people treat you like fish?

You can apply this question during conversations between you and your ex. Every time he says something that makes you feel angry, hostile, or spiteful, stop and visualize him dangling some lovely bait in front of your little fish mouth.

He might say, "I know what the divorce papers say, but I'm taking our son on his birthday this year," or, "I'm going to stop your child support payments if you don't . . ." Now for the moment of truth. Are you a person or a perch? If you take the bait, the fight is on. Your ex will hoot and holler as he sets the hook. He'll thrill at the unmistakable sound of the fishing line spinning from his reel as you run to deep waters. Yes, the fight is on. It may last five minutes or five months, but eventually you'll be boated, breaded, and frying-pan bound.

Whatever the situation, make a conscious decision not to take the bait. Let it drift by without a nibble. Remember, if you take the bait every time it is cast, guess who is always in the driver's seat? Right, the fisherperson. Remember, it's more fun being the fisherperson than a hooked halibut.

RESOLVING AND AVOIDING CONFLICTS

We need to learn how to resolve postdivorce conflict, because such conflict is unavoidable. Divorced or married, you will eventually experience conflict. It is part of human nature. Let's examine what the survey stated were the hottest, postdivorce issues. Let's play Dysfunctional Family Feud!

The question goes over to the Jones family. "For 200 points, what do single moms say is the biggest problem they have with single dads following divorce?"

Well, Richard, we're torn. We'll go for "Who'll get custody of the kid's hair piece?" (Yeah, good answer, good answer.)

If "hair piece" is up there, you win the car and the deluxe home version of Dysfunctional Family Feud! Survey said?

"Following the rules!!!!" (Buuuuzzzeeeerrrrr))

Ooooh, sorry, but grab a lovely parting gift on the way out the door!

THE PROBLEM:
ONE CHILD, TWO SETS OF RULES
The number one problem single parents report is "confusion created when the child tries to follow two sets of rules after a divorce." In my last book, *How to Avoid Alienating Your Kids in 10 Easy Steps* (Moody 1993), I examined how children manipulate their parents—and these were two-parent families, which gives you an idea of how serious the problem can be when kids are being bounced from one parent to the other.

Some of the more common areas of conflict are:

- The child's allowance
- Overindulgence
- Discipline (to spank or not to spank . . .
  is there really any question?)
- What's appropriate to watch on TV
- What friends the child should be hanging out with
- Curfew
- Bedtime

Complications involving dual rules arise because (1) there will always be differences (some subtle, some major) between parents and (2) children tend to exploit those differences.

You've probably heard it. "Well, Dad says I could watch MTV whenever I wanted to when I'm with him, and he even lets me take a sip out of his bottle of beer." That makes you feel great, doesn't it? First, build up a good head of steam. Next, hammer your ex about his lack of morals. Then after about five minutes of ranting, you'll finally hear what his dad's policy really is: "I don't let him watch MTV, and I haven't had a beer in about six months."

At this point, you'll need to dig through the old fishing tackle box for the fishhook removers, because your child has caught on to the fine art of baiting the hook.

The fix. If you are feeling particularly masochistic, you may want to try to establish some uniformity between your and your ex's rules for the children.

You may want to start with a casual conversation with your ex about how most children manipulate single parents because they know there's much less chance of being discovered than in a two-parent family. Let your ex know that a good response to that kind of manipulation is for the two of you two to agree upon basic rules for situations such as the ones listed above. An effective way of doing that is to discuss the rules over the phone, or if that might create too much opportunity for conflict, then perhaps by letter.

Both of you should keep a copy of the rules handy for future reference. For instance, if you feel strongly that your teenagers shouldn't be allowed to watch PG-13 movies but your ex thinks it's okay, you might be able to resolve the difference this way: your ex agrees to accompany the children when they go to PG-13 movies so that he can monitor the films for appropriateness and be there to discuss areas of confusion or controversy.

Now, I'm already hearing some of the more negative readers looking at this example and saying, "No, that's not okay. They're my kids, and if I don't want them to go to PG-13 movies, they shouldn't go." I understand your feelings, but keep in mind, your ex will probably do what he wants to do when the kids are with him—with or without your permission. The trick is to anticipate that possibility and reach a reasonable compromise over likely problem areas and then stick with it.

The final element of this approach is to share your plan with your kids. Let them know in no uncertain terms that you and their dad have discussed and agreed upon many issues. Also let them know that when confusion arises, you and your ex have committed to calling one another for clarification. Even if that doesn't happen all the time, it's still good for your kids to see unity and agreement in how the boundaries apply to them.

THE PROBLEM:
VISITATION

When I was a police officer, Saturday mornings and holidays were "the pits." Not because everybody else in the family was home. Not because the best football and baseball games were usually played Saturday mornings. Not even because I had to go to bed early on Friday night. It was because working Saturday morning meant having to deal nonstop with single moms and dads and their visitation issues.

Saturday meant a slew of calls to settle disagreements over whose day it was for visitation. And the courts didn't make it any easier.

"Let's see, Mr. Smith. This is the third Saturday of a month beginning with the letter 'J' so that must mean that you can have your left-handed child between the hours of 7:00 and 9:00 P.M."

"Yes officer," Mrs. Smith chimes in, "but it's only 6:55 A.M. He can't legally be on my property for another five minutes."

You laugh (actually I'm hoping you're laughing), because you know it really gets that crazy. When it comes to visitation, some single parents pull out all the stops. Don't be five minutes early and don't be five minutes late, or it's back to court.

Some go to extremes for seemingly good reasons. Some were

taken advantage of for years prior to the divorce and they see visitation rights as a golden opportunity to seek a measure of revenge. The problem is, it's often at the children's expense.

Children aren't blind. They already know there are big problems between their parents. They don't need to see bickering, arguments, and even fights over who has legal custody at 6:55 A.M. today.

Like all of us, kids desperately need to be wanted. Even if you don't understand or like it, most children look forward to visiting with their noncustodial parent. If you create an atmosphere where each visitation brings about pain, bitterness, and conflict, the children will begin to feel unwanted by both parents.

The Fix. Try to keep the following points in mind when it comes to your child's visitation needs:

1. Be more concerned for your child's happiness than anything else.

2. Remember that you're not doing this for your ex. You're doing it for your child.

3. Go the extra mile for your child. If that means being flexible, so be it. Your reward will come when he's older and is able to look back and see your selfless effort.

4. Keep visitation as consistent and hassle-free as you can from your end.

5. Be flexible and trade visitation days if possible. Your willingness to give will come back to you some day.

6. Don't make decisions that affect your ex's visitation time without first consulting him or her first (e.g., vacation Bible school, trips, lessons, summer jobs).

7. Process the child's visit once he gets home. Listen to what he did and what kind of time he had. Your child needs to see and feel your acceptance of the fact that he can have a good time with the other parent as well as with you.

8. Be understanding and flexible of your child's feelings as you are planning visitation. Cutting into his scheduled plans and activities can cause resentment if you don't include him in the planning.

9. Resist the temptation to grill your child for information about the noncustodial parent. If you do grill him he will

clue into this quickly and resent you for using him as an indirect way of communicating with your ex.

10. Don't be a "Disneyland Dad" or a "Marineland Mom." Remember what we learned about quality time. Sure, a kid likes to go to places like that, but he needs your time and direct attention even more.

THE PROBLEM:
TIME AND DISTANCE HURDLES

What I'm about to say may cause some of you to want to throw this book out of sight, although eventually I think you'll come to agree with me. Many single parents find themselves in situations where the custodial parent lives far away from the noncustodial parent. In most cases, that is fine with both parents. They would just as soon not run into each other at the soccer field or at the 49-cent hamburger counter at the local Mini-Mart. The only one who pays the price for this time and distance dilemma is the child.

I am strongly opposed to either parent moving any great distance away from the child after a divorce. The only exception would be if the child is old enough to hop on a plane and travel to dad's or mom's, but even that is rarely a viable option. After all, how many single parents are so well off that money is no object and they can afford to send the child back and forth twice a month?

Sure, staying relatively close is uncomfortable. It may even present a hardship if one or both of you have to turn down a transfer or job opportunity. Sure it's sad. But don't try to justify your moving by saying something silly, such as "I'll make more money in my new position, so I'll be able to give my kids more." Wrong! What your kids need has very little to do with money. What they need you to provide is *you!*

The Fix. Why don't you simplify visitation as much as possible by saying to your ex, "I'll do whatever it takes to make visitation as consistent as possible if you'll do the same." If that means passing up the job opportunity of a lifetime, then you pass it up. If that means you don't get to use your season tickets, so be it. If it means that, for the first time in your adult life, you don't get to go golfing every Saturday, too bad . . . so sad.

Too many single parents view their visitation time with their children as an obligation instead of what it really is, a privilege. Face it, you'd drop everything and drive all day and all night if it were for something you really wanted to do. But how many single parents drop everything to spend time with their children? One answer is "quite a few." Another answer is "not enough."

My intention is not to throw a guilt trip at you or cause you to hang your head in shame. (Besides, if you're reading this book, you're parenting priorities are probably squared-away.) No doubt, it's the other parent who lives three-hundred miles away, has a new job, a new truck, a new spouse, and is generally late with child support payments.

My prayer is that you'll share this information with the one who really needs it. After you share it with him (or her), pray fervently that your ex will realize what aspects of life are truly important. Pray that he or she will want to keep visitation as frequent and consistent as the children want and need.

THE PROBLEM:
THE CHILDREN SEE OUR MUTUAL ANGER

The other day I was ribbing Paul Meier about the titles of two of his books, *Happiness Is a Choice* and *Love Is a Choice*. I asked him if he were going to write another book called *Choice Is a Choice*. I did that because I especially appreciate Paul's assertion in his books that God has empowered us, through free will, to make the critical decisions in our lives. He doesn't give that authority to anybody but us.

If anger is such an unpleasant feeling and it makes us do such unpleasant things, why do we hold onto it so tightly? Why do some people use their anger as a weapon against the other parent?

I spoke with a single mom who asked a wonderful question. "How can I stop seeing red every time my ex comes over to pick up the children? As soon as he walks through the door, I get angry all over again and start taking it out on him—and it's been three years since our divorce."

The answer is that this mom is stuck in the grieving process. She's gridlocked in a position termed *anger turned outward*. What that means is that every time she sees her ex-husband, she is reminded of how hurt she felt over her losses. A peculiar fermentation process takes place when hurt is left to itself. It can turn into resentment and then into anger. The only way to neutralize hurt, resentment, and anger is to allow those feelings to be experienced and grieved. We'll cover this process in greater depth in chapter 7.

The Fix. There are certainly many reasons for single parents to feel angry. I'm not going to try to talk you out of a single one of them. You have a right to be angry over lost dreams. You have a right to be mad that you are starting over financially. And that's just the beginning of the list.

Your children also have rights. They have the right to grow up in a house where their mom and dad aren't outwardly hostile. They don't need to experience your anger. You need to get over it.

What does all this mean? It means that if you want to do what's right for your children, you're going to have to put some effort into being civil toward your ex. What did getting hostile and angry ever get you except anger and hostility in return?

Anger is a choice too, so take the lead and make a choice to change.

THE PROBLEM:
KILLING THE MESSENGER

I can see the ad campaign now. "PARENTAL EXPRESS . . . When it absolutely, positively has to irritate your ex. Overnight."

Sad to say, some single parents turn their children into a messenger service to deliver the frustration and anger they feel toward the ex. "Sweetie, would you call your father and remind him he's late with the check?" This question is heard in far too many households throughout the world, not just from the standpoint of the ex's not being on time with the check but from the standpoint that the question puts the child in the middle, right where he doesn't belong.

Or how about "You tell your mom that I don't appreciate her dropping you guys off late." That kind of dig works both ways, which is to say that both parents use it, with the result that the poor kid gets a double dose. Kids should come with a sign that reads, "Don't kill me. I'm only the messenger."

There are other hurtful games that go on between single parents. One is to turn the child into a modern day James Bond and send him into the enemy camp to gather intelligence. "Is he still drinking as much as he used to?" "Is your father still dating that blonde?" Those two oldies never seem to go out of style. But they should.

The Fix. The fix for manipulating others to do your dirty work is to stop it by becoming more direct. If you want to know if he's still dating that blonde, ask him. If he doesn't tell you, that's not a signal to put the spies in motion. It's a signal that it probably isn't any of your business.

When you place your kids in the middle, you are teaching them several destructive lessons. One is that people shouldn't be direct with the questions or problems they have regarding other people. Another is that it's okay to manipulate others into doing your dirty work. The result of passing these lessons on to your children is that it will tend to make it hard for them to trust adults. They will learn only manipulating skills and not how to have their needs met directly.

THE PROBLEM:
HE MAKES NO EFFORT TO SEE THE KIDS

It never ceases to amaze me how many parents there are who don't want to have anything to do with their children after the divorce. I wonder if these same people throw away their cars when the ashtrays are full too.

Parents who resist seeing or refuse to see their children are saying volumes about their character. They are likely self-centered and egotistical, placing themselves and their happiness above all else.

The Fix. You might first ask yourself the question, "Do I even want to encourage (or to demand that) my ex follow through with visitation orders?" If you decide in the affirmative, how do you deal with a parent who has demonstrated that he doesn't care enough to make the effort to see his child? I believe you take your best shot, one time, and one time only. And you do it with the assistance of ongoing counseling.

I would communicate the rule this way. "Since you're now wanting to see your child, I agree it would be beneficial for him to spend time with you as well as with me. Since you and the child have been apart for _____ amount of time, an adjustment period is needed. I think it would be helpful for you to receive some counseling while you are integrating back into your child's life." You might even offer to split the cost of counseling if that is within your budget.

If your ex resists or refuses counseling, I'd make a stand for full custody. If his intentions are honorable and he realizes he has made a mistake in not seeing his child, he should be willing to go to counseling, at least during the initial period.

THE PROBLEM:
YOUR CHILDREN AREN'T YOUR COUNSELORS

When we are feeling hurt and alone, we naturally want to share our problems. We want to talk about how tough the divorce has been, how poorly we've been treated, how we're not sure how the family is going to get by financially, or how we're not sure we are going to be able to afford living where we currently live.

There's nothing wrong with sharing those concerns. In fact, it's downright healthy—unless you are sharing them with the wrong people —namely, your kids.

The Fix. Your children are not your counselors. You don't have the right to go to them and share your deepest fears and frustrations, irrespective of their ages. They are not emotionally equipped to handle their parents' problems.

An illustration of how wrong it is to put a child into the role of counselor lies in the realm of the professional ethics required of psychologists. Most states have rules that outline the dos and don'ts of a therapeutic practice. A major "don't" is that you don't counsel family members or people with whom you have a personal relationship. It's called avoiding a conflict of interest.

Isn't that the same thing you're asking your children to do? Don't they have an even greater conflict of interest here? They not only know and love the person doing the complaining, but they also know and love the person being complained about. Give them a break and let them share their problems without being overwhelmed with yours.

JUST WHAT IS OUR RELATIONSHIP NOW?

After divorce, many couples struggle with identifying, establishing, and placing boundaries around a new relationship with the ex-spouse.

You're not sure whether you should treat each other as you used to, treat each other 180 degrees differently, or find someplace in the middle. The only absolute is that there is at least one little person hanging around who is banking on your ability to work it out.

Perhaps the best place to start resolving this issue is with the foundation that things can never be the way they were before. Too much has happened and too many changes have taken place for both of you to try to act as though nothing's changed.

Some single parents may at first try to reestablish the same familiar ways they and their ex used to communicate. They may talk about intimate thoughts, feelings, and secrets in hopes of keeping things as much as possible like they once were. They might even see this renewed relationship as as a fallback position, should their new life not work out as planned.

Although that tactic is understandable, in the end it frustrates most people, as it is inconsistent with the way the relationship has evolved. A better way to handle your uncomfortable feelings concerning the evolution of the relationship is to follow the advice given by the apostle Paul when he wrote, "Speak the truth in love" (Ephesians 4:16).

Speaking the truth in love allows you to communicate your concerns, confusions, and anxieties over this latest chapter in your lives. Though you each have your own new lives, you both share a life: you are still parents to the same child or children, which provides you with a common bond forever. Openly discuss what both of you want and need of each other. That will be a good first step to feeling more comfortable and supported in your changing roles.

Another wise tactic is to try to deal with one another on a professional, adult, ethical basis. That approach may seem cold and impersonal on the surface, but most single parents report that dealing with the ex-spouses in that way actually fosters a spirit of cooperation and a single-mindedness when it comes to providing for the welfare of the children. Not only does treating your ex professionally and ethically make the relationship easier, but the harmony that results is something your children will appreciate as well.

LONG-DISTANCE ENCOURAGING

The common goal of both single parents should be to help the other parent be as effective as possible. If that principle is always kept foremost in mind, there will be considerably less room for error and conflict. One way the custodial parent can help the noncustodial parent is by encouraging him to practice active single parenting. To the noncustodial parent active single parenting means taking initiative to seek often and in many different ways to make a positive impression on the child. Let's take a look at some commonly used methods.

PHONE CALLS

As simple and easy as it sounds, telephone contact is grossly underutilized. It takes just a few minutes to call a child to tell him about something new in your life or to "tune in" to him.

The simple act of calling your child to tell him that you love him and are thinking about him is worth a million times what you paid for the call. Go ahead, splurge.

CASSETTE TAPES

A few single parents I've met have stumbled across the idea of recording messages for their children on a cassette tape. Tapes are considerably more personal than letters because they allow your personality to come through.

LETTERS AND CARDS

Why is it that moms can do the letter and card thing in spades, whereas dads shy away from it? Come on guys, isn't it time to dispense with this macho hang-up? Go hang around the Hallmark aisle at the store. Start engaging your children in an open and loving relationship—*today*.

VIDEOTAPES

Even better than cassette tapes are videotapes. They allow you to send your kids a message as well as to be there when they receive it.

FLOWERS

Kids love to receive flowers. I know they are expensive to send, but it's worth it to hear your ex describe your kids' expressions when they got them. This is an especially effective way for dads and daughters to connect on special occasions, such as birthdays, proms, first dates, and graduations.

PHOTOS

I've met a few noncustodial parents who have found that sending photos (and even photo albums) to their children is an effective way of staying connected. They take and send pictures of their homes, family pets, stepchildren, and job sites—essentially anything that will help their children feel as though they are still an important part of dad's (or mom's) life. Photos are also helpful in integrating the child into the environment when he comes to visit.

·7·

TAKE CARE
OF YOUR OWN
EMOTIONAL NEEDS

"Don't you walk away from me when I'm talking to you, you disrespectful, back talking, little . . ." With that, Linda angrily hurried toward her son, who was hastily beating a retreat to the smallish makeshift bedroom that used to be Grandma's sewing room.

Since Linda and her son had moved in with her parents, Devon's room was continually a sore subject for the eight-year-old. His chief complaint seemed to be the vintage 1966 decor, featuring pink and green plaid wallpaper with matching lace curtains. And to make matters worse, Devon's grandmother had left her sewing machine along with two overflowing baskets of clothes that were queued-up, just waiting for Grandma's available time. Devon was sure many of those clothes had been there since the room itself was built.

Devon constantly groused about not having room for his Michael-Jordan-Meets-Bugs-Bunny, one-on-one, personally-autographed-by-Bugs-himself poster. There was no allowance for throwing his old, beat-up size eight Nike's anywhere they happened to land after he flipped them from his feet. And nowhere to keep Waylon and Wynona, his hamster roommates.

"This place stinks and so do all the people in it!" yelled Devon, as he made his way past the rows of perfectly hung family portraits that lined both sides of the hallway. "I'm sick and tired of living here. I'm sick and tired of lace doilies everywhere I look, and I'm sick and tired of all of you, especially you, Mo—"

At that precise moment, everything seemed to go into slow motion for Linda. She was barely conscious of her thoughts as she charged furiously down the hallway in pursuit of her son. She caught up with Devon just as he reached the heavy wooden door, laden with several peeling coats of off-white paint. She watched herself from a distance as she grabbed his arm, spinning him around, knocking him off balance. "Don't you ever talk to me that way!" Linda screamed at the top of her lungs as she slapped Devon across his face several times with her right hand. Devon's surprised and pained expression registered his disbelief over what was happening.

Linda regained her composure as she heard the familiar sound of her father jingling his keys in the locked front door. Her face went flush when she realized how out of control she had gotten. "Devon, I'm sorry honey. I'm so very sorry. I promise I won't hit you like that ever again, honey." For what seemed like hours, Linda cradled Devon in her arms, rocking back and forth as the two cried and grieved over their respective losses.

Normally, Linda would give Devon a quick kiss on his cheek and send him off to bed. But not tonight. Tonight, Linda felt worse than she ever remembered feeling in her life. *How could I have become one of those moms you read about in the newspapers?* Linda asked herself as she gently rubbed Devon's back. *I've never even had to spank him, and now I lose complete control of myself to the point where I'm abusing him. I'm not just angry at Devon. I'm angry at Kenny for not being a better husband. I'm mad at my folks for being just like they were when I wanted to get out of here when I was eighteen. And I'm really mad at myself!* Linda thought as she clasped her hands so tightly together that the fingernails of one hand dug deeply into the other.

I'm a twenty-eight-year-old single mother who's put on twenty-five pounds and is living with her parents. It's not bad enough that I messed up Kenny's and my life. Now I'm messing up Devon's life. I'm so depressed, I just wish I'd go to sleep and never wake up. At least then Devon could live with his dad.

Linda bent down and gently kissed Devon's cheek, whispering "Good night, sweetie." She rose softly from the side of his bed and tiptoed across the hardwood floor toward the partially open door and reached down to turn on the night light. Linda paused. She stood motionless in the open doorway, illuminated only by the faint aura of the small light. It was at that moment that Linda prayed a prayer she'd never forget.

"Dear Father, please give me the strength to decide what to do." Linda prayed in a hushed tone as she leaned against the doorjamb.

"Father, only You and I really know how desperate and suicidal I'm feeling. Father, I'm tired of running and I'm tired of feeling confused and sad all the time. I think I would just prefer it if You would come and take me home tonight in my sleep. I don't want to live anymore, Father. If that's Your will, so be it. Please don't ever let Devon forget how much I love him. Please help him to find forgiveness for what I've done to him and his life. I know he'll be better taken care of when I'm gone."

Linda had never felt this way before. She was completely numb. It was as though she were watching herself on a movie screen. She walked slowly down the hallway, past her parent's closed bedroom door and into the bathroom. She stood in front of the old porcelain sink with rust stains and stared into the oak-framed mirror, the very mirror she had stared into as a little girl and later as a teenager. Only now, she neither saw nor felt any hope in her pale reflection.

She slowly opened the medicine cabinet and reached inside. She knew right where to reach. The third shelf up, all the way to the right, next to the Q-Tips. That's where Mom always kept her sleeping pills. Linda didn't even have to look. She knew they'd be there. Linda cautiously and quietly took the sizable, amber-colored prescription bottle from its usual spot and held it firmly in her hand. She looked around quickly, half-wishing, half-dreading that she'd be discovered. "Nobody," she whispered, as she filled the pink Tupperware cup with water, the same cup that had occupied that spot by the sink for the past twenty years.

Linda poured the entire contents of the medicine bottle into her left palm. "I hope these aren't her hormone pills. With my luck, I'd go to sleep and wake up with a mustache and an urge to read the sports' section." The smirk on Linda's face disappeared as she raised the handful of white and blue capsules to her mouth. As she reached for the Tupperware cup, an eerie feeling crept over her.

"Mom, what are you doing?" came a soft, little voice from behind her. Linda dropped the handful of capsules and whirled around to find Devon standing in the doorway, rubbing his sleepy eyes with both fists.

"I couldn't sleep 'cause I had a bad dream," he said. "I dreamed we were in this big ol' crowd of people and somehow got separated. I got real scared 'cause I don't like it when I'm not with you, Mom."

Tears streamed down Linda's cheeks as she hugged Devon. "Don't worry, honey, we'll never be separated again."

LIVES IN TRANSITION

Creatures of habit. That's what we are. We bristle at the idea of changing a routine. We get ready for work the same way each morning. Take a shower, blow-dry our hair, finish getting dressed, brush our teeth, grab a cup of coffee, and we're out the door. We drive the same way to work each day and usually eat lunch at the same place at least two times a week.

Since we are naturally resistant to change, making the dramatic adjustments necessary following a divorce can be a shock to the system. Change must be coaxed a step at a time. Single parents find their world turned completely upside down, because nothing is the way it used to be.

The internal drive to go it alone also makes it difficult for many newly single parents to make important changes in their lives. Christian single parents are especially prone to disengage themselves from friends, family, church, Bible study groups, and even their relationship with Christ—essentially anyone or anything that makes them feel stigmatized.

The reason single parents most often give for emotionally distancing themselves from others is that they believe their Christian friends and acquaintances will not accept them in their new "fallen" state. And it's true that divorce is not what God wants for our lives. In more than one place in the Bible God speaks against divorce. But there is a place in the Bible, too, for those whose lives have been shattered by sin—either their own sin or the sins of others. Wouldn't it be wonderful if, instead, pastors and church friends came gladly to the assistance of those reeling from a divorce, asking what they need or how they might help? If they were there for them emotionally? And, to be fair, that sometimes is the case.

Far more common, however, is a body of believers that is not so accepting, but rather looks at the newly divorced as though they had a communicable disease. "Stay away from Jeannie, she's divorced," the whisper goes, as though simply being around Jeannie might somehow expose one to divorce, that dreaded virus for which there is no vaccination.

Don't be fooled. It's not that they feel they might catch what infected your marriage that keeps some Christians at arms' length. It's that you represent something that forces them out of the security of denial. "We're Christians. We're not supposed to be faced with divorce and adultery. That's for those heathen, secular people."

I'm reminded of what Jesus teaches us in Matthew 9:10–12. That passage tells of a dinner party Jesus was invited to at Matthew's house. Among the guests with Jesus were tax collectors and what the Bible calls "sinners" of every variety. When the Pharisees saw Jesus at the dinner, they asked the disciples, "Why does your teacher eat with tax collectors and 'sinners'?" When Jesus heard them gossiping, He said, "It is not the healthy who need a doctor, but the sick. But go and learn what this means: 'I desire mercy, not sacrifice.'"

I like to imagine that somewhere in that group of "sinners" and tax collectors eating dinner with Jesus, there must have been at least one single parent. She probably had trouble getting a sitter that night, but she still managed to sit down for a bite with the Messiah. The Pharisees no doubt were shocked that she was there. But that is where she should have been—as close as possible to the Lord.

Don't let your single state push you from Christianity, God, or other people. Just the opposite. Begin (or continue) your single parenting journey as near to the Lord as you can be, and yet with eyes wide open to the reaction you may face in the church. It's true, many Christians will avoid you after your divorce. But there will also be many Christians who will still love you and welcome you into the fold. The trick is in finding the "safe" Christians.

PLEASE SECURE YOUR MASK FIRST

The other day I was traveling across the country to conduct a single-parenting seminar. As I took my seat, the stewardess's voice came over the intercom system. She was going through the usual spiel about what to do in the event of an emergency, and all that stuff that nobody ever listens to.

"In the event of a water landing, you may use your seat cushion as a floatation device," she said blandly, as though there were such a thing as a "water landing" for a jumbo jet. She might just as well have said, "In the event that we crash into the ocean, you can try using your seat cushion to keep yourself afloat, but I wouldn't make any dinner plans."

Then the stewardess described what would happen if there were a sudden drop in cabin pressure. "An oxygen mask will drop from the overhead compartment." I had heard the message a hundred times. But this time the rest of what the stewardess said caught my attention, perhaps for the first time. "Please secure the mask around your own mouth and then assist any small children you may be traveling with with theirs."

What a rat this stewardess must be, I thought. *Does she really expect that the parents on board will calmly adjust their own oxygen masks while their children gasp their last breaths in the oxygen-depleted cabin as papers, tray tables, and plates fly by?*

She did intend that parents do just that—and what she said applies to single parenting. Newly single parents might think they should put their own emotional needs in second place behind the emotional needs of their children, but in reality the exact opposite is true. Although they are operating on the basis of an honorable motive, the oxygen mask concept is valid. They must first secure their own "oxygen masks" if they are going to be able to help their children survive. If they fail to do that, they might die from lack of emotional "oxygen" while they're frantically fumbling with the "oxygen masks" for their kids. Single parents will be better able to take care of their children's needs if they take care of their own as well.

WHAT DOES TAKING CARE OF ME LOOK LIKE?

As odd as it may seem, some single parents really do forget to see to their own emotional needs. The reason they usually give for this omission is that they have so many obstacles to maneuver around before they can even consider personal time.

Consider the list. School. Going over homework. After-school activities. Seeing that the children are fed. Spending time with the children. Shopping for them. Cleaning up after them. The truth is, if you allow the list to govern your life, you truly will never have any time for yourself.

In counseling, one of the things I try to empower single parents to do is to give themselves permission to relax, even if it is just once in a while. Sadly, in subsequent counseling sessions, many report, "I tried, but I really didn't know what to do," or, "I felt too guilty, so I chickened-out."

That is when a single parent needs to resort to making a list of things she used to enjoy doing (if she can even remember). Some single parents will have to think back to the days before they were married.

I suggest to all single parents that they strategically plan (and schedule) personal quality time. Although the optimum time varies from parent to parent, I've found that even a short getaway (two to four hours in duration) once a month works wonders. Some activities that fit into this time frame are:

- Going to a movie or even a double feature
- Going shopping at the mall (for themselves, not the kids)
- Meeting with friends or family over a leisurely lunch
- Getting a massage
- Having your nails done (mostly the single moms, but these are the nineties, so who am I to question)
- Going horseback riding or sailing, or engaging in some other recreational activity (perhaps a fitness class)
- Going to the park and reading a book while soaking up some sun (minimum SPF 30 recommended)
- Taking in a local sporting event

As you're reading this list, you may be saying to yourself, "I haven't done any of these things in years. And besides, I'd never have the time even if I had the desire." That's just the point. You have to *make* time in your schedule for yourself, or you won't do any of these things.

The second part of this all-important time equation is planning a quarterly escape. Those escapes can be weekend getaways, or they can be longer. They might feature such activities as:

- A weekend trip alone or with friends
- A church retreat
- If money is tight, spending a weekend with a friend or relative

The importance of designating quality time to look after your own emotional needs can't be overstated. I understand you might have to deal with roadblocks ranging from guilt to child care. But the truth is, if you are resourceful enough, you'll work it out. It's that important.

EMOTIONAL BANKRUPTCY

When everything in our lives begins to change, we get thrown off balance. Things that we used to take in stride now take on overwhelming proportions. We begin to unravel and gravitate toward a condition I call *emotional bankruptcy*. It's a term that single parents need to understand.

It's easiest to understand the principle of being emotionally bankrupt by thinking in terms of banking. Let's say you went to the bank and opened a new checking account with the minimum $200 deposit. After leaving the bank, you stopped and bought some things, writing checks for each purchase.

The following day, you wanted to do some more shopping, but you knew you were close to your balance. So before going to the mall, you stopped by the bank to deposit more money. Now you were able to go shopping because you knew you could cover your checks. What's inside your account was equal to, or greater than, what was being withdrawn.

Being emotionally bankrupt is like having too little money in your checking account. Consider the following list of withdrawals being taken from your emotional account daily.

Substantial Penalties for Early Withdrawals

- Your children's neediness and relentless demands on you
- Trying to be a mom and a dad
- Pressures from your ex
- Pressures of a new lifestyle
- Functioning pressures (e.g., sleep, weight loss or gain, anxiety)
- Financial pressures
- Loneliness
- Work-related pressures
- Adapting to the social changes that come as a part of being a single parent (e.g., at church, with friends, in dating relationships)

DEPOSITS INSURED

You may have been able to add five, ten, or one hundred items to the list of withdrawals. The things that can sap you of your time, energy, love, desires, and sleep are endless. In stark contrast, there are only two conditions that will enable you to make deposits to your emotional account, anytime, day or night. They are:

- Your ability to feel loved and connected to God
- Your ability to feel loved and connected to others

That's it. There isn't a secret formula for adding vast resources to your emotional bank account. This is God's plan for all of us.

Without feeling loved and connected to God and others, we are all destined to be emotionally bankrupt, no matter what our circumstances.

HOW DO YOU KNOW
WHEN YOU'RE BANKRUPT?

Perhaps you can remember when you first tried to learn about the concept of checking accounts. Wasn't it hard to understand the principle behind the fact that if you had checks in your checkbook, you needed as well to have money in your account?

Some of us still operate our emotional lives with the same vague mind-set. We reason, "I've got friends. I get dressed up every Sunday and go to church. My kids love me. I must be doing all right." Right?

Not necessarily. You may be bouncing emotional checks all over the county and not realizing it. Although you look okay on the outside, that doesn't necessarily mean you are doing okay emotionally.

The telltale signs of emotional bankruptcy can be as subtle as a pine needle settling onto a roof or as violent as a tidal wave. The difference lies in our respective levels of tolerance. Some people can tolerate tons of pine needles settling overhead and collapse only when the weight is very great. Others are unable to handle the slightest increase in pressure without feeling as though they are teetering on the brink of emotional ruin. The secret of survival lies in understanding the limit of your coping abilities.

I know that you're expecting some wonderful scriptural example here that will illuminate the point. Suffice to say, there are dozens of Bible references that address this issue to a tee. But instead I'm going to resort to a line from an old Clint Eastwood movie: "A man's got to know his limitations."

How simple can you get? Granted, Clint Eastwood will never be thought of as a Socrates or a Plato, but what more is there to be said? The line goes to the core of the issue. *You've got to know your limitations.*

You must know when you are reaching the point of emotional fatigue. The point where you feel frazzled and at your wit's end. The point where you start to feel as though you have nothing to give those many persons standing in front of you with their hands out. The point when you feel like screaming, running away, lashing out in anger, or giving up. That's what being emotionally bankrupt feels like.

THE EMOTIONAL
BANKRUPTCY SELF-TEST

In order to begin addressing your need for emotional support, you need first to identify some of the signs of emotional bankruptcy.

Look over the list of fourteen true-false statements below. Respond to them as openly and honestly as possible. You may even want to ask someone who has known you both before and after your divorce to you to help you take the test.

1. I often feel down in the dumps or even depressed.   TRUE / FALSE

2. I seem to be more easily irritated lately.   TRUE / FALSE

3. I've noticed that I don't seem to have the energy I used to have to do things such as cleaning, laundry, or cooking.   TRUE / FALSE

4. I find that I have little or no motivation to start new tasks or to complete those I've already undertaken.   TRUE / FALSE

5. I have noticed a decrease in my ability to concentrate. This is most easily seen when I try to read or stay on task at work or school.   TRUE / FALSE

6. I find myself avoiding social settings.   TRUE / FALSE

7. I've noticed an increase in my use of or desire for alcohol or medications.   TRUE / FALSE

8. I've recently asked my doctor for a prescription to help me feel less depressed or anxious or to help me get to sleep.   TRUE / FALSE

9. I've noticed that my normal sleep patterns are disrupted. I either sleep more or less than I used to.   TRUE / FALSE

10. I seem to avoid being around people whenever
    possible.   TRUE / FALSE

11. I seem to be angry or short tempered with friends,
    co-workers and family members.   TRUE / FALSE

12. I'm doing more things compulsively, such as
    spending, eating, shopping, cleaning, or saving
    seemingly useless things.   TRUE / FALSE

13. I don't seem to have fun doing the things that used
    to be fun for me.   TRUE / FALSE

14. It seems as though everyone wants something from
    me, yet nobody is willing to give.   TRUE / FALSE

SCORING YOUR TEST

If you answered "True" to more than three questions, then you should consider yourself "on notice." You are likely struggling with, or already burdened with, emotional bankruptcy. One thing for certain about being emotionally bankrupt: depression isn't far behind.

Your next step should be to seek some form of counseling, either from a pastor who has counseling training or from another mental health professional.

Read on. There's hope.

HOW TO OPEN A NEW ACCOUNT

If you took the test above and learned that you are either on the verge of emotional bankruptcy or are already completely bankrupt emotionally, the following suggestions should be of utmost importance to you. They will initiate a routine that will help you make more frequent deposits into your emotional bank account.

Step One   Acknowledge that you are emotionally bankrupt. The first step to emotional wholeness is to break out of your denial and openly acknowledge that you are in need of some help.

Step Two   Confess your helplessness to God and to others. Pray regularly for help, encouragement, and support in coping with your frustrations and hurts.

Begin attending a church where they welcome single parents. Churches that do that are usually churches who sponsor divorce recovery workshops and have counseling available.

Be careful to steer clear of churches that do not seem to reach out to single parents.

Step Three   Make a commitment to take better care of your needs. Not only do you need to commit to change, you need to invite a close friend or family member to help hold you accountable to making changes.

Step Four   Start setting boundaries around the needs and demands of others who are constantly draining you of your time, energy, and love.

Step Five   Identify people in your life who are safe. Those are usually people who can empathize with where you are emotionally because they've been in your shoes.

Take a chance by letting friends in. Sure, you run the risk of getting hurt, but those risks are insignificant in comparison to the consequences of staying disconnected.

Begin looking into divorce recovery workshops, single-parenting seminars, and support groups.

Step Six   Get actively involved in your recovery. Participate one to two evenings each week with other divorced people or single parents. Stay active for a minimum of one year.

Step Seven   Work toward forgiveness. As we have learned in previous chapters, the forgiveness you are counting on from God is linked to your ability to love and forgive those who have hurt you.

THE CONSEQUENCES
OF HOLDING ONTO ANGER

You have every right to be angry. You've been hurt, let down, and placed in a vulnerable position. The last thing I or any other psychologist would ever try to do is to talk you out of your anger. It's your choice. In fact, if you want to hold onto your anger even up to your deathbed, it's up to you.

But if you decide to hold onto your anger and grudges against those who have wronged you, you should be aware of a few important facts.

Certain emotionally damaging chemical changes take place in the brain when we hold onto our anger and unforgiveness. There is well-documented evidence that harboring grudges, storing anger, or repressing anger will cause the depletion of two important chemicals, *serotonin* and *norepinephrine,* from the brain amine supplies. When the brain is depleted of normal levels of those chemicals, clinical depression is likely to follow.

The process takes a period of time and many different factors enter into the question of how long it takes before depression takes over. The only thing we are sure of is that eventually it will.

If this sounds like you, then you need to make another choice. If depression has gotten the better of you since your divorce, I recommend three steps for retrieving the situation.

1. Begin praying that God will help release you from your anger and resentment toward the persons who have hurt you. That step is often made easier if you move toward a position of forgiveness. You may want to contact the people in question, either in writing or in person. Explain your feelings and your desire to get past your anger.

    You may also want to consult with your pastor, therapist, or a close friend while you are engaged in this process. A fresh perspective can be very helpful.

2. Seek counseling, both biblical and clinical, if necessary. The reason clinical counseling may be necessary is that although depression often starts out as a condition that can be managed through behavioral changes, if it is left unchecked it will affect the natural chemistry of the brain. When that takes place, medication may well be necessary to put things right. Although the time frame for depletion of the brain's natural antidepressants differs from person to person, the common belief is that the brain can deplete itself of its own antidepressant chemicals somewhere between 90 days to 180 days.

3. If the depression has gone beyond what can be managed only through behavioral or environmental changes, a clinician should evaluate whether short-term, antidepressant medications would be beneficial. Often those medications are helpful in allowing the brain to begin replenishing its levels of serotonin and norepinephrine. While the chemical aspects of the depression are being addressed, the therapist can more easily address the behavioral or environmental aspects.

Depression seldom, if ever, goes away on its own. But as I said, the choice is yours.

LONELINESS IS A CHOICE

The other day, I was watching my children playing hide-and-seek. My son, Matt, who has the misfortune to have inherited my humor and warped way of looking at things, was the seeker. My sweet, adorable daughter, Tracy, was the seekee.

She ran out of view and hid while my son closed his eyes and began to count. When he reached 100, he shouted, "Ready or not, here I come," and proceeded to get on his bike and ride down the block to his friend's house to play Nintendo.

I must admit, part of me admired the technique, but then the therapist side of me kicked in. If it weren't for that big smile on his face as he peddled off into the distance, I could've gotten angry.

Do you ever feel that your life is a game of hide-and-seek, and nobody's trying to find you either?

Many newly single parents, as well as the veterans, often choose to isolate themselves following the divorce. They quit participating in things that used to be fun, such as Bible studies, recreational activities, and social groups. They may even change churches, or quit going to church altogether.

Then, as if that weren't bad enough, an even stranger phenomenon occurs. Once others have left them, they feel resentment because they aren't being sought out and rescued. In therapy, that is called a *rescue wish*.

Why do some single parents quit activities and choose to isolate? We've explored several of the reasons in this and other chapters, but one reason overshadows all others: shame. Shame over failing to be the perfect parent. Shame over being different from others in the family or within the circle of friends at church. Shame over what the children are experiencing now. The list goes on.

Isn't it sad that it is a parent's shame that drives him into a position of hiding—hiding from the very thing that would make him feel better: bonded, attached, healthy relationships.

This chapter is intended to help single parents identify what they need to do in order to be more emotionally happy. (As a word of advice: all suggestions are absolutely useless if they're not put into action.)

STARTING YOUR OWN SUPPORT GROUP

A while back, a dear friend, Gary Richmond, the Singles and Single Parent Pastor at the First Evangelical Church in Fullerton, California, invited me to speak to his group. Upon arriving, I was astounded to be greeted by more than three hundred single parents who had gathered for this regularly scheduled session. Now granted, Gary's church is the exception, but there are probably more single parent or divorce recovery support groups out there than you'd believe. All it would take is a few phone calls to a few churches to find out what's available. In the event that none of the churches in your area offers a single parent support group, don't give up. Why not start a group yourself?

The best way to do that would be to identify one or two other single moms and dads in your church. Contact them and see if they would be interested in meeting to discuss participating in your support group. If they express an interest, strike while the iron is hot. Contact the pastor and ask him if the church would be willing to make a meeting room available. See if he would be willing to make an announcement concerning the group and its meeting place and time or allow you to place a message in the church bulletin or newsletter.

If you're worried about not having any materials to use for discussion guides, how about the book you're reading now? I've also written *Helping Single Parents with Troubled Kids* (Colorado Springs: NavPress, 1992), which was designed to provide material to be used by single parents in support groups.

Even without any study or discussion guides, you'll find no difficulty getting single parents to open up and share their problems, concerns, and successes.

GAINING PERSPECTIVE

There is a vast difference between *having relationships* and being *in relationship*. Too often, we get the two confused.

Having relationships is being healthily connected to others. That connection is what keeps us from feeling isolated, lonely, and depressed. But being *in relationship* with another person is to deal with that person on a level of emotional intimacy that requires a deeper level of trust, energy, and commitment.

Both *having relationships* and being *in relationship* are healthy steps on the path to becoming emotionally happy, although the latter level of interaction is sometimes risky. Single parents might consider reconnecting first in friendly, mutually supportive relationships, especially with other single parents, before even considering developing intimate relationships.

At some point down the road, intimate relationships are certainly recommended, but before you enter an intimate relationship, step back a bit and take an inventory of where you are emotionally.

Taking such an inventory requires insight and patience and the capacity to be comfortable with aloneness. Don't panic! That doesn't mean you have to take a vow of silence and join a monastery. Learning how to be alone means allowing yourself to experience the full range of emotions, from grief to relief. It means learning how to address your own neediness while being alone. Learning how to be comfortable with aloneness will help to create in you a self-confident, inner-dependency that will in turn make it easier for your future relationships to take on a more mature profile.

As part of learning to be comfortable with "just you," work your way through the following questions dealing with postdivorce issues. When you can answer each question with a degree of personal satisfaction (and more important, a degree of maturity in yourself and in the Scriptures), then perhaps you are ready for more intimate relationships.

EMOTIONAL INVENTORY

1. Who am I really, and how would I define myself to a total stranger?
2. What do I stand for, and what are my beliefs?
3. What are my values when it comes to the things of major importance, such as religion, politics, sex, abortion, and drugs?
4. What are my likes and dislikes?
5. Am I confident in who I am, or do I adapt to fit those around me?
6. Am I hiding my bad sides from God or others?
7. Am I easily pushed around, or do I stand up for what I believe in?
8. What do I want out of the rest of my life?
9. When I look in the mirror, do I like what I see? If so, why, and if not, why not?
10. Do I feel as though I need to be with somebody in order to feel good about myself or to feel more valuable?
11. Am I happier today than I was six months ago? Why or why not?
12. What has been the hardest part of being single?
13. What has been my lowest point since my divorce, and what steps have I taken to move forward?
14. Am I still angry or harboring grudges toward others, or have I begun to move to a position of forgiveness?
15. Where do I see myself in one year, three years, five years? What is my plan for attaining this vision?
16. How has my relationship with God changed in the last ninety days? The last six months? The past year?
17. What types of people do I seem to gravitate toward in relationships?

   □ Passive
   □ Broken people I can fix
   □ Sullen or moody
   □ Outgoing
   □ Those who like to be in control
   □ Emotionally unavailable

   □ Aggressive
   □ Upbeat
   □ Quiet or shy
   □ Abussive or uncaring
   □ Those who like to be submissive

18. Do these people represent personality types similar to that of my ex-spouse? In what ways?
19. What role do I like to take in close relationships?
    □ Victim   □ Aloof and distant
    □ Dominant and aggressive   □ Submissive or passive
20. Why do I seem to like this role? Was there someone in my life (perhaps a parent) with whom I identify this role? Which parent?
21. What have I done in the past year to help myself to grow spiritually and to get closer to God?

The Emotional Inventory Test isn't the type of test you can sit back and grade. This kind of test gives you a gauge of where you are in the healing process. You may see from your answers that you are feeling more in control and that you indeed have a clearer sense of who you are and what you stand for. Or you may see that you have a pervasive sense of insecurity or an uncertain identity.

Either way, if the emotional inventory caused you to think or to redefine yourself, your boundaries, and where you see yourself in the future, it has served its purpose.

I recommend taking this test every month or so. You'll find that you'll change rapidly during the early stages of single parenthood and then change somewhat slower later on. Retaking the test allows you to keep a pulse on who you are in relation to your evolving personality.

THE DATING DILEMMA

Many pastors and therapists counsel people to wait at least one year after the divorce before dating. I'm hesitant to put such a time frame around when it's safe to get back into the water—it's too much like trying to sanction happiness on a calendar. I don't believe that can or should be done.

However long you choose to wait before dating, you should make wise use of the time before you date. Use the time for personal growth, for making new friends, and for developing a closer relationship with God.

Once you are secure in who and what you are, then perhaps you may want to consider dating. But please, do yourself a favor and don't date until you have met that criteria. Jumping into being *in relationship* before you have identified and established your identity almost certainly will cause you problems. For example, if you were a passive, get-taken-advantage-of, codependent type of person in your marriage, you'll likely reprise that role in the next relationship if you haven't taken corrective action. As George Santayana put it, "Those who do not study history are condemned to repeat it."

SLEEPOVERS

Let's go on record as stating that except for a few moments of pleasure, there is nothing positive about having sex outside of marriage. I'll spare you a recital of the many scriptural, moral, and medical reasons premarital sex should not occur. Instead, I want to focus on the effect your having premarital sex will have on your children.

When you were a child, a sleepover (read "slumber party") was an entirely appropriate activity. It was fun for you and a friend to stay up late and laugh and talk and play games—and wake up the next morning completely wasted.

But when you are an adult and your friend is really your date and the activity consists of spending the night in bed together, the concept of "sleepover" takes on a whole new aspect. It is morally wrong on its face and, down the road, will send an entirely wrong message to your children.

Having a girlfriend or boyfriend sleep over will cause a multitude of mixed feelings in your children. At the very least it will create angry, hostile feelings in your children because of their desire to protect the "other" parent—the parent they perceive as being wronged, or sinned against, by what you are doing. It can also create confusion in your children as to why you promulgate abstention for them but not for yourself.

Letting your date sleep over also exacerbates your child's fear of being a third wheel. Remember, your children have already experienced the loss of one parent. Sleepovers exhume the still raw feelings they have about the divorce and can make them fear that another loss is imminent. Only this time, there will be no more parents left to fall back on.

And, lest you imagine that it is enough to stave off problems with your children by being discreet about an affair, consider the moral implications of your behavior. Extramarital sex is wrong, period. Even if your children never found out about the affair, you would know—and so would God.

SOME PRIORITIES
FOR SINGLE PARENTS

If you were once a part of a reasonably well-balanced parenting team, your priorities might have looked like this:

1. Spending time in your relationship with God
2. Spending time with your mate
3. Spending quality time with your children
4. Providing an income (or an additional income)
5. Making time for yourself

Things were moving along on cruise control for the most part. Church on Sunday. Bible study on Wednesdays. Get the kids off to school in the mornings. Go to your part-time job. Be home before they get home. Fix dinner or go out once in a while. It was simple. A no-brainer!

Now, as a single parent, the deck has been shuffled, and all previous bets are off. Now your priorities stack up more like this:

1. Work full time
2. Keep the kid's lives in order (school, soccer, Brownies, homework, Cub Scouts)
3. Keep the house in order (cooking, cleaning, laundry, chores)
4. Church on Sunday (when convenient)
5. Little or no quality time with the kids
6. No time left for yourself

Let's reshuffle the hand you've been dealt to see if you can't find a way to put your life back into balance.

PRIORITY #1:
KEEPING GOD FIRST
A truly balanced life is only attainable through a committed, personal relationship with Jesus Christ. For most people that means being faithful in daily prayer, weekly church attendance, and fellowship with other believers.

PRIORITY #2:
QUALITY TIME WITH YOUR KIDS

No spouse to worry about, so single parents should naturally move their children into the number two spot, right? Not necessarily. Some single parents get so caught up in their loneliness they move dating, social activities, or the pursuit of a new father for their children ahead of the children themselves.

Remember what was said in chapter 5 about spending quality time with your kids? Quality time with your children is too important to relegate to a lower priority. Cooking, cleaning, laundry, working overtime, dropping the car off for service—and all the other things you do during the week—can wait at least a half-hour. Your kids can't. Remember, there will come a time when they'll be gone.

PRIORITY #3:
PROVIDING A SAFE, LOVING ENVIRONMENT

It's up to you to ensure that your kids' emotional needs are taken care of, even while you are outside the home earning a living.

Do your level best to ensure that your children don't become latch-key kids—kids who come home after school to an empty house, cook their own meals, make their own lunches for school, and occupy themselves alone until their mom or dad gets home. That is no lifestyle for a child. It may be extremely difficult to find some way to ensure that your child won't be home alone after school is over, but the effort will be worth it.

Some alternatives you might consider: for a younger child, enlist relatives, neighbors, or friends to serve as after-school care givers; for an older child, investigate after-school activities (YMCA sports programs, band practice, Scouting, drama group) that would give your child something positive to do when school is over and at the same time keep him from having to be home alone.

PRIORITY #4:
EARNING A LIVING

Being a single mom is almost synonymous with being a working mom. Unless you have independent wealth (or an ex who can afford very generous alimony and child support payments), you are going to need to develop a source of income. So earning a living is going to have to be one of your major priorities.

But a word of caution: Don't get caught up in the away-from-home rat race men have been running ever since the Industrial Revolution. When (or if) you work outside the home, keep that work in perspective. Work so that you

- can provide the necessities for your family's well-being;
- have enough money to allow you and your children to participate in fun activities, such as family vacations;
- have enough money in savings to guard against short-term financial problems.

That is not to say that you should necessarily give up the idea of a career or that you should give your employer only half-hearted service. It simply means that because you are the only parent at home you'll need to put your children high on the priority list. If you discover that your work tends to shove your children aside, then maybe you need to realign your priorities.

PRIORITY #5:
FRIENDS, EXERCISE, AND HOBBIES
Nobody lives by work alone. A balanced life includes time with friends, exercise, recreation, hobbies, and just plain having fun.

·8·

UNDERSTAND RISKS AND SPOT WARNING SIGNS

"Hey Noah!" the tall, thin boy with scraggly, dirty blond hair yelled from across the football field. "Wait up, dude, I got some!" Noah squinted his eyes to see who was calling his name from across the football field. He didn't recognize the voice. Nor did he recognize the face from that distance. But he did recognize the baggy, green shorts that crept past the teenager's knees and the black tank top emblazoned with a silver skull and the words "Grateful Dead Head."

"Check it out, Noah dude," the teenager said. "I got me an eight ball. Time to smoke out," which Noah had come to understand meant in doper terms, "I am in possession of an eighth of a ounce of marijuana. Would you care to smoke some of it with me?"

Scotty really hadn't been friends with Noah for very long. In fact, they weren't the type of boys you would expect to hang around together. Noah, a junior at Marshall High, was always considered pretty straitlaced. He had lettered the past two years on the varsity football and baseball teams. He had a part-time job as a delivery boy for Pizza Pete's and had even saved up enough to buy a motorcycle. He had pulled a solid B average all three years of high school and was active in his church high school group.

Scotty, on the other hand, was the poster boy for the word "remedial." He was the reason detention hall was invented. He was dirty-mouthed, disrespectful, disheveled, and disinterested in school. He seemed to care little for anything except smoking pot, drinking beer, and hassling his stepdad, or RoboMouth, as he sarcastically called him.

The teenagers seemingly had nothing in common—except that both had parents who were divorced, a link the two boys had not even been aware of until that day. Noah just seemed to gravitate toward Scotty. Maybe it was because Scotty was a senior. Indeed, Scotty had been a senior for the past two years.

"Where'd you score the weed, Scotty?" Noah asked as he reached inside the right front pocket of his Levis and pulled out his Bic lighter.

"I got it from that guy in the Corvette who cruises the parking lot in the mornings," replied Scotty.

The two boys looked around the field carefully. "Any sign of that butthead, coach Manship?" asked Noah.

"Dude, if that bald-headed Manship messes this up by taking one of his stupid walks around the track during lunch, I'm going to break into his office, steal his hairpiece, and glue it to one of the pigs over in the 4-H Building," Scotty replied.

"I am not going back to sixth-period remedial English without a few bong hits, man." He chuckled. "I hate that class, and Mrs. Zimmer is a complete space alien. You know, dude, she's flunked me three years in a row! I think that's the school record."

"Man, that evil woman's really got it in for you, dude."

Noah busily loaded the bowl portion of the marijuana pipe—the same pipe Scotty had carefully disguised to look like a vase when he made it in ceramics class. Every few seconds he paused, looked around the track and football field nervously for any signs of danger, and then concentrated again on the task at hand—getting stoned.

As Noah expertly packed the fine-grained, green, leafy substance into the bong, he glanced up at Scotty, who was standing in front of him, moving impatiently from one to leg to the other, smiling broadly. *Man, I'm never going to be that bad,* Noah thought as he looked at Scotty. *What a total "stoner." He'll probably still be a senior when I'm on social security.*

Noah handed the bong to Scotty, who took great pleasure in inhaling the ceremonial first hit. Noah wondered how in the world he had gotten connected with Scotty in the first place. *I always thought Scotty was a total geek-doper. I don't even like those hoodlum friends of his, but here I am, sneaking around under the bleachers, smoking dope—trying to decide if I'm going back to class later or not.*

The two boys kicked back under the bleachers in back of the football field and took turns passing the ceramic implement back and forth. "Your parents know you smoke-out at school Noah?" asked Scotty, his speech already starting to thicken.

"Are you crazy, dude? My dad doesn't even live with us, and my mom wouldn't know a 'joint' if it walked up to her and bit her on the nose." The two boys laughed hysterically, even though neither could have said what was so funny.

"What happened to your—what do you call it?" Scotty asked. "Dude, I can't think of what you call that dude who runs the family."

"You mean my old man?" asked Noah.

"Yeah, that's what I meant to say," said Scotty as the two boys broke again into uncontrollable laughter.

It was at that moment, for some unknown reason, that a Bible verse flashed into Noah's mind. "He who walks with the wise grows wise, but a companion of fools suffers harm" (Proverbs 13:20).

Oh, great, thought Noah. *When some guys get loaded, they see the* Sports Illustrated *swimsuit models. Me, I do Bible trivia.*

"Hey, you boys," came a loud, stern voice from a few yards away. "Johnson, is that you? What is this, about the one-hundredth time I've caught you smoking dope under the bleachers? What an idiot," chided Coach Manship. "Who's this with you? Hey, I don't seem to know your—"

The coach stopped in midsentence. "Is that you, Erickson? I haven't seen you here since you dropped off the football team midseason. What are you doing out here smokin' dope with the likes of Johnson?

"Okay, guys. Johnson, you know the routine. Let's take a little walk to Principal Williams's office." With that, Coach Manship grabbed both boys by their collars and began walking them from underneath the bleachers, across the football field, and through the campus quad area.

This is the most humiliating experience of my entire life, Noah thought as the trio passed what seemed to be the entire student body, who were gathered in groups throughout the quad, eating their lunches. And Noah was right.

The unmerciful teasing began almost immediately. There were countless cries of "Way to go, Scotty," and "Ooooooohhhhhh busted," just to name a couple. Not to mention the undistinguishable sounds and catcalls too numerous to mention.

Unfortunately for Noah, his problems were just beginning. The next thing he knew, he and Scotty were standing in front of Mr. Williams's desk.

As Mr. Williams looked up from his paperwork, Scotty slurred, "You're probably wondering why I called this meeting, Mr. Williams.

Well, sir, it's about Coach Manship. We believe he's spending entirely too much time walking around the track, and I, for one, am worried about his feet. We thought it was only fair that we stake him out from under the bleachers. Everything was fine until one of the hogs snitched us off."

"Oh no, not you again, Johnson. I think we'll call a special school board meeting just to rename the term 'suspension.' We're going to call it a 'Johnson' from here on out. Son, you have got to be the biggest dope-smoking mutation I've ever met in my life. What's wrong with you, boy?" asked Mr. Williams, the veins bulging out of his forehead and neck.

"I was framed, Mr. Williams. The baggie of marijuana and bong are Coach Manship's. I tried to get him to stop, but you know how he is. You're going to have to deal with him now. I'm at my wit's end with this coach," Scotty said, both hands firmly planted on hips.

Noah couldn't hold it in any longer. Even though he knew laughing was probably the worst thing he could do under the circumstances, he couldn't help himself. He burst into laughter, which immediately drew the ire of Mr. Williams.

"Thousands of comedians out of work across the country, but not you, Scotty. And you even brought your own private audience with you. So what do you have to say for yourself, Noah? I can't believe you're hanging around with the likes of this one," said Mr. Williams, gesturing toward Scotty. "Let's call your parents and get them down here. Who's home at your place, Noah, your mom or your dad? Isn't he a fireman or something like that?"

"My dad doesn't live with us anymore. He and my mom got a divorce a year and a half ago. He's remarried and lives up north with his new family," replied Noah soberly.

"Oh. Sorry to hear that, Noah. Is your mom home, or is she at work?" asked Mr. Williams.

"She's at work, but I know the number."

Tammy couldn't believe what she was hearing. "He was smoking what at school?" she asked incredulously. "I'll be right down."

Tammy raced across town to Marshall High, parked in the no-parking zone, and scurried the short distance to the office. She paused at the front counter only long enough to find out where Mr. Williams's office was before hurrying through the reception area toward the closed door with the sign on it: "Mr. Williams. Principal."

Tammy could feel her face flushing red with anger and embarrassment as she knocked at the large, maple door. She wondered what she should say or do when she got inside. *Should I keep my cool or should I walk up to Noah, turn him over my knee and paddle his behind right in front of the principal?* Then reality hit home as she remembered that Noah was some two feet taller than she, outweighed her by sixty pounds, and hadn't had a spanking since long before his dad left.

"Come in," answered Mr. Williams, responding to Tammy's light raps on the door.

Noah stood motionless and silent as Mr. Williams and Coach Manship took turns describing the boys' escapades. Tammy was shocked. "Smoking marijuana underneath the bleachers? Noah, what in the world were you thinking of? How could you let this boy talk you into taking drugs?"

Noah glanced at Scotty, then at his mom, and muttered, "I started smoking marijuana months ago, Mom. I've only known Scotty a few weeks.

Then Tammy turned the conversation to something that had been bothering her for several weeks. "Does this have any connection with the money that's been missing from my purse?" she asked.

"Yeah. I suppose it does, Mom," Noah replied, looking down at the floor.

The rest of the conversation centered around the suspension procedure that would follow: one week of suspension followed by two months of detention hall and campus clean-up for Noah, as it was his first offense. Scotty, on the other hand, was expelled from school.

A usually short trip home turned out to be a long, awkward ride for both Noah and Tammy. *How could I have missed the signs?* Tammy wondered. *He's been taking money from my purse and smoking marijuana for months. And I didn't even notice. I had a hunch about the money, but why didn't I say something? If I'd confronted him, he would have told me he needed help, and we wouldn't be in this jam now.*

WHAT THE SINGLE-PARENT
FAMILY SURVEY TAUGHT US

Surveys in general are boring. Some are less boring than others, but for the most part, I find them more appropriate when used to line bird cages.

That's why, in December of 1986, when I set out to conduct my first single-parent family survey, I did so with reservations. What exactly was the survey going to prove? Was it going to produce relevant information that could impact lives and foster change, or was it going to end up wrapped around a fish on its way to somebody's frying pan?

One of the main focuses of the survey was to discover information that could help single parents understand more about the risks they and their children face and how they could deal with those risks more effectively. It was designed to learn more about the common behavioral patterns that show up in children and teens, boys and girls, following divorce.

The purpose of this chapter is to use the information from that survey to equip you with the answers to these three questions:

- Who is at the greatest risk, children or teens, boys or girls?
- When should you go on hyperalert with your children?
- How can you avert a crisis by learning what to look for?

BOYS AND POTENTIAL RISKS

A common observation made by counselors who work with children and teens in both inpatient hospital programs and in outpatient counseling offices is that boys far outnumber the girls in those programs. The single-parent family research validated that informal conclusion. At a ratio of almost three to one, boys are more likely to be referred for counseling following their parents' divorce. One reason that is so is that boys are far more given to aggressive disorders, which in turn makes them much more likely than girls to call attention to themselves as persons needing counseling.

CONDUCT DISORDERS

Conduct Disorders were the most commonly diagnosed emotional problems found in boys following their parents' divorce. Here is a sample of the most frequently cited of those disorders:

- Two or more incidents of stealing
- Running away from home
- Frequent lying
- Deliberate fire-setting
- Frequent truancy
- Breaking into others' property
- Deliberate destruction of others' property
- Physical cruelty to animals
- Frequent initiation of physical fights

- Stealing, with confrontation of the victim (I would have included shoplifting)
- Physical cruelty to people

ALCOHOL AND DRUG DEPENDENCY

Boys are more likely to become involved in drugs and alcohol use following their parents' divorce. The exact reasons are not entirely clear, although it appears that the girls are gaining ground rapidly. I do know from past experience that males (both teens and adults) are more often arrested for drunk driving and alcohol-related crimes than are women. The survey revealed that teenage boys are also more likely to experiment with drugs than girls. We could discuss the reasons for this forever, but for the sake of expediency, let's just attribute it to a difference in the sexes.

If you think the way I do, you have probably taken the stance that any alcohol use by a minor is alcohol abuse. It is important, however, to know the difference between alcohol use (or experimentation) and abuse. Here are some factors that will help you determine if your child is addicted to drugs or alcohol.

- Resistance (or tolerance) is becoming a factor, and the alcohol or drug is being taken in larger amounts or over a longer period of time.
- The teen shows a desire to cut down his use or tries unsuccessfully to control the alcohol or drug abuse.
- A great deal of time and/or energy is spent getting the drug or alcohol, taking it, or recovering from it.
- Important social, school, religious, or recreational activities are given up or reduced because of the drug or alcohol use.
- The teen continues to use the drug or alcohol even though he knows its continued use is creating emotional or physical problems.
- The teen displays a marked tolerance for the drug or for alcohol.
- Withdrawal symptoms occur when the teen discontinues or reduces the use of the drug or alcohol.
- The drug or alcohol is taken to relieve or avoid symptoms of withdrawal.

OPPOSITIONAL DEFIANT DISORDERS

A relatively common trait among postdivorce children and teens, and especially boys, is what the medical/counseling profession calls *oppositional defiant disorders*. That's a fancy psychological term referring to a class of behavioral problems. Let's see if you are able to recognize any of these traits in your child.

- Loss of temper
- Arguments with adults and especially those in authority
- Defiance of adult requests or rules
- Deliberate antagonizing or annoyance of others (sibling rivalry excluded)
- Blaming of others for mistakes
- Anger and resentment
- Spitefulness or vindictiveness
- Swearing or obscene language

A CONCLUDING THOUGHT

An important message for single parents to understand is that the post-divorce emotional problems usually found in boys are easier to recognize than those affecting girls.

The reason for that can be seen in the list of behavioral problems given just above. Each of the symptoms tends to be more aggressive in nature—and let's face it, boys are usually more aggressive than girls. It stands to reason, therefore, that they are more likely to be singled out for treatment than girls. They were simply more often involved in behavior that was easier to spot as reflecting emotional problems.

That doesn't mean that single parents of girls can lean back, prop their legs up, and relax.

GIRLS' EMOTIONAL PROBLEMS

Girls' emotional problems are less obvious. Unlike boys, girls tend to exhibit their anger, pain, and anxiety in a less aggressive, and more inward, manner. Because their problems express themselves in more passive ways than those of boys, they are also less easily spotted.

EATING DISORDERS

Eating disorders are associated almost exclusively with teenage or pre-teenage girls. Only recently have counselors and medical personnel begun to see teenage boys with this problem.

Eating disorders are some of the toughest emotional problems to deal with. That is partly because the disorder is relatively easy to conceal and partly because there is a great deal of shame and guilt associated with having this problem.

Three of the main eating disorders, with their characteristics, are listed below. If you suspect your child of having an eating disorder, contact a child or adolescent psychologist or a pediatrician for advice before you confront her over this problem.

Anorexia nervosa. The first of the three major eating disorders, anorexia nervosa is characterized by the following tendencies:

- A refusal to maintain body weight above the minimum normal weight for the child's age and height
- Failure to gain weight routinely during periods of growth, which leads to a body weight at least 15 percent below average
- An intense fear of gaining weight or becoming fat, even though the child or teenager is underweight
- Talking about feeling or being fat even though the child or teenager may be too thin
- In teens and adults, an absence of at least three consecutive menstrual cycles that would normally occur

Bulimia nervosa. The second of the major eating disorders is characterized by the following:

- Compulsive overeating in an effort to compensate for love and relationships that have never been present or have been lost
- Recurrent binge-eating episodes (i.e., out-of-control eating)
- A feeling of lack of control over eating behavior during the binge cycles
- Self-induced vomiting as a regular practice (also common are the use of laxatives or diuretics, strict dieting or fasting, or vigorous exercise to prevent weight gain)

187

- A minimum of two binge-eating episodes per week, planned or impulsive, for at least three months
- Persistent overconcern with body shape and weight

Compulsive overeating. The characteristics of the third most common eating disorder follow.

- Compulsive overeating, especially when the person is under stress
- Out-of-control eating
- Hiding-out to eat
- Feeling a sense of security, pleasure, or contentment while eating
- Obesity (a common but nonessential element)
- Despondency or depression over her physical appearance, generally accompanied by feeling powerless to change the eating behavior.

DEPRESSION

Another group of emotional problems that tend to appear in girls more often than boys are sometimes called depressive neurosis, dysthymia, or just depression.

Although certainly both boys and girls can become depressed following their parents' divorce, boys tend to act out their depression. Girls, on the other hand, mask their depression by turning it inward. Here are some common signs of depression in both boys and girls.

- Poor appetite or overeating
- Sleep-related problems (i.e., inability to sleep, sleeping too much, fitful sleep, or nightmares)
- Low energy, lack of motivation, or fatigue
- Low self-esteem or poor self-image
- Poor concentration in the classroom or during homework preparation, or difficulty in making decisions
- Feelings of hopelessness and helplessness
- Isolation or withdrawal from family and friends
- Tearfulness or sometimes uncontrollable emotions
- A lack of regard for physical appearances (e.g., clothing, hair, cosmetics, cleanliness)

TEEN PREGNANCY

Our list wouldn't be complete without discussing teen pregnancy. Teen pregnancy is obviously somewhat different from the other emotional problems that we've examined. I consider most teen pregnancies to be a symptom of a greater problem rather than independent problems unto themselves.

I have found, for example, that teen pregnancy is often related to the teen's poor self-esteem, which often stems from a girl's lack of relationship with her father. Because of this low self-esteem, she may unconsciously feel she can't maintain a relationship with a boy unless she gives in to his sexual advances.

Support for this theory is found in a study by Johns Hopkins University where researches found that "young," white, teenage girls living in fatherless homes were 60 percent more likely to have premarital intercourse than those living in two-parent homes.[1]

This study points out that teenage girls are becoming quite aggressive in their pursuit of love and acceptance from boys. It attributes this need for male acceptance to the lack of a loving, consistent, and attached male figure (i.e., dad) in their lives.

The result of this need for male acceptance has led many teen girls into a lifestyle of premarital sexual relations, which they falsely misinterpret to mean intimacy. From my experience as a therapist, I believe this misinterpretation is based on the fact that most of these girls grew up without a healthy concept of appropriate male-female interaction.

A CONCLUDING THOUGHT

As single parents, it is vitally important that you become at least casually familiar with each of the warning signs presented in this chapter. It is important that you do that irrespective of whether you have boys or girls, children or teens.

It is also of great importance that you understand that all of these emotional roads can lead to depression. Whenever severe emotional problems occur with children and teens, rest assured, depression is either present or lurking just around the bend.

Depression is certainly a dominant element in any crisis, and especially in cases of suicide, which is the third leading cause of death among teens. A recent survey by the U.S. Centers for Disease Control revealed that out of 11,631 ninth- through twelfth-graders in this country, 27 percent had seriously thought about killing themselves in the preceding year. Sixteen percent stated they had made a specific plan, and one in twelve said they actually tried to commit suicide.[2]

From my experience as a police officer and as a therapist, I can assert that at least one of these warning signs were present in every instance of suicide involving teens and children. Sadly, the warning signs were often missed or misunderstood.

THE DIFFERENCES BETWEEN THE SEXES

Here is a list of some of the similarities and differences in the way boys and girls deal with the stress of a traumatic event such as divorce. Reference is also made to the frequency of these problems respective to each sex.

Stress Trait	Boys' Frequency	Girls' Frequency
Depression	frequent	frequent
Running away from home	somewhat frequent	less frequent
Use of alcohol and drug use	frequent	slightly less frequent
Loss of temper	frequent	slightly less frequent
Stealing from others	somewhat frequent	infrequent
Shoplifting	somewhat frequent	somewhat frequent
Lying	frequent	frequent
Profanity	frequent	slightly less frequent
Interruptions in sleep patterns	frequent	more frequent
Truancy	more frequent	frequent
Deliberate fire-starting	infrequent	seldom or never frequent
Destruction of property	somewhat frequent	seldom frequent
Poor concentration	frequent	frequent
Physical cruelty to animals	infrequent	seldom or never frequent
Decreased self-image	frequent	more frequent
Forced sexual activities	occasionally frequent	seldom or never frequent
Tearfulness	seldom frequent	very frequent
Fighting/aggressiveness	frequent	less frequent
Poor school grades	frequent	frequent
Likelihood of sexual activity	frequent	slightly less frequent
Eating disorders	seldom frequent	more frequent
Conduct disorders	frequent	slightly less frequent
Suicidal thoughts	frequent	more frequent
Suicide plans	relatively infrequent	slightly more frequent
Attempt or commit suicide	relatively infrequent	slightly more frequent

THE HIGH-RISK AGES

There's no way to avoid it: divorce takes its toll in the lives of all children and teens. Some weather their parents' divorce more smoothly, whereas others are thrown into emotional tailspins.

Studying children and teenagers who had difficulty dealing with their parents' divorce and ultimately needed professional assistance provided valuable insights. One such insight was to identify the ages of the kids who fell into the high-risk groups (which in this case refers to the age or ages children and teens are most likely to be seen for counseling). The theory behind studies of this kind is that if we can better understand how age affects stress, then we can take positive steps to address the special needs of children whose parents are divorced.

Here are the findings pertaining to divorce and a child's age.

THE HIGH-RISK TEENS

From a therapist's perspective, the findings developed in this section of the survey were one of the more fascinating aspects of the study. The results clearly revealed that teenagers fifteen and sixteen years of age were the high-risk kids. Of all the teen years studied, those two years accounted for nearly one-half of the instances of stress traits. Simply put, fifteen- and sixteen-year-olds had the most trouble coping with their parents' divorce.

The next step was to identify the factors that accounted for the numbers. The reasons for the higher risk factors among the two ages are multidimensional. The research points to a broad range of changes (ranging from hormones to emotional growth) that are at their peak during the two years. Those normal transitions, coupled with the stress of the changing family, may send a teen's life into crisis. Let's take a closer look at the influences lying behind the surface troubles.

Hormonal changes. Sometimes I think the term "screaming hormones" was coined for fifteen- and sixteen-year-olds. This age is commonly recognized as being the most turbulent, as it is the period during which the body is undergoing major psychological changes. Hormonal factors are at their peak.

Increased sexual pressures. Increased sexual pressures are brought about by a combination of increased sexual awareness and the body's hormonal changes. Even a glance at various groups of high schoolers points out the wide span of sexual awareness among teens. Some teenagers still look and dress like children, whereas others have taken on that sixteen-going-on-twenty-six look.

Separation and individuation. Another factor that moves fifteen- and sixteen-year-olds into the high-risk group is that they are emotionally and socially in transition. Stress and crisis takes its emotional toll on all of us, irrespective of age. It may be that the stress of the divorce pushes teens to grow up faster, or it may be that they are just acting older as a coping mechanism. Whatever the reason, these kids demonstrate an ability to act, dress, look, and talk older. They gravitate away from age-appropriate friends and activities and move with an older crowd and lifestyle. And that's not good.

During these years, teens typically realize they're not children any longer, but they're not really adults either. They're actually in an emotional no-man's-land. Many teenagers expressed the thought that, following their parents' divorce, they wished they were a kid again. They longed to feel the nurturing that kids receive more freely from moms and dads after a crisis. Many reported feeling pressure to handle the divorce more like an adult and less like a child.

Those pressures caused them to separate emotionally (or distance themselves) because they saw it as a more grown-up response to the divorce. Sadly, they also found themselves trapped. Once they assumed the emotional role of an adult, they felt compelled to keep the act going. Returning to the neediness of a child, although that was what they desired, was no longer an option.

THE HIGH-RISK YOUNGSTERS

As with their teenaged counterparts, it was important to identify the high-risk age groups of children. Whereas the high-risk teens were in the middle teen years (fifteen and sixteen), the high-risk children's group tended to be in the upper end.

The survey revealed that, of all ages and sexes, the group most affected by their parents' divorce were eleven- and twelve-year-old boys. The group next most affected were girls of those same ages.

Again, as with teens, these kids are in between developmental stages. They're not really children any longer, nor are they teenagers yet. They are at an awkward, emotionally volatile time in their lives, a time when their hormones are driving them away from childhood and toward maturity.

It was also interesting to note that children act out their post-divorce feelings differently than teenagers. They are often more subdued, passive, or withdrawn in their emotional expression. Parents must be careful, however, not to miss these still waters while looking for the more severe acting-out behavior. As the saying goes, "Still waters run deep."

THE WARNING SIGNS OF CRISIS

Now that we've taken a look at the age and gender factors related to postdivorce emotional problems, let's examine another significant finding of the survey, that relate to the warning signs, specifically symptoms, or behaviors, that are often present when a child or teen is struggling with emotional problems.

In the spirit of Jeremiah 5:3, "O Lord, do not your eyes look for truth?" those warning signs should be viewed as road maps to the truth of the emotional pain the children and teens are experiencing.

Following each of the eleven warning signs listed below are some precautionary procedures, or helpful hints, designed to put your child's recovery into motion.

WARNING SIGN #1:
LONELINESS AND MOODINESS
The terms *lonely, quiet,* and *moody* are commonly associated with depression. As such, they should be viewed as classic, precrisis warning signs.

I learned from many single parents that these symptoms were more obvious following the child's visit to, or phone conversation with, the noncustodial parent.

Although a general feeling of loneliness, quietness, or moodiness might be considered normal after the emotional stress of visitation, these feelings should be monitored. Prolonged symptoms (lasting several days or weeks) are definitely cause for concern. Short-term symptoms (lasting one or two days) are generally viewed as a child's way of processing his feelings.

Helpful hints. Sit down with your child or teen and let him know you've noticed some of these changes. Tell him how you imagine he might feel when he returns from a visit with dad.

For instance, you might say, "Boy, it must be tough to be just one person but feel like you want to live in two places. I've been noticing that you seem more quiet and lonely when you come back from visiting dad. I'm concerned that you might be feeling sad or angry on the inside about things, and I just wanted to let you know that I'm here for you if you'd like to talk."

Remember to validate their feelings. Catch yourself before saying anything even remotely resembling a minimization, such as "Oh, you shouldn't feel that way," or, "You're really making more out of this than there is." The child's feelings are never wrong. It's up to you to understand how he is feeling, not the other way around.

Ongoing points to monitor. Closely monitor how the child is doing in these areas:

- Is his loneliness or moodiness a sign of a deepening depression? Look for increases in tearfulness, sleeplessness, lack of motivation, loss of energy, decreased or increased appetite.
- Is he connecting with you, friends, siblings, or any other children?
- Is he continuing to isolate from his peer group and others?
- Is the child displaying any of the other warnings listed in this chapter?

WARNING SIGN #2:
DEPRESSION

Some level of depressed mood has to be considered as common following a parents' divorce. The truth is, I'm often more concerned with kids who don't show signs of depression than those who do. (That doesn't mean it's okay to let the depression go unchecked, however.)

Here are some typical depressed feelings reported by children and teens in the postdivorce time-frame.

• Hopelessness	• Helplessness	• Poor concentration
• Low energy	• Little or no emotion	• Low motivation
• Low self-esteem	• Tearfulness	• Sleep problems
• Impulsive feelings	• High stress/agitation	• Difficulty in making everyday decisions
• Reduced affect, or emotions (laughter, smiling, crying)	• Feeling like hurting oneself or others	

Here again, after a divorce you'd expect to see some of these responses in small to moderate amounts. Depressed feelings start to become warning signs of an impending crisis when they go on for extended periods of time. A safe rule to follow is that if any of the symptoms listed above lasts longer than a few weeks, it should be addressed professionally.

One fact about depression is that the longer it remains the harder it is to treat. It is imperative that you learn how to identify the symptoms of depression quickly, as the depression may otherwise lead to long-term problems or even suicidal thoughts.

Helpful hints. A good approach is not to overemphasize your child's depressed mood or your observations, but not to minimize them either. Try to be as matter-of-fact about them as possible. As you enter these conversations, look for subtle changes in the child's facial expression, body language, or the words he uses. Is he quick to defend or deny? If so, that is an indication that the depression is present and that he knows it at a subconscious level. Depressed feelings are often accompanied by elements of shame and guilt. That is why both children and teens, as well as adults, often try to hide their depression.

When you initiate the conversation about what you are seeing, make a brief opening statement, but then let the child do the talking. Use the empathic method we discussed earlier to draw him out of hiding about his depression. You might begin by saying, "I'm wondering if you're feeling some sadness and depression because I've found myself feeling the same way at times."

Get a grip on your frustration and your desire to "fix" the child's feelings right away. The best thing you can do is to draw out his feelings and thoughts and then listen intently. Reflect back what you are hearing so that he can examine them from an outside perspective. For example, you might say, "So, what you're telling me is that you've been feeling like your life has been turned upside down and you're kind of confused. Is that what you are saying?"

Always go after the underlying feelings beneath the symptoms. Symptoms are just a sign of something deeper, and your goal is to find out what that "something deeper" is. You'll also want to screen for signs of any suicidal thoughts that may piggyback depression.

I've found that a good way of asking about this is to say, "I'm wondering if you are feeling so confused or helpless that you've considered doing something drastic?" Most children and teens will know what you are asking if they've actually been feeling this way. A common reaction to this question might be tears. If so, you should take that as a yes. If the child doesn't understand what "drastic" means, you might say, "Like you might feel like hurting yourself or someone else." Don't worry about putting thoughts into his head that wouldn't have been there otherwise. This isn't a time for burying your head.

Whenever your child talks about his feelings, thank him for being so open, honest, and trusting. If one of those feelings involves suicidal thoughts, suggest to him that it may be time for some outside help. Don't try to handle a situation of this kind on your own. It's risky, and there's too much at stake.

WARNING SIGN #3:
LOW SELF-ESTEEM
Let's face the facts. Self-esteem during the teen years is fragile under the best of circumstances. Feelings of inadequacy seem to bleed over into nearly every aspect of a teenager's life. Teenagers already feel insecure over their changing bodies, but when a divorce occurs they have the added insecurity of a changing family system.

Following divorce, a child or teen's self-esteem and self-image may take a nosedive. The child or teen may secretly think, *If my parents didn't love me enough to stay married, I must be unlovable or unimportant.*

A poor self-image can also affect the way a child or teen feels about God. Often the concern voiced by these kids following a divorce is, "I must not be very important to God if he allowed this to happen to my parents and me. My life is ruined."

Helpful hints. Gauging self-esteem and self-image in your children is a difficult task. For the most part, you'll want to learn more about how they are feeling about themselves in these areas:

- His likes
- His dislikes
- Who his friends are
- How he is doing in school
- Does he think he's smart?
- What is he good at
- Does he think God loves him?
- Does he think he is good-looking?
- Does he feel any responsibility for your divorce?

Most young people with low self-esteem will answer these questions about these matters negatively. They will tell you that they do okay in school, that they really don't have many friends, and that they don't think they are very nice looking. In other words, nearly everything that helps to define who they are is viewed with uncertainty and negativity.

A decline in self-esteem in a teen or child usually starts with feelings of being broken or different. You may want to start by understanding and possibly relating some facts. Somewhere around 59 percent of all children born last year will spend some time growing up in a single-parent home.[3] Also, there is a divorce in the United States every twenty-seven seconds, and each year 2 million kids under eighteen will be caught in the middle of their parents' divorce.[4] Although this information doesn't make divorce good, knowing these figures will help the child or teen see that he has a lot of company.

With younger children it is helpful to put this information into conceptual terms that will help them understand that they are not all that different from other children they know. Point out that some one-half of the kids in his school, or one-half of the kids in his Sunday school, are just like him. Some of these kids have new families, whereas others live with just one parent. Help him see that these kids are normal and that they live good lives.

Take extra time to help your kids build their self-esteem. Spending quality time with them will have a positive affect in this process —but remember, it's a process, not an overnight wonder. Whether you are working or playing with them, send them positive messages, but be careful not to exaggerate or be obvious. The best way to do that is to encourage them when they do things well, and then encourage them to do these good things even more.

On a final note, be cautious of and monitor your own negativity and low self-esteem. Children will pick up on it and translate it into their own low self-esteem.

WARNING SIGN #4:
SLEEP-RELATED PROBLEMS
Many children and teens report that they experience sleep-related problems following their parents' divorce. Most of them said they had problems just getting to sleep. Fitful sleep, nightmares, interrupted sleep, and oversleeping were also common.

Sleep-related problems are the subconscious mind's way of telling us something is wrong. Parents should pay attention. Disrupted sleeping patterns can be telltale signs of depression, anger, excessive pressure, or anxiety. Sleeping problems are also a critical symptom of post-traumatic stress disorder (PTSD). (We'll discuss PTSD shortly.)

Quite often, disrupted sleep patterns can be traced to the absence of the other parent. Children in particular are creatures of habit, and as such, feel insecure when both parents are not sleeping together in the next room. When parents divorce, the change in sleeping arrangements can cause disturbances in the child's sleeping patterns. Usually those problems manifest themselves when the child is trying to go to sleep or if he awakens during the night.

Helpful hints. For children up to age ten or so I sometimes recommend making concessions in the sleeping arrangements common in your home. An effective method is to let the child start out sleeping in your room, perhaps in a sleeping bag next to your bed. Or you might let him know that if he awakens in the night, he can bring his sleeping bag into your room and bed down next to you.

It's often helpful to read bedtime stories to children in their own rooms until they fall asleep. Be forewarned, some kids will stay awake as long as they possibly can just so you won't leave.

It's also not unusual for children, and sometimes teens, to sleepwalk or have yelling episodes in their sleep. This is often a sign of overwhelming anxiety. As soon as it is practical after one of these episodes, get the child or teen to open up about his fears. Doing so should allow him to vent in a waking state what his mind is releasing while he's asleep.

If his sleep disruption involves nightmares or frequently recurring dreams, ask your child to describe them. By encouraging the child to talk about his dreams, you are allowing him to release subconscious thoughts, feelings, and anxieties.

Be careful about making dream interpretations unless they are obvious. Dream interpretation is a study in itself, and many books are available at the public library that may help you understand your child's dreams.

Many older children and teens find it comforting to read (or have read to them) a few Bible verses when they awaken from a bad dream. You may consider walking them through Scripture that points out how God loves and comforts us. Help them to remember that they are never alone when they believe in Him.

We frequently hear of children and teens who have difficulty getting to sleep. This is often due to a thought process called *racing*. Racing occurs when many thoughts (often sad and anxious ones) move very quickly from the subconscious to the conscious, leaving behind feelings of being overwhelmed. You can make the following suggestions to help your kids get to sleep:

- Suggest that the child or teen keep a diary or tape recorder next to his bed. Have him make notes of thoughts and feelings when he experiences racing.
- Help the child or teen to set aside a "worry period" of only ten minutes just before going to bed. Set a timer and let him know that he should begin worrying immediately. When the timer goes off, tell him it is time to stop worrying, think of pleasant things, and go to sleep.
- Set aside some time just before going to bed for the child to read some Bible verses (or read to him) and then pray. This is a time to share secrets and distressing thoughts with God. Teach children and teens to ask God to take control over their lives, including their problems. Don't be afraid to take the lead and let them hear your prayers first. And don't push them to pray if they resist for a while.
- Take a few minutes to chat with your child about anything that may be bothering him. Try to have a positive subject to talk about just before it's time for him to go to sleep: his little league game on the weekend, an outing that is being planned.
- Avoid sweets or drinks that contain caffeine for at least four hours before bedtime, preferably longer.
- With younger children, you may want to consider light exercise or other play activities to help them unwind.
- Consider letting your child go to sleep listening to music or talk radio.

WARNING SIGN #5:
ISOLATION

The single-parent survey revealed that isolation was present in varying degrees in 80 eighty percent of the cases. In fact, the urge to isolate is almost universally present in all emotional problems. Perhaps this tendency, like depression, takes place because of feelings of shame and guilt.

Some of the more common problems where isolation is present are:

- Depression
- Anxiety disorders
- Stress
- Learning disabilities
- Eating disorders
- Conduct disorders

Children and teens often isolate because it helps them feel more secure and less vulnerable. They may feel that if they isolate from others they cannot be hurt again by failed relationships, such as what happened in their parents' divorce.

Helpful hints. Whenever you see, or merely suspect, that your child is beginning to isolate from others, look for the underlying cause. Try to determine which of these feelings best describes him:

- ☐ Feeling he doesn't belong
- ☐ Feeling unworthy of love
- ☐ Feeling resentment toward others, especially those with seemingly happy home lives
- ☐ Feeling cheated, hurt, and angry over his circumstances
- ☐ Feeling bad, ashamed, or guilty about himself

As you gain a better understanding of what the underlying causes of his isolation are, begin a systematic approach to get him reconnected.

Reconnecting is an emotional process. It doesn't involve simply forcing a child to be around others. You need first to help the child connect with his true feelings; that, in turn will help him reconnect with others. Remember, it is human nature to see things under the worst possible light. Bringing his concerns into conversation and relationship makes them tolerable again.

Sometimes it's effective to contact the youth pastor where your child attends church to ask him to assist you in your project. The project involves his efforts in helping pull your child out of solitude by encouraging him to participate. He may also solicit the assistance of another child or two within the group to draw your child out of his shell and into relationships.

WARNING SIGN #6:
ANGER AND ABUSIVENESS

Studying the responses from the children and teens regarding their feelings of hurt, frustration, and anger during the postdivorce period provided some interesting facts. More than 70 percent of the teenagers and 60 percent of the children said they were very angry and felt as though they hated everybody and everything during the divorce. And over half of the teens said their anger made them feel like hurting themselves or somebody else.

Many older children and the teens were characterized as being verbally abusive or as lashing out at friends or family members. The symptoms were viewed as "just blowing off steam" until the seriousness of their emotions were better understood. Unfortunately, this better understanding sometimes involved a serious event or crisis.

Children and teens reach the point of having to release their anger when they are unable to deal with those feelings any other way. Their anger escalates until it is unintentionally (and sometimes quite intentionally) released.

That anger is often misdirected at innocent bystanders because most children and many teens lack the insight to know why they are feeling the way they do and do not know what to do with their anger. Like our friend the bear, in chapter 2, the child or teen's feelings will continue until someone gets close enough to help him understand and work through his feelings.

Helpful hints. I suggest that a parent use *identification* techniques when dealing with his child's anger. The process involves learning whatever one can about the anger before considering addressing it. Specifically the parent should note such things as:

- The time of day when the child's anger is most obvious
- The events, conversations, circumstances, and relationships that brought about the child's anger
- What the child did with his anger
- What helped the child calm down after the anger outburst
- How and why the anger seems to control the child

Once you have an understanding of where your child's anger is rooted, you can begin talking to him about it. One of the basic differences between children and adults is that children act out their anger, whereas adults talk about it. (That's ideally speaking, of course.) This is not to say that in helping your child to deal with anger you are somehow trying to make an adult out of your him. Rather, you are trying to teach him to confront and work through his angry feelings without acting them out.

Teenagers often inappropriately act out their anger. Some will swear; others will scream, break things, or punch doors or walls. Before you jump on your teenager about it, find out if he's learned the behavior from someone you know. Make sure you, your ex, or another adult in his life has stopped expressing anger inappropriately before asking him to do so.

Children and teens will use their anger to manipulate you and others. Look carefully at how you handle his anger. If you give in to or shrink away from him, then you have reinforced his anger and assured its presence in the future.

WARNING SIGN #7:
CHANGES IN EATING HABITS
The survey revealed that more than one in ten teenagers developed some type of troublesome eating-related problem (i.e., anorexia, bulimia, or compulsive overeating) following his parents' divorce.

As a general statement, crisis often brings about changes in appetite and/or eating habits. For instance, when children or teens become depressed, they tend to overeat or undereat. It is when teenagers feel out of control emotionally, that they try to gain control over their lives through their eating habits. I won't try to cover all of the complicated dynamics of eating disorders in this book, but you need to be informed about the subject. There are many good books about eating disorders, and it would behoove any parent who suspects his child has an eating disorder to conduct extensive research.

It is important that you know what to look for when eating disorders are suspected. Here's a checklist of typical eating disorder symptoms.

- ☐ Significant weight loss or gain
- ☐ Emaciated appearance
- ☐ Preoccupation with food contents (e.g., calories or fat grams)
- ☐ A ritualistic routine with food (weighing or only eating certain types of foods)
- ☐ Binging on high-calorie or high-fat foods
- ☐ Use of laxatives, diuretics, or diet pills
- ☐ Compulsive overexercising
- ☐ Eating small portions or skipping meals
- ☐ Spending excessive time in the bathroom following meals
- ☐ A yellowing or dulling of the tooth enamel
- ☐ Resistance to eating out or with the family
- ☐ Bulging veins or muscles around the neck and face
- ☐ A hollow or dull appearance in the eyes

While you are learning and communicating with your child about a suspected eating disorder, I suggest you seek professional help. Eating disorders are a special problem that take considerable expertise to adequately address.

It would be beneficial, in the meantime, to understand that your child's underlying problems are likely hidden somewhere in the following checklist. Remember, the eating disorder is only a symptom of what's going on underneath.

☐ Out-of-control feelings   ☐ Anger   ☐ Depression

☐ Anxiety/stress   ☐ Poor self-image   ☐ Insecurity

☐ Feeling victimized   ☐ Feeling abandoned

WARNING SIGN #8:
POOR SCHOOL PERFORMANCE
School-related problems were identified in nearly all of the children and teens involved in the survey. Most of these issues revolved around:

- Poor or failing grades
- Poor attendance
- Acting out in classrooms
- Getting into fights at school
- Defiance of authority
- Refusing to complete or turn in assignments

In support of these findings, the National Center for Health Statistics reported in 1988 that children ages five through seventeen who live with both biological parents had to repeat a grade in 12 percent of the cases, whereas 22 percent of children living with a divorced mom needed to repeat a grade.

Helpful hints. When you begin to notice a decline in his school performance, check out these areas first.

☐ Has the distraction of the divorce severely affected his concentration and motivation?

☐ Is there now less time and attention devoted to monitoring his education?

☐ Did he change schools or is he anticipating doing so?

☐ Is he reacting to or projecting anger onto authority figures (i.e., school teachers, coaches, and administrators)?

☐ Is this an act of defiance toward you and/or your ex because of the divorce?

☐ Is some emotional factor, such as depression or anxiety, causing these problems?

Before you take steps to correct the situation, you should rule out other conditions, such as a learning disability. Sometimes children are able to manage their disabilities until something like a divorce sends them into a tailspin.

That aside, you should sit down with the child and calmly discuss each of the areas listed above. Addressing those areas lets him know that you understand (although you do not approve of) what's going on. Don't forget to ask for his cooperation in improving his school habits. Sometimes simply paying attention to a problem is enough to solve it. If change doesn't seem to be taking place, don't let him get too far off-course before considering a tutor or some other resource program.

WARNING SIGN #9:
LOSS OF PLEASURE IN ONCE-PLEASURABLE ACTIVITIES
When faced with conflict and trauma, teens and children often loose interest in once-pleasurable activities. Some of the more commonly reported activities were:

- After-school sports
- Music lessons
- Scouts
- Church youth groups
- After-school social activities
- Other lessons/hobbies

A classic interpretation is to say that children and teens quit such activities following their parents' divorce because they are angry. In their subconscious minds they may feel a sense of retaliation in quitting activities that their parents had previously encouraged.

Another interpretation is to say that children and teens may look at these activities as commitments. When they see their parents break something as important as the marriage commitment, they may subconsciously see that as making it all right for them to break their lesser commitments.

Still another group of children and teens quits activities as a response to depression. Remember, depression often brings about a decrease in activity, motivation, and energy. When that is coupled with the urge to isolate, quitting activities becomes almost inevitable.

Helpful hints. It's important to help your child understand why he or she is wanting to quit an activity, especially one he used to have fun doing. You may want to use the old standby approach of saying, "If you can give me one good reason why you should quit, then it's okay." There's a slim chance he'll have a good reason, but it's likely not.

Sometimes quitting an activity is related to something the other parent used to do with him, or something that brought the whole family together. Each time the child participates in the activity an emotional reinjury occurs. Helping the child understand that those feelings are understandable (and normal) may help him to continue the activity.

WARNING SIGN #10:
ALCOHOL AND DRUG USE

Parents (especially moms of teenagers) often reported that they found alcohol, drugs, or drug paraphernalia while cleaning their kids' rooms. Alcohol is often the first level of escape for teens and sometimes children, just as it is for adults who would prefer to avoid painful realities.

A secondary problem with alcohol use by teens and children after divorce is that it is a depressant. When taken by kids who are already depressed, it can compound and intensify their feelings. Many scenarios involving teen suicide include the use of alcohol and drugs on top of an existing depression.

The cycle of alcohol use and drug abuse commonly begins when the teen drinks to numb his or her painful feelings. When the effects of the alcohol or drug wear off, the old depression returns, along with the new depression brought on by the alcohol. Since that results in the teen being in even more pain than before, he drinks again to escape the new pain. That is how people get stuck in cycles of drinking or taking drugs to escape.

We discovered through the single-parent family that an alarming 82 percent of the teenagers and 48 percent of older children drank during the time of the divorce and the period immediately following. That behavior, the researchers stated, went on until the teenagers and older children were caught, decided to quit, or received treatment.

In September 1991, the Associated Press reported that 51 percent of the nation's 20.7 million junior and senior high school students had had at least one drink in the previous year, and 8 million students drank weekly. The story added that 454,000 students said they binge on alcohol weekly.

Helpful hints. There are two stages to helping a child or teen break free of addictive substances. The first is the detection stage; the second, following closely after the first, is the intervention stage.

The detection stage involves familiarizing yourself with the objective symptoms of drug and alcohol use—in other words, with what your kids might look like if they are using drugs and/or alcohol.

The chart below lists the most commonly used illicit drugs along with their respective symptoms. Street names are given on the left.

Chemical	Signs of Usage
ALCOHOL	Decrease in levels of functioning
	Increased aggressiveness
	Change in sleeping patterns
	Avoiding the home and family members
	Moodiness (often agitated during use)
	Change of friends
	Lack of eye contact
	Decreased motivation
	School-related problems
	Redness; bloodshot and watery eyes
	Decreased appetite
	Odor of alcohol
	Unsteady gait
	Slurred or thick speech
	Dilated pupils
COCAINE	Flushed appearance
Coke	Sniffing/runny nose
Cola	Irritated mucous membranes in nose
Crack	Dilated pupils (ongoing four to six hours after use)
Ice	Paranoia (sometimes including hallucinations)
Snow	Mood swings
Blow	Anxiety or panic attacks
Stuff	Bloodshot and watery eyes following use
	Hyperactivity (followed by depressed mood)
	Avoidance of family, church, and old friends

Paraphernalia used in taking cocaine
Straws cut into small sections
Razor blades
Mirrors (generally purse size)
Small amber or clear glass vials with caps
Rolled-up dollar bill used as a straw
Small spoons
Small folded pieces of paper (approx. 1 inch square,
  often magazine pages, called "bindles")

MARIJUANA   Decreased motivation
  Weed   Increased appetite
  Smoke   Bloodshot and watery eyes
  Joint   Slightly noticeable incoherence (staring)
  Reefer   Slightly slurred or thick speech
  "J's"   School problems
  Dope   Strong odor even hours after use
  "Ses"   Laughing inappropriately

Paraphernalia used in taking marijuana
Small metal alligator clips called "roach clips"
Lighter or matches
Cigarette rolling papers
Glass, metal, or wood pipes called "bongs"
Ziplock plastic baggies

METHAMPHETAMINE   Agitation (anger, aggressiveness)
  Speed   Paranoia (occasionally hallucinating)
  Crystal   Trouble sleeping
  Meth   Irritated mucous membranes and runny nose
                   Dilated pupils (several hours after use)
                   Mood swings
                   Anxiety or panic attacks
                   Hyperactivity (followed by depressed mood)
                   Avoidance of family, church, and old friends

Paraphernalia used in taking Methamphetamine
Straws cut into small sections
Razor blades
Mirrors (generally purse size)
Small amber or clear glass vials with caps
Rolled-up dollar bill used as a straw
Small spoons
Small folded pieces of paper (approx. 1 inch square,
   often magazine pages, called "bindles")·

If you have determined that your child is using alcohol or drugs, it is time to move into the second phase, intervention and finding help. I generally suggest that your best immediate response when you discover your child is drinking or taking drugs is no immediate response at all. Stop and collect yourself. Regain your composure and consult a few experts in the field of teen substance abuse. You can generally find someone by asking your youth pastor for a referral or by calling one of the many Christian referral agencies.

Depending on the situation, you may opt to conduct a formal intervention (which will involve outsiders, such as counselors), or you may decide to address the problem alone.

It's generally not as important to act immediately as it is to act relatively quickly and responsibly.

WARNING SIGN #11:
CHANGES IN APPEARANCE
Well over one-half of the parents who participated in the survey commented that prior to their child's serious problems, they noticed changes in two areas, personal hygiene and style of clothing.

Personal hygiene. After divorce, many parents noticed that hygiene was not as important to their children as it once was. For instance, several parents commented on how difficult it became to get their children or teens to comb their hair, brush their teeth, or bathe regularly.

The most likely reason for these changes is the trauma—and resulting depression—of the divorce. A common statement of someone who is depressed is "Why should I take care of myself? It doesn't matter anymore."

A child or teen's lack of interest in hygiene can also be interpreted as a subconscious rebellion. After all, don't most parents continually remind their children to take a bath and brush their teeth?

Style of clothing. The second change frequently noticed was in child's style of dress. Younger children (ages five through ten) are often attracted to a particular set or type of clothing. Many children (and even some teens) will try to wear the same outfit day after day. They may even unconsciously choose an outfit that at one time was a favorite of one or both parents, or was disliked by one or both.

Changes in dress for teenagers tend to take on more defiant aspects. If you were to venture to your local mall and take a look at the groups of teens hanging-out, you would see two primary groups. One group is dressed normally (granted, a relative term) and uses the mall as a nineties version of the corner malt shop. For them, the mall is a place to socialize. But there would also be a second group. These kids stand out like a sore thumb. For them, the style de jour tends toward dark clothing and unusual-looking hair styles. The boys are likely to be unshaven, with both the boys and the girls sporting multiple earrings and smoking.

If you were to take an informal poll of how many of the kids from this second group are from divorced families, would you be shocked at the high number? Probably not. Many seem to be looking for support and relationships with others whom they perceive as being safe, like them. Safe kids often identify other safe kids by similar clothing, mannerisms, and language. In that way, they are better able to protect their inferior feelings.

Helpful hints. The rationale teens and children have for adopting changes in clothing following their parents' divorce probably falls into one of three categories:

1. They are passively seeking attention.
2. They may subconsciously be trying to punish their parent(s) or themselves.
3. They feel a sense of confusion and a loss of self-esteem and self-identity.

Try to determine the reasons behind the change in dress. You may decide to take action and insist that they dress differently, or you may decide that the issue is not important enough to draw the line here.

POST-TRAUMATIC
STRESS DISORDERS AND DIVORCE

We cannot thoroughly discuss warning signs of crisis without discussing post-traumatic stress disorders, or PTSD.

The single-parent family research clearly revealed the presence of PTSD in children and teens following their parents' divorce. PTSD is a relatively new area of psychological interest and study. Following the Korean War, soldiers returning home who had difficulty adjusting to a normal lifestyle were classified as having what was called *delayed stress syndrome*. In the post-Vietnam War era, returning soldiers who had psychological problems stemming from their combat experience were diagnosed as having PTSD, the new and improved version of delayed stress syndrome.

What doctors have found in studying PTSD is that soldiers do not have exclusive claim to this disorder. In fact, PTSD is now found in *Diagnostic and Statistical Manual of Mental Disorders DSM-III-R*, 3d rev. ed., American Psychiatric Association Staff (Washington, D.C.: American Psychiatric, 1987) and is becoming an increasingly used diagnosis for persons who are not adjusting well to a traumatic experience, such as a death in the family, rape, child abuse, an unusually serious accident, or divorce.

A child or teen who goes into a deep emotional crisis following his parents' divorce may be linked to a PTSD diagnosis, although not necessarily, because there are specific criteria for the diagnosis. It's important that parents understand the symptoms and elements of the syndrome in order to better understand their child's emotional problems and to facilitate healing.

A critical element of PTSD is that it can have a delayed onset. That means that a child can experience a traumatic event, such as divorce, and appear to be adjusting well to it. Six months or more later, when all seems to be well, the child may begin having emotional problems such as the ones we've been examining.

Some key elements of PTSD, and its delayed onset in children and teens after divorce, are the following:

- In younger children, often a diminished interest in developmental activities, such as language skills (reverting to baby talking) or toilet training may be seen. Perhaps they won't sleep alone, whereas before they were comfortable in doing so. Somewhat older children may resume sucking their thumbs or wetting the bed, even though they had given up that behavior long before.

- A restricted range of affect (i.e., the outward appearance of emotions.
- Difficulty in falling asleep.
- Depression.
- Anxiety.
- Irritability or outbursts of anger.
- Difficulty in concentrating.
- An exaggerated startle response (for example, if you were to walk around the corner and startle a child suffering from this syndrome, he might respond by screaming, nervously trembling, or running.
- Recurrent, troublesome, and distressing memories of the divorce. These may occur during periods of daydreaming.
- Distressing dreams or nightmares of the divorce, especially if there were angry or violent aspects to it.
- Feelings of intense distress when exposed to places or events (such as birthdays, anniversaries, or old neighborhoods) that symbolize or resemble an aspect of the divorce.
- Avoiding thinking, feeling, or talking about any aspects of the divorce.
- Making an effort to avoid people, activities, or situations that make him remember the divorce.
- Giving evidence that he has blocked-out memories of the divorce and its accompanying trauma.

Whenever you suspect your child is exhibiting any of these characteristics, address the matter right away. PTSD is a difficult and complex disorder that needs to be handled immediately by a professional.

THE WINDOW OF OPPORTUNITY THEORY

Perhaps the most interesting result of the survey was that it led to the formulation of what I call the "window of opportunity theory." This theory states that there is a fairly fixed length of time between the onset of divorce and the point at which a child is likely actually to go into emotional crisis.

First, we should define the term *onset of divorce*. As you know, the emotional and relational aspects of your divorce likely occurred months prior to the actual filing of the papers and certainly well before the final decree. As such, *onset of divorce* refers to the point in time when the family unit emotionally collapsed. The onset, in most families, takes place when (a) things have deteriorated relationally, (b) divorce papers are filed, or (c) when one parent moves out.

The Window of Opportunity Theory states that in both children and teens, the vast majority of emotional problems occur within twenty-four months of the onset of the divorce.

It's easiest to grasp this theory if you imagine a twenty-four month calendar with one page per day. The first page represents the onset, or beginning of the window period. Each day that passes, you remove one page from your calendar until you have reached the last page, two years from the onset. Most of your children's emotional problems related to the divorce will occur somewhere between the first page and the last.

Breaking down the Window of Opportunity Theory even further, I was able to discern individual blocks of time that would allow parents to gauge their energy and attention strategically.

The time when warning signs are most likely to be seen (and missed) starts with the onset and ends at around six months. During this period parents need to *be hypervigilant*. They need to be on constant alert for any and all warning signs of impending emotional crisis.

In the second block of time, from six months to one year, things seem to be settling down somewhat. But don't be fooled. You still need to *remain hypervigilant* as the added dimension of PTSD comes into play. Remember there's often at least a six-month delayed onset factor.

After a year has passed within the Window of Opportunity (assuming there have been no emotional warning signs), parents are able to *step down from hypervigilant status*. It's sort of like taking an Air Force fighter squadron off combat status and placing it on *alert*.

During the second year following the breakup of the family, parents may also stay on *alert* status, that range between hypervigilance and their once normal routine. This stage lasts throughout the second twelve months of the window, unless severe emotional problems crop up. In that case, guess what? You *go back to hypervigilance*.

Once the Window of Opportunity passes, the highest degree of risk has passed. That is not to say that you can hang up the track shoes in favor of golf shoes, but it does mean you've made it through the densest part of the jungle.

THE SINGLE-PARENT CHILD WELLNESS CHECKUP

I always enjoy anonymous quotes that sum up how we sometimes handle being hypervigilant or "on alert." How about this one? "It doesn't do any good to sit up and take notice if you keep on sitting."

In the spirit of addressing that issue, I've come up with a checklist I often give to parents, single or otherwise. "The Wellness Checkup" is designed to be completed weekly for each child during the first year following divorce. The items on the report correspond to many of the emotional warning signs of crisis we examined earlier in this chapter. I've found that if a parent completes this form each week he has a much greater chance of spotting an oncoming crisis. Compare any changes you see with past reports to establish patterns or problems in the offing. The Wellness Checkup is intended to be a diagnostic resource.

Child and Teen Checkup Form   Date of this checkup   _____

Date of last checkup   _____

Does the child or teen appear to be:

1. Lonely, quiet, or moody?   YES ☐   NO ☐

---

2. Depressed? (low energy, poor
   concentration, low motivation)   YES ☐   NO ☐

---

3. Suffering from low self-esteem?   YES ☐   NO ☐

---

4. Having difficulty sleeping?   YES ☐   NO ☐

---

5. Negative about everything and everybody?   YES ☐   NO ☐

6. Isolating himself or herself?   YES ☐   NO ☐

7. Angry or abusive to others?   YES ☐   NO ☐

8. Argumentative and/or deceitful?   YES ☐   NO ☐

9. Exhibiting changes in eating habits?   YES ☐   NO ☐

10. Fighting at school or at home?   YES ☐   NO ☐

11. Doing poorly in school (grades/conduct)?   YES ☐   NO ☐

12. Dropping out of school or other activities?   YES ☐   NO ☐

13. Violating curfew?   YES ☐   NO ☐

14. Using alcohol or drugs?   YES ☐   NO ☐

15. Refusing to come to church or church functions?   YES ☐   NO ☐

16. Lazy or often procrastinates?   YES ☐   NO ☐

17. Choices in friends have changed?   YES ☐   NO ☐

18. Is suspected of being sexually active?   YES ☐   NO ☐

19. Changes in appearance?   YES ☐   NO ☐

20. Not making good eye contact (shame)?   YES ☐   NO ☐

Comments or action taken: _____

Second opinion needed?   YES ☐   NO ☐

Notes

1. As quoted by Josh McDowell and Dick Day in *Why Wait?* (San Bernardino, Calif.: Here's Life, 1987), 60.
2. Quoted in Gregory S. Cynaumon, *Helping Single Parents with Troubled Kids: A Ministry Resource for Pastors and Youth Workers* (Colorado Springs: NavPress, 1992), 83.
3. The Bureau of Labor Statistics, 1984; and *Demography* 21, 71–82.
4. *Special Report*, August-October 1990, 7.

•9•

APPRECIATE THE IMPORTANCE OF ROLE MODELS AND RESOURCES

Tammy was sick of sitting at the computer, fingers frozen on the keyboard, waiting for something to happen. Nothing had, of course; there was only the soft, blue glow of the monitor slowly lulling her to sleep. "Wait a minute," she said as she shook herself, switching off the computer in disgust. "My PC isn't on deadline. I am." Taking matters (along with ballpoint) into her own hands, she decided to try it the old fashioned way—in longhand.

She dug out a legal-sized, yellow pad and began writing her final restaurant review for the week, a complete rundown of the county's best hot dogs. *Now that's a glamorous gig,* she thought. *Nothing like critiquing bad food in dumpy places prepared by men with names like Al or Mel. No wonder I've got writer's block. I can't believe they bumped me from the editorial department to the weenie beat.*

At last, the sentences began flowing again, albeit from a badly gnawed pen. "Did you see that, Mr. IBM Clone," she taunted, waving the ragged BIC in front of the screen. "I can get by without your trillion megabytes of RAM and floppy drives. Men, computers, and hot dogs—who needs 'em!"

Newspaper work was a snap compared to the perils of parenting solo—a job Tammy was starting to get the hang of since her husband left for the great Northwest sixteen months ago. *"Sales manager leaves family to find roots as a forest ranger." Has the makings of a made-for-TV movie,* Tammy thought, jotting down the idea in her notebook.

The entire family, or so it seemed, had gone into hormonal

overload. Noah, thirteen, was now possessed by the dreaded puberty monster, not to say that excused his recent suspension from school for smoking marijuana. His big sister, Ruthie, sixteen, the child Tammy lovingly called the "PMS poster child," was feeling ugly, awkward, and in desperate need of reassurance. Even six-year-old Jackie, mom's little fire-starter, was displaying the raw talent in big demand by the nation's finest institutions—correctional institutions.

Even the stray cat Ruthie had smuggled into the house under her big, yellow raincoat, was now in heat. *Swell.*

After a year and a half of single parenthood, Tammy was thoroughly frustrated and drained by the experience. *It could be worse, I guess,* she thought, trying to stay positive. *At least Walter isn't a deadbeat dad. I mean, he's never missed a child-support payment. And he does phone once every couple of weeks—around lunch time when nobody's home. But at least he leaves a message.*

Tammy was dealing with the divorce, even her ex's new girlfriend and her kids, but how could he put so much geography between himself and the children? The answer was only too obvious, she angrily concluded. *He placed his wants and needs ahead of those of his children. What a pea brain!*

Lately, even her job at the paper was beginning to sour. She was growing weary of evenings out alone, reviewing restaurants that were all beginning to look and taste alike. She didn't realize the newspaper's tight budget would limit her beat to establishments with drive-through windows, or signs that said "Eat Here."

Worse, she was losing her tiny gymnast's waistline—the one she had worked so hard to preserve since high school. It was disappearing under a constant barrage of cheesecake, cheeseburgers, and chili-cheese dogs—in increasing portions. *Wonderful,* she sighed. *The only things larger than my expense account are my thighs.*

What had gone wrong? She had always been such a "together" person: a modern, professional, working woman of the eighties able to juggle career, love, and kids—and even play a decent game of tennis without breaking much of a sweat.

She had gone from being the envy of her friends—solid marriage, handsome husband, and ridiculously well-behaved children—to a divorced, dateless, bloated person with stigmatized kids who were getting harder to handle by the day. *What a mess!*

Bottom line? She needed help. Her kids needed a positive and consistent male role model, and she knew it. Somebody other than mom they could share their feelings with—although truth to tell, she worked overtime (usually without success) to get them to share their feelings.

Thank heaven for Grandad Dan (she always liked the way that sounded). He was the one ray of positive male sunshine readily accessible to her kids. Fortunately, he had remained close to the disenfranchised family throughout the divorce. He visited the children frequently, and he was a willing volunteer whenever a baby-sitter was needed. Not surprisingly, he and his wife had also divorced recently after many miserable decades of marriage.

"You know, Tam, a lot of your problems can be laid at my doorstep," he confided, still angry over his son's decision to leave the state. "I'm afraid I didn't set much of an example for Walter. When I wasn't out drinking, or womanizing, or fighting with my wife, I was fishing or hunting with my friends. I'm not making excuses for my son's behavior, but I didn't give him a very straight path to follow, either.

"Just being with your children," he continued, "is like a second chance for me—an opportunity to be a positive influence, to make a difference. The kind of difference I never made for my own kids."

Tammy was only half-listening to grandad's heartfelt confession. She was preoccupied about Noah and why he wasn't home yet. "I'm sorry, Grandad Dan, what were you saying? I'm just a little concerned about Noah, that's all."

He just laughed. "It's okay, dear. I'm almost glad you weren't listening."

Noah finally wandered in about 9:10, still within his fifteen-minute grace period. He quickly apologized for being late—too quickly for Tammy's liking. But there were no telltale cigarette or marijuana odors on his breath, hair, or clothes. His eyes were clear and bright. "The movie was a little long," he said, interrupting his mom's inspection. "I'm going to bed now. Good night. 'Night, Grandad."

"Grandad, if it's not beer or drugs—what is it? He's much too happy. What if it's a girl? That's it! What if he gets her pregnant? I hope he's being safe. What am I saying? I don't want him fooling around at all. He's never asked me anything about sex. How 'bout you, Grandad?"

Granddad Dan just shook his head and smiled sheepishly, "What do I know about women? I've made a mess of every relationship I've ever had. I didn't even talk to Walter about that kind of stuff."

Well, so much for Grandad as the ideal role model for the children, she said to herself, as she gently pulled the heavy comforter around Jackie as she slept. *Why is it they're so cute when they're asleep? I've got to give some more thought to this role model thing.*

Just then the phone rang. It was Jerry, one of the copy editors from the paper. "Sorry about calling so late, Tam," he said nervously. "I scored some great seats to the new musical in town. Orchestra, I think. Got 'em before the editor could snap 'em up. Would you like to go? Friday night?"

"Jerry, I'm genuinely flattered. I really am," she said softly. "But you know how hectic things have been for me lately. What with deadlines, restaurants, kids, dogs, and now, cats in heat . . . What time should I be ready?"

"Eight? Fine, see you then."

Now I've done it. A date! She worried about what the kids would say. *What's the big deal? I haven't allowed myself to this point. I deserve a little fun!*

Jerry arrived right on the dot, as you might have expected from an exacting copy editor. Noah was home at the time; Grandad was doing the baby-sitting honors.

"Now, be a big boy, Noah, and take care of your Grandad Dan." Tammy smiled. "I'll be calling around ten to make sure everybody is doing okay. And thanks again. Oh, here's the number of the theater. I don't care if it's during tune-ups, in the middle, or while the fat ladies sing—have me paged if there are any problems."

Tammy had a great time, even if those "hot" orchestra seats turned into back row, balcony. She had to admit it felt good being catered-to for a change.

Jerry took her out on several more dates over the course of the next month. He even accompanied her on one of her restaurant assignments. Things were going nicely, slowly. Just the way that Tammy wanted them to go. Her first and foremost responsibility was to her children. Her priorities were well established.

Jerry called up one Saturday morning, saying he just got a pair of football tickets for the game that night. "I know you consider the sport barbaric, Tam. So I'd love to take Noah along, if you don't mind."

She immediately started to say yes, before catching herself and changing her decision to no.

"That's very sweet of you, Jerry, but I think it's a little early in our relationship for that kind of involvement with my children. Thanks for thinking of them though." Jerry seemed to understand.

The second she set down the receiver, she began kicking herself. *Stupid, stupid, stupid! A nice, normal (well, for an editor), decent-looking guy. All he wants to do is take a kid to a football game, not out skydiving. And you say no. Nice call, Einstein.*

As she calmed down, her decision began to make some sense after all.

Jerry seems like a great guy. I'm probably going to continue seeing him. But it's just too early to allow him to get too close to the kids. It wouldn't take much. They're so needy. There's plenty of time for football games if our relationship becomes really serious. And I'm in no hurry for that.

Still, the question remained. How was she going to provide her kids with a good example of a happy marriage? She didn't even know of any. She was afraid that if she couldn't come up with some role models for her children to emulate they would eventually wind up divorced, just like Grandma and Grandad and now her.

She felt a sense of relief. At least she had a mission. A game plan of sorts: find a role model for the kids. *First, however, I've got to finish this column. Let's see . . . "Fat Alby's Dog House, famous for its 'Fat Fries,' has taken the hot dog to new heights by introducing the Fat Dog. If you like sauerkraut, chili, cheese, and anchovies on your hot dogs, then this is the place for you . . ."*

WANTED: ROLE MODELS

Most people are familiar with the infamous "love triangle" when it comes to describing a certain type of relationship. However, relationships come in every conceivable combination of geometric design. *Dyads* are two-way relationships—mom to dad, dad to child, mom to child. There are also *triads,* or triangular relationships, which, unlike the relationships depicted on daytime soaps, refer to mom to dad to child, and countless other combinations.

Relationship, love, communication—the very basics of life—are a lifetime learning process for the majority of people. Most of us were lucky. We saw some positive forms of those elements as children.

With that in mind, ask yourself these questions:

- How are your children going to learn and observe what a healthy marriage looks like?
- Where are your children going to learn and observe how parents interrelate with children in typical two-parent families?
- How are your children going to learn and observe positive role models, particularly if they seldom see the other parent?
- How are your children going to learn and observe how women and men show appropriate affection to one another?

Coming by answers to these questions perplexes even the most adept single parent. That's why I encourage all single parents to consider seeking role models for their children.

This idea of role models is met with resistance by some single parents. For some unknown reason, there are a significant number of single parents who believe in going it alone. They see themselves as both mom and dad, the family unit rolled into one. Perhaps they're trying to demonstrate their self-reliance to an ex. Or maybe it's their way of "whistling past the graveyard." We met this type of parent early in the book. Remember the Superparent?

Scripture tells us that it's not advisable to go it alone. Jesus certainly had the ability to successfully walk alone, yet He chose to enlist the assistance of twelve trusted friends to help Him in his task (Matthew 10:1–42).

Prudent people identify their goals and assess the resources they will have to accomplish them. That is an important point for single parents to understand. What do you truly need? Even the best single parents in the world still need role models for their children.

Can you think of anyone suitable to serve as a role model for your kids? Look around. Only 25 percent of single parents are truly at a complete loss for role models. There are married aunts and uncles. Grandmothers and grandfathers. Brothers and sisters. Second cousins, third cousins, ninety-fifth cousins if need be. If you shake your family tree long enough, chances are you'll find a suitable and willing role model.

Let's say, however, you're part of the group that truly doesn't have any family. Or, perhaps your family is out of state, or bears a close resemblance to the Adams Family. Okay, maybe family isn't always the answer, but don't give up yet.

THE PARAPARENTING SOLUTION

When I was a policeman, I was actively involved in a "big brother" type of program. I was asked to get involved in the life of a young man whose parents were divorced. Although I truly enjoyed my experiences with the young man, I realized that I was limited in what I could teach him. Sure, we could go to ball games, shoot baskets in the park, and other "guy" stuff. But what could a twenty-two year old, single cop teach a nine-year-old about moms and dads, good husband-wife relationships, and how parents interact with their children?

This lack of experience would eventually lead me to the Para-Parenting concept. The prefix *para* has several definitions, but the one that applies to this situation includes the concepts of assistance and close association. Paramedics assist doctors, paralegals assist attorneys, and ParaParents are intended to assist parents.

Potential ParaParents are everywhere. Your son's soccer coach and his family. Your next door neighbor and his family. Your child's best friend's family. The pastor and his family, or another in your congregation. The list is endless. The requirements are relatively simple, but shouldn't be taken lightly.

Here is a generic list of what you should look for in potential ParaParents. You should customize this list to incorporate what you feel are essential to you and your family.

- They should be mature and of sound moral character.
- They should have children close to the same age as your child—but that doesn't mean you should automatically rule out parents with children of different ages than yours or even couples with no children.
- They should hold ethical standards and values similar to yours.
- They should have a secure marriage and appear to be raising good kids.
- Most of all, they have to have a desire to help and be willing to include your child in their lives.

In the absence of more traditional candidates with younger families, married seniors can make great ParaParents.

HOW TO APPROACH A POTENTIAL PARAPARENT

Once you've identified the families who seem to match up with what you are looking for in a ParaParent family, try the direct approach. It's generally the best.

Sit down with the ParaParent candidates (just the husband and wife) and let them know what you're considering. Take any pressure away by letting them know, right up front, that you are not expecting (or wanting) any financial commitments from them. Also let them know that you're not asking for large amounts of their time or energy. What you are asking of them is that they occasionally integrate your child or teen into their lives on a gradual basis. Tell them that you are only asking them to be "themselves." That's why you chose them.

WHAT DO PARAPARENTS DO?
ParaParents don't need to do anything out of the ordinary or deviate from their family routine. That's the beauty of the whole program. They just have to be themselves.

What we're actually talking about here is a commitment to integrating your child into their family for about two hours a week.

Face it, two hours is easy. Especially when you don't have to do anything special. However, consistency is the key to the entire program.

Communicate to the ParaParent candidates that those two hours a week might be as simple as inviting your child to come over for dinner and a video. Occasionally, they might also include your child on family outings, a trip to a ball game, a visit to the park for a picnic, or any of a host of other activities.

Let the ParaParent know that the impressions they are leaving with your child could make a profound difference in his life. Through the Paraparenting family, children from single-family homes have a chance to witness the subtle interactions of a two-parent family.

The impressions etched on your child's mind by these experiences as he matures will be invaluable. When he begins dating, he can play back images of how adults relate. He will have in mind positive images of a married couple. As for children, he'll play back the images of two parent-child relationships, the relationships he has in your family, and the ones he observes in the ParaParent family. That doesn't mean he will have less respect for what you've done as a single parent. Quite to the contrary. I've found most children have greater respect for their single moms and dads when they've discovered, firsthand, how difficult the job is for even two parents working together.

If there is one point to make clear to the ParaParents, it's that consistency is essential. ParaParenting can't be an on-again, off-again proposition. There's already been too much of that in your child's life.

OTHER BENEFITS OF HAVING PARAPARENTS
I recently spoke to a group of twenty-five single parents who have connected with ParaParents. Their enthusiasm for the program was heartwarming. In each case but one, the ParaParents had done a wonderful job. Not only had they lived up to their commitment to integrate the children into their lives, they had also helped out the single parents themselves.

In many of the cases, the ParaParents and the single parent

attended church and home Bible studies together. The ParaParents provided friendship, companionship, counsel, and even baby-sitting on occasion.

In short, the ParaParenting program had provided the single-parent families with more than they had imagined. Not only were their children receiving the impressions that are so important, but the single moms and dads had gained friendship, fellowship, and support as well.

STEMMING THE TIDE OF DIVORCE

Since 1971, single-parent families have increased by about 1 million each year to the point where they account for 24 percent of all American households.[1]

The single parent survey also produced evidence that if your parents were divorced, you stood a 5 percent greater chance of being divorced than the national average. Because your children are part of a single-parent home (divorce only), they will also assume the same risk for divorce.

It is essential that you set out to stem this tide by providing positive images for your children, such as the ParaParenting program. It also means avoiding negative images, such as having dating relationships where your children see new people moving constantly in and out of their lives.

FINDING CONFIDANTS FOR KIDS

In the single-parent survey, more than 65 percent of all children and teenagers said they had no one they could confide in about their true feelings. Virtually the same percentage said they didn't feel comfortable expressing their feelings with their parents, for a number of reasons.

Many felt that their being fully candid might touch off an already explosive situation with a mom (or dad) who was already stressed-out. Instead, they kept their feelings, frustrations, and fears to themselves or took them elsewhere. All too often, "elsewhere" was not an appropriate source for solutions to their problems.

Refer back to the chapter on communication as often as necessary. Try your best to be that "safe person" in your child's life—a person he feels he can open up to and someone he can depend on to listen, as objectively as possible, without fear of a judgmental, minimizing, or punitive response.

Don't condemn yourself if you're not your child's personal counselor. That doesn't happen very often, and it's not a reflection on your abilities or inabilities. Think back on your childhood. Would you go to your parents with your deepest, darkest secrets and problems? When you did, did you go back a second time? I thought not.

The ParaParent partnership may ultimately develop into the type of relationship we are discussing here—one in which your child will open up and discuss his feelings. But it's not guaranteed.

I strongly suggest single parents go on the offensive immediately following the divorce and find their children appropriate resources, people with whom their children can share their secrets, fears, and questions.

If you attend church, there are often several resources available. Start with the youth pastor or someone who has some counseling training and experience. Don't be shy or ashamed to ask the pastor to take a special interest in your child. Let the person you approach know that you would like your child to feel safe in coming to him in the future when and if he needs to talk to someone other than yourself. The pastor may even recommend another staff person who is better qualified to help. Don't take the referral as a rejection. Pastors are busy people too, so just stick to it until you connect with the right person.

There are usually counseling resources available at your child's school as well. Pay a visit to the school resource counselor or principal and ask him if he could suggest someone to help your child.

Again, single-family support groups and divorce recovery groups are often the best resources available. Why reinvent the wheel when there are countless single parents who have already been where you're going? Look everywhere for these support groups. Here are some ideas of where you might start looking for help:

- Churches in your area (probably the larger ones)
- The school system (both Christian and secular)
- PTAs
- Christian counselors
- Social Service departments of your local city and county
- Service organizations (e.g., Women's clubs or YMCA)

Note

1. *The World Almanac*, Bureau of U.S. Census Report (New York: World Almanac Publishing, 1989), 834.

·10·

UNDERSTAND THAT YOU'RE NOT DAMAGED GOODS

I had just enough time to duck into a convenience store after my radio show, pour myself a Big Gulp, grab a bag of pretzels, and make it to my office for my 1:00 P.M. session. In other words, it was a typical day.

In clinical terms, this is called "a rut," I thought, as I hurried to the check-out stand.

"Where do you keep the fruit snacks?" I asked the store clerk, Mr. Abu, nearly forgetting my son's last-minute request this morning. "If I forget the treats for their lunches again, I'm dog meat. They'll probably file for a parenting malpractice suit against me—again."

He smiled, although I could see he didn't have a clue as to what I was talking about. "Every day you come in and buy the same thing, Dr. Greg. Why don't you try something different? Like a Slushie? We have Tangerine-Grape, Papaya-Lemon, and Banana-Peanut Butter," he said in his best broken English.

"As tempting as those flavors sound, Mr. Abu, I think I'll stick with the Big Gulp today. Maybe next week I'll live dangerously, but I have a motto, 'Never mix food groups together in the same cup.' Besides, I bet Banana-Peanut Butter Slushie stains are murder to get out."

"No problem, Dr. Greg," Mr. Abu replied, smiling. "But if you don't mind me saying so, I think you are in a rut."

Oh, wonderful. Even the counter clerk at the stop 'n rob says I'm in a rut. "Thanks for the diagnosis, Mr. Abu. Send me a bill."

As I drove across town to my office, I was careful not to spill my Big Gulp. Pulling into the parking lot, I quickly scanned myself and the front seat for any sign of damage. Not bad. Only a small, unsightly stain on my pants this time.

"Hi, Carolina," I said, as I walked through the door at exactly 12:55 P.M. "Are the ladies from my one o'clock single-parent group here yet?"

"Yes, Greg. They're in the small group room ready and waiting, except for Connie. I haven't seen her yet."

"Good afternoon," I said as I walked into the room, looking at the group with pride. It wasn't a personal, boastful pride that I know we Christians aren't supposed to feel. It was more a sense of pride in what they had accomplished over the past six months. Who am I kidding? To be completely honest, maybe I did feel a twinge of personal satisfaction. But they've all worked so hard.

"We're going to have to get started here in a minute," I said.

"Wait a minute," Tammy interrupted. "We can't start without Connie. Did she call anyone to say she'd be late for today's session?"

"You know Connie," chided Linda. "She'll probably be late for her own funeral. Actually, she did call to say it was her week to drive the infamous car pool—you know, her two kids along with six others. I told her about my little car pool secret. If the kids are really bad on the way to school, you just threaten to honk your horn and yell, 'Have a nice day—and by the way, did you remember to take the Dino Flintstone vitamin?' as you're letting them off in front of all their friends. You'd never believe how compliant kids can be. Yup, keeps them right in line."

This was the first women's support group exclusively for single moms I had conducted. However, I had no hand in its planning. The group started when Connie, who was in individual therapy, asked if Donna, a neighbor of hers who was also a single mom, could join her in therapy once in a while. Donna was having anxiety attacks as she tried to cope with the stress of her husband's leaving her with six children and no child support. Donna was a great student.

The group took off from there. Connie and Donna invited Linda and Tammy, two single moms from their church, into the support group. Word spread of a single mom's support group; and before I knew it, the group grew to ten, with a waiting list.

"Okay, let's get started," I said, taking my usual place in the large floral chair. Today, we're going to focus our attention on your postdivorce feelings. We'll examine why many single moms begin to feel like damaged goods—as if they're somewhat different, somehow less of a person since the divorce. We'll talk about how some moms look at their single status as a death sentence. Remember, you were a parent before the divorce, and you're still a parent. These are the same children you loved and cared for before the divorce. Your circumstances have changed, not you. Let's start with a working definition of the term *damaged goods.*"

At that point, Connie slowly opened the door and closed it softly. Hoping nobody would notice, Connie crept toward the last open chair. One by one, all the single moms greeted Connie as she took her seat next to Linda.

"Boy, you sure look happy, Connie. I wish all my patients enjoyed therapy the way you seem to," I said sarcastically. What the other ladies didn't know was that Connie had let me in on a secret. She was late to the session because she and Darren, her fiancé, were going to the mall to pick out wedding rings.

Connie had met Darren one day at church. He had been sitting a few pews away, watching her throughout Sunday service. After service, he walked up and introduced himself and they talked for a few minutes. The next week, Darren waited for Connie to take a seat and then sat beside her. After church, they talked for a short while.

Connie had learned by experience to work her three kids into the conversation early-on to allow for as much maximum squirming time as possible. It always amazed her how the mere mention of kids can refresh the memories of single men. The excuses were many, but the prize for the lamest had to go to the guy who said, "Oh, hey, I just remembered. I can't go out next Friday. That's the night of my great aunt's funeral. I'll call you."

Darren was different. When he learned that Connie had three children he immediately invited them all to visit his place of employment. Darren is an executive for a rather well-known theme park whose mascot is a large mouse. As you might have guessed, he was an instant hit with Connie's kids. Even Aaron, now fourteen, approved of Darren. The rest, as they say, is history.

"Connie," I said, holding back a smile, "would you do me a favor and put something over your left hand? I'm getting a blinding glare from whatever it is you are wearing on that finger."

With that, Connie broke into a giant smile as all the ladies from her support group rushed over to "oooo" and "ahhh" over the diamond engagement ring she was wearing.

"Does this mean I have to leave the group, Greg?" Connie asked with a smile on her face and tears of joy running down her cheeks.

"Leave the group? No way Connie, I've got a feeling you're going to be leading single-parent support groups some day."

REMBRANDTS, PICASSOS AND SINGLE PARENTS

We're all in transition. Whether we are parents, single parents, or nonparents—we are all humans in transition. That's simply the nature of God's plan for each of us.

A more emotionally responsible way of living would be to manage only what is manageable. Next, resolve to live with that which is unmanageable, through God's grace. For some reason, however, we keep struggling for perfection, seemingly oblivious to the obvious—we can never achieve it here on earth.

One day, while studying perfectionism for a Sunday school class, I stumbled onto a wonderfully revealing passage that helped me to better understand the meaning of God's truth and grace in our lives. God gives us truth in order to keep us moving in the right direction, the path that leads toward maturity (Ephesians 4:13).

The Scriptures teach us Christian ethics and values. With those in mind we should be moving toward being better people tomorrow than we are today, and better today than we were yesterday. It is the grace characteristic of God that ultimately makes it okay for us to fail. Without His grace, our failures would certainly lead to condemnation.

We are a people under construction, a work in progress. That may seem like a lowly place to be until we understand the road has been traveled by many greater than ourselves—even He who was greatest.

In Luke 2:52 we learn that Jesus Himself was in a sense "under construction" as He walked among us. How can that be? How could Jesus possibly have had any room for improvement? The answer is that although He was perfect and therefore not needing improvement of any kind, during His life on earth He grew from an infant to a man and, as Luke 2:52 puts it, "grew in wisdom and stature, and in favor with God and men." As He grew into adulthood, Jesus Himself was changing, was becoming wiser and growing in stature in everyone's eyes, even God's.

The application of this passage is clear. If Jesus moved through the various stages of human growth during his life on earth, shouldn't we reconcile ourselves to the fact that we too are under construction?

Perhaps we could bolster our understanding of what it means to be under construction if we saw ourselves as unfinished masterpieces.

My mother has always been a talented artist. As a child, I would watch her paint beautiful oil paintings that would often take months to complete. She is truly a master of her craft.

Occasionally, an art collector would bring an old masterpiece to be restored. I marveled as my mother painstakingly prepared the canvas for the arduous task ahead. I wondered how the human eye could match modern-day oil colors to the primitive paints used centuries ago, paints that had long since cracked, flaked-off, and faded with age.

Over a period of months, the masterpiece would appear in various stages of completion. While one area of the painting was being scraped from the canvas with various mixtures of linseed oil and turpentine, another area was receiving its finishing brush strokes. At first the changes came rapidly, only to slow to a crawl in the particularly delicate and detailed areas.

When the masterpiece was finally restored, though it was nearly identical in every respect to the original, it was actually a new creation—a creation to be admired and cherished for the time, love, and attention to detail that went into its restoration.

People are like artistic masterpieces. We spend our lives in various stages of restoration at the hands of the real Master.

GOD'S VIEW OF DIVORCE

Let's take the concept of our lives being under construction a step further to try to see how God might view divorce and single parenting.

If you are a divorced Christian, you probably studied the Scriptures repeatedly and counseled with numerous pastors prior to making your final decision. You are aware of Bible passages concerning divorce, the church's historical position on divorce, and the view of divorce most church members have. As a result, you have likely experienced enough grief, shame, and embarrassment to fill the AstroDome.

You undoubtedly have read in the book of Malachi what God says about divorce (Malachi 2:16). You have scoured the Old Testament to see what it gives as permissive grounds for divorce (e.g., Genesis 3; Leviticus 18; Jeremiah 3; and Deuteronomy 24). And you have probably come to the same conclusion I have: God hates divorce.

What does that mean in terms of your life? You have already made your decision. You weighed the options and decided divorce was preferable to the way your were living. To use my favorite three words in therapy: So now what?

"So now what?" You've chosen divorce, or it was chosen for you. What implication does that have for your relationship with God and with other Christians? How will the divorce impact the rest of your life?

You could start by asking yourself these two questions:

- Because of my divorce, do I consciously or subconsciously feel that I am no longer acceptable to God?
- Because of my divorce, have I experienced condemnation from Christians and do I somehow feel I don't fit in anymore?

If you answered yes to either question, or to both of them, let's bring your feelings into the light where we can begin restoration work right away.

When Christians divorce, it has been my experience that they focus their anxieties on three questions.

- Will God hold my divorce against me the rest of my life?
- Will my divorce have an impact on how much grace and forgiveness God will provide me while in the body?
- Can my divorce impact my salvation?

At the time of this writing, God has not yet visited me with direct answers to these questions, nor do I expect Him to place a tablet on my sofa anytime soon. God does, however, give insight in the Scriptures into this and other life issues.

Until such a time as we're fortunate enough to get an audience with Him, the Scriptures will do just fine. (Although, I *would* also like to ask Him the meaning-of-life question. He probably hears that one about 8 million times a day. Next, I'd like answers to questions about a few personal things in life. For instance, why do I put on five pounds just looking at a cheesecake, whereas my biological brother is a rail? And I'd be remiss in not asking Him "What's with penguins? Were you just kinda having an off-day, or what?" And I promise, I'll ask Him the three questions regarding divorced Christians.)

Based on what Scripture tells us about God, here is what I have been able to come up with in response to those questions:

Question #1: Will God hold my divorce against me?

Answer: Hold us accountable? Yes.
Hold divorce against us? Open for interpretation, but I suspect not.

Remember, God allows us free will in our lives. Mistakes and poor choices carry consequences. Second Corinthians 5:10 tells us that we are to appear before the judgment seat of Christ in order to receive what is due to us for what we have done while in the body—whether good or bad. That is the accountability aspect of God's message.

Be careful not to confuse the word *accountability* with the word *condemnation*. Yes, we will be held accountable for our actions. Yet nowhere does God say accountability supersedes grace and forgiveness.

Question #2: Will my divorce have an impact on how much grace and forgiveness God will provide me?

Answer: I believe the answer to be no. Although we believe we understand most of God's feelings regarding divorce, we also know how He feels about grace and forgiveness.

We have a clear picture of how grace and divorce intermingle in Jesus' example in John 4. That is where Jesus talks openly with a woman who has had five marriages. Not only that, she was currently living in an adulterous relationship. Jesus showed this woman care, concern, and respect for her emotional struggles. He continued to minister to her regardless of her sins or marital status. That gives us a clear example of how God's grace and forgiveness override judgment and condemnation.

Question #3: Can my divorce impact my salvation?

Answer: I believe the answer to be no. I am unable to substantiate anywhere in Scripture that a person's salvation is in jeopardy based solely on divorce.

God provides us many chances to atone for our sins. He instructs us to forgive others, even up to seven times seventy if necessary. The Scriptures are alive with passages demonstrating God's gentle hand of grace and forgiveness in situations that make divorce look like a walk in the park.

I believe the key to this issue can be found in Matthew 12:31, where Jesus confirms that all kinds of sins will be forgiven, except for blasphemy against the Holy Spirit. God has seen it all. There really isn't anything that you could do or say that would shock Him. And yet we sometimes act as though He is like our childhood friends, who would take their ball and go home because things weren't going their way.

I interpret Matthew 12:31 to mean that there is truly nothing you or I could do, other than blasphemy against the Holy Spirit, that would motivate God to withhold His grace and forgiveness.

Where does the Bible teach that once you have a problem or sin in your life, it's time to throw in the towel? If that were the case, and a mistake or sin brought about instant rejection from God, then I fear few would have any reason to go on trying to do things the right way—according to God's will.

In 1 Timothy 1:15, Paul writes: "Christ Jesus came into the world to save sinners, of whom I am the worst." Paul has fully acknowledged the sins of his past and continues to move ahead. He presses forward toward God. Paul then advises us likewise to "fight the good fight, holding on to faith and good conscience."

As a Christian and a therapist, I am naturally opposed to divorce. But I am also a realist. I understand that circumstances sometimes exist that make marriage an impossible situation. When those circumstances lead to divorce, I find it equally impossible to believe that God casts single parents aside.

LIVING IN THE PAST, PRESENT, AND FUTURE

I have come to the realization that people get stuck in problematic ways of living (or in a "dysfunction," as it's often called) because they are either living in the past or living in the future. They aren't living in the present.

Let's take a look at these two errors and how they influence the lives of single parents.

TRAPPED IN THE PAST

How may times do you find yourself feeling melancholy about "the good old days"? You look back fondly on your childhood, your high school years, your first love. You remember when your kids were small or when you and your spouse were happy. That's right, back before your house became a toxic waste dump and you became the janitor.

The function of the memory, like a computer, is input and output. It records your personal historical data. Its primary function is to log the sum total of your life experiences. Its secondary function is to allow the other parts of your mind to access its "hall of records" upon request. No ID or security clearance necessary. Remember, your memory is just that—a part of the past. It is important not to stay "logged on" to the past for too long.

We often view our past as though we are are looking through those thick blocks of glass used for interior decorating. When I learned they are called *depression glass*, I thought that was an appropriate name. Our perspective of our past is often distorted by clouded recollections. We often bring that about ourselves by seeing things as we wished they were, rather than how they actually were.

We may also use our past to convince ourselves of how miserable we truly are in the present. "If only I hadn't . . . ," or, "If only I would have . . ." Those are the battle cries of the depressed. They are indicative of being trapped in the past:

- "I wish . . ."
- "If only . . ."
- "I should have . . ."
- "Things would be different if . . ."

Memories of the past, whether idealized or despised, make up an ineffective, or trapped, way of living. Idealized memories keep us from enjoying the present by constantly comparing it to "the good old days."

On the other side of the coin, negative memories keep us in an isolated and frozen position of anger and unforgiveness. Either way, we lose.

We'll take a look at how we can escape being trapped in our pasts, but for now, keep in mind that eventually the "good old days" will be today.

TRAPPED IN THE FUTURE

An equally dysfunctional style of living is to trap oneself in the future. A person who has done this is constantly looking over the horizon for signs of something better. Living for today is completely unacceptable, because tomorrow holds an artificial promise of happiness.

Single parents who are trapped in the future will likely say or feel such sentiments as these:

- "I won't really be happy until . . ."
- "Once I get . . ."
- "Things will be better when . . ."

A common trap for single parents has to do with how they view themselves. Their subconscious thoughts may sound like this: *I'm a divorced Christian with children. That's not a good thing to be, so I won't really be a whole person until I remarry.*

This distorted reasoning keeps many single parents in an *unsatisfied-pursuit* mode. Instead of focusing their attention and efforts on what it will take to make life better for their children and themselves, they are off to tomorrowland. There, they consume themselves with trying to find a new husband or wife, a new father or mother, or proving to others that they're still okay—in spite of the divorce.

Tomorrowland is also identifiable by motion detectors. Many single parents go into hypermotion as a way of dealing with their discomfort. That drives them to attend every group, activity, conference, and retreat they can find. Although that may seem like a good idea at the time, it's really creating a jumbling-up of priorities. The pursuit of a spouse (aka *parent*) gets top billing, while learning to be alone with the kids takes a backseat.

I've observed that most single parents are happiest when they accept their singleness and then seek others who accept it as well. Accepting singleness means realizing that it's okay to be a single parent. You're not broken, discarded, or destined for the scrap heap. It means understanding that the distorted images you have of yourself aren't reality. It means getting comfortable with *you,* and you with your children.

As we've discussed, a good way of doing that is to become in-volved with a single-parenting support group. Again, that's *one* group, not all of them. If you find you aren't comfortable with the group you initially attend, shop around a bit. You'll eventually find one where you feel comfortable.

Living in the future is like traveling down a long stretch of open highway. You look ahead for an identifiable landmark, perhaps a windmill or a tunnel off in the distance. You think, *Boy, once I get to that point, I'll be a lot closer to my destination.* But when you finally reach the landmark, you notice that you aren't really that much clos-er to your destination than you were before, so you fix your sights upon another object in the horizon.

The problem with viewing happiness as a far-off object is that that keeps happiness just beyond the horizon. Fixing our eyes on the horizon prevents us from noticing and experiencing the happiness that might be right next to us.

I stumbled across an anonymous quote that sums it up: "Fear of the future is a waste of the present."

LIVING IN THE PRESENT

This may seem overly simplistic, but try to look at today as a precious commodity, more precious even than money, jewels, or your Visa Gold Card.

Take a second to look at your calendar and your watch. What is today's date and what time is it? Do you realize that you will never have this particular day back? Once it's gone, it's gone forever. It's not like a once-a-year white sale that, if you miss it, comes around again same time next year.

Living in the present means separating yourself from being trapped in idealized or despised memories of the past as well as your wishful future. I'm not saying "Don't dream." I'm saying you shouldn't rele-gate your happiness to some point down the road.

Let's take a look at a highly complex set of instructions for changing your life from a focus on the past to a focus on the present. Are you ready? Okay, here it is: *Stop it!* (How did it feel to hurl the book across the room?) As simple as it sounds, that's the key.

Addressing any obsessive or compulsive behavior, whether it is gambling, drinking, smoking, overspending, or living life outside the present eventually comes down to *Stop it!*—whatever the *it* is. Stop-ping this *it*—any troublesome behavior—requires following some ba-sic steps.

- Acknowledge you are doing *it*.
  Break free of the denial system that has you trapped. If you are living in the past or in the future, acknowledge that as a problem in your life.
- Make a decision to change *it*.
  If living your life outside of "today" has caused you grief by preventing you from really enjoying yourself, your children, your relatives, your friends, and your relationship with Jesus Christ, make a decision to change.
- Identify and ask for the help needed to change *it*.
  Giving up any troublesome habits or behaviors leaves an emotional void. That void will likely cause you to feel anxious, sad, guilty, or lonely. If you don't choose to fill the remaining emptiness through relationships with God and others, your troublesome habits are likely to return.
- Practice changing *it*.
  Any muscle, especially the "free will" muscle, needs to be exercised or it remains weak. If you exercise it once or twice and then sense frustration or failure right around the bend, you'll be tempted to give up.
  Practice living your life in the present by catching yourself whenever you venture into the past or the future. Above all, take it easy on yourself. Understand and make allowances for setbacks. They are simply part of the learning process.
- Stop doing *it*.
  Remember, it all comes down to those three words. All the book knowledge, street smarts, and therapy in the world won't help if you don't just stop doing whatever you know you shouldn't be doing.

Living in the present requires you to focus your attention on living life to the fullest each and every day. The longer you live your life in the present, the easier staying there becomes.

DOS AND DON'TS
FROM SINGLE PARENTS

If your dream is to sail around the world in a sailboat, the first thing you'd want to do is talk to somebody who's done it. You'd ask questions: Which route is the fastest? Is it safe? What do I need to take in the way of supplies? There are hundreds of questions you would want to have answered before setting out on your journey.

The vast majority of single parents didn't have the luxury of being able to chart their course before being thrown into the ocean. They had to use the trial-and-error method. Besides, how many of us can navigate by the stars?

A major portion of the single parent survey was dedicated to asking single parents what advice they would give to newly single parents. In other words, how might they direct single parents through uncharted waters to avoid the problems they encountered. Here's their advice.

- Don't take your anger at your ex out on your kids. The divorce wasn't their fault.
- Make sure your kids don't think the divorce was their fault.
- Don't miss the signs that things might be going wrong with your kids.
- Don't try to play your kids against your ex. It will backfire on you and only makes matters worse.
- Don't let your kids stop talking and hide.
- Begin socializing in single-parent groups right away. The worst thing you can do is sit around the house getting depressed.
- Don't try to be both parents to your child.
- Don't be afraid—or too proud—to ask for help from friends, family, or the church.
- Pay attention to your kids' friends. See if they are hanging around with a different crowd.
- Get active in a church right away. If the people seem to be treating you differently since the divorce, find a new church.
- Encourage your kids to make friends with other kids of divorced families so they can see that they're not alone.
- Get your kids involved in church youth activities right away.
- Don't get buried in the feeling that your life is ruined because of the divorce. It does get better—really.
- Don't back off from or increase your discipline of your kids. Try to keep it similar to the way it was prior to the divorce.
- Find a role model for your kids, especially if you are a single mom with boys.
- Don't hesitate to find a good divorce recovery group, or single-parenting workshops or groups. Join, don't hide.

YOU'RE NOT DAMAGED GOODS

If you and I were sitting in my office, this is probably the moment when I would ask, "So, how are you feeling about all this? Are you feeling okay? Are you feeling happy or sad? How has what's been said impacted the way you see yourself as a single parent?" If we were successful in presenting the material covered in this book, then you came away with a new perspective on single parenting. If we were successful in reaching our goal—to write a true-to-life, single parenting book that provides real answers, instead of just rehashing the problems, then we would have convinced you of the following:

- That it's important to know what your children are thinking in relation to your divorce. Knowledge is strength, whereas a lack of knowledge creates risks and vulnerability.
- That you are only responsible for being the best single parent you can be. You don't have to be a Superparent in order to compensate for the lack of a cooperative ex-spouse.
- That the importance of establishing rules and boundaries cannot be overstated.
- That learning how to communicate as a single parent may be very different from what you've been used to.
- That making the most of quality time is the best way to help your kids at the same time keeping your sense of personal guilt to a minimum.
- That even though there seems to be a million obstacles to working through all the issues and problems between your ex, your kids, and you, it can be done.
- That overlooking your own emotional needs while tending to everyone else's will eventually lead to self-destruction.
- That kids of single parent families are at higher risk of emotional problems, but understanding those risks can neutralize them.
- That the value of role models in your child's life can't be underestimated—and that role models can be found, even when it seems impossible.
- That you are not damaged goods following your divorce. Your life has taken a detour, but you can choose to get back on course. To you, the single parent, I say this: Take heart. God is on your side.

Dr. Greg Cynaumon is a therapist in private practice with the Minirth-Meier Clinic West, Newport Beach, California. He is also the host of "Family Forum," a radio talk show focusing on Christian counseling issues facing families today. Dr. Cynaumon directs the Counseling and Support Group Ministries at Rose Drive Friends Church, in Yorba Linda, California. He received his master's degree and Ph.D. in Psychology from Sierra University. Dr. Cynaumon, his wife, Jan, and his two children, Tracy and Matt, reside in Orange County, California. For more information regarding tapes, speaking engagements, or staff training sessions, write or call:

Dr. Greg Cynaumon
c/o Minirth-Meier Clinic West
260 Newport Center Drive, 430
Newport Beach, CA   92660
1-800-877-4673

Moody Press, a ministry of the Moody Bible Institute,
is designed for education, evangelization, and edification.
If we may assist you in knowing more about Christ
and the Christian life, please write us without obligation:
Moody Press, c/o MLM, Chicago, Illinois 60610.